THE CONSCIOUS ROAD HOME

THE CONSCIOUS ROAD HOME

A REVOLUTIONARY APPROACH TO HEALING YOURSELF AND YOUR LOVE RELATIONSHIP

MARVIN ALLEN
with Jenny Allen

gatekeeper press
Where Authors are Family
Columbus, Ohio

The Conscious Road Home: A Revolutionary Approach to Healing Yourself and Your Love Relationship

Published by Gatekeeper Press
2167 Stringtown Rd, Suite 109
Columbus, OH 43123-2989
www.GatekeeperPress.com

Copyright © 2019 by Marvin Allen

All rights reserved. Neither this book, nor any parts within it may be sold or reproduced in any form or by any electronic or mechanical means, including information storage and retrieval systems without permission in writing from the author. The only exception is by a reviewer, who may quote short excerpts in a review.

ISBN (hardcover): 9781642376180
ISBN (paperback): 9781642370188
eISBN: 9781642376197

Library of Congress Control Number: 2019949746

This book is dedicated to my sister, Anna Allen and my wife, Jennifer Allen, the two best friends I've ever had.

Contents

Dedication v
Introduction ix
Chapter 1: The Struggle to Love 1
Chapter 2: A Little History 9
Chapter 3: Why We Do the Things We Do 13
Chapter 4: Understanding the Brain 17
Chapter 5: Internal Family Systems Therapy 23
Chapter 6: The Parts of Our Mind 27
Chapter 7: The Exiles 31
Chapter 8: The Protectors 41
Chapter 9: Reactive Firefighters 51
Chapter 10: The True Self or Captain 59
Chapter 11: Parts Blending With the Captain 65
Chapter 12: Summary of the Captain and the Parts ... 69
Chapter 13: Parts and Captains in Action 73
Chapter 14: A Therapeutic Session with a Captain and Parts 83
Chapter 15: Anatomy of Arguments and Fights 97
Chapter 16: Attachment in Love Relationships 103
Chapter 17: Four Types of Attachment 111
Chapter 18: Attachment Cues 123
Chapter 19: Anger in Relationships 129
Chapter 20: Hurt Feelings 167
Chapter 21: The Natural Tendency to Blame Others .. 179
Chapter 22: The Healing Apology 195

Chapter 23: Understanding Usable Love 209
Chapter 24: Men and Their Struggles with Love 223
Chapter 25: Men and the Struggle to Be in Relation 235
Chapter 26: Men and Their Emotions 239
Chapter 27: Men and Sex 265
Chapter 28: Healing Your Wounds and Opening Your Heart 271
Chapter 29: Understanding Healing 281
Chapter 30: Getting Started 285
About the Author 292

Introduction

As most of us know firsthand, committed love relationships expose our level of maturity, our psychological development and our emotional intelligence. Without even trying, love partners test limits, push buttons, and provoke each other in countless ways. While the power of love can bring us joy and happiness like we've never known, trying to achieve it with another person can also reveal our defenses, our sensitivities, our rage, our fear, and the darkest sides of our egos. Authentic, efficacious love can provide us with the greatest gifts available on this planet, but it can also demand more of us than any enterprise we will ever undertake.

Sadly, it's highly probable that the majority of men and women in the United States are not sufficiently prepared to deal with the complexities of romantic love after the romance has ebbed. There's just so much that they don't know and don't understand about how love works between two people who live together.

The first part of this book touches on the challenges that face wounded couples who try to love each other. The second part offers a look at the mind/brain and why the past can have such a profound influence on our present lives. Also included in the second part of *The Conscious Road Home* is an explanation of

IFS Therapy and how its processes can help to change the way love partners think, feel, and behave in their interactions with each other.

The third part of the book examines how various styles of attachment deeply affect how we see our partners, how we react to them, and the level of emotional security we feel in a committed relationship. Also included in the third part are chapters on anger, blame, hurt feelings, and apologies. The fourth part of *The Conscious Road Home* reveals the challenges that men face when trying to become emotionally intimate and connected with their partners. Finally, the fifth part provides examples and processes that can help partners learn to deal with and even heal old emotional and psychological wounds that get in the way of loving and feeling loved.

This book is designed to provide not only essential knowledge, but the wisdom to *apply* that knowledge to a variety of situations in love relationships. It was also written to help you through the personal changes you might need to make so that you can live and love with an open heart. Although this part of your journey might be difficult, with enough desire, a little courage, and a heaping of patience, you can do it.

Someone once asked me, "Why should I have to work and grow just to love my partner and feel loved by them? If I love them, shouldn't that be enough for things to work out?" Well . . . there are a million couples in the United States that divorce each year because "things didn't work out." It is critical to understand that successful relationships with a love partner do not come naturally for most people. Love relationships are like classes that require learning, practicing, and doing your homework. Make no mistake about it, your partner's way of being with you in the relationship will provide you with lessons and opportunities for growth that you'll find nowhere else.

I've been on this journey for a while and have had to do

a lot of learning and pruning along the way. It's been tough at times, and occasionally still is, but what are my choices? I can argue and fight, settle into a dead, soulless relationship, or get divorced. Or, I can go against my programming and try to become the best husband and human being I can be.

Recently, I've been reaping some incredible rewards in the form of increased emotional safety, intimacy, connection, and especially, *felt-love*. The utter joy, happiness, and sense of well-being would never have been possible without the lessons I've learned in my relationship. I'm sure there will be more struggles and challenges along the way, but that's OK, because I know it will be well worth whatever I have to go through. And if you choose to follow this special path of growth and healing, I'm very confident that you too, will never regret it. Make your relationship into a powerful classroom where you can work, learn, and play in what is simply the best game in town. Please don't let such an opportunity get away from you.

Chapter 1:

The Struggle to Love

"Your task is not to seek for love, but merely to seek and find all the barriers within yourself that you have built against it."

—Rumi

IF YOU ARE looking for relationship advice, you can find it in dozens of books in libraries, bookstores, and of course, on the virtual shelves of Amazon. These books often tell you what you should *do* in love relationships. Readers quickly learn, however, that consistently doing those things with a partner is far harder than reading about them. And even after some behavior changes, many couples discover that they're still plagued with the same loneliness, conflicts, and misunderstandings. Regrettably, for most of us, intimacy, connection, and love require more than just *doing* the right things; they require *being* the right person.

Remember that you and your partner are acting and interacting exactly according to the programming you received from parents, siblings, peers, your culture, and various experiences. You are both doing the best you can with your current level of development and self-awareness. To make meaningful changes in your relationship, either you or your partner, or both of you, will have to do some re-programming. As you read this book, you will learn to see fights, arguments, and other painful interactions as mere symptoms of underlying issues and wounds that have never been resolved. These symptoms can provide you and your partner with valuable opportunities for self-awareness and growth. Instead of taking it personally, you can both learn to explore the hidden world of feelings, beliefs, and attitudes beneath the conflicts, anger, passivity, withdrawal and other hurtful ways of relating that plague your relationship. This is critical because if you don't take care of the fundamental hurts beneath the issues, you will never rid yourself of the painful, recurring symptoms.

When exploring underneath the symptoms, it can be helpful to understand that there are two different types of psychological wounds. What might be called *fundamental wounds* often result in feelings of anxiety, depression, obsessive-compulsivity, low self-esteem, or excessive anger. These basic wounds cause us intrapersonal turmoil, suffering, and unhappiness that usually persist throughout adulthood.

Relational wounds suffered in childhood result in empathic failure, insecure attachment, guarded hearts, narcissism, defensiveness, and the inability to trust. These wounds can also plague us throughout adulthood unless they are healed through emotional and psychological work. Unlike fundamental hurts and scars, relational wounds rarely bother us until we enter a committed romantic relationship. Once we move in with a romantic partner, these wounds gradually emerge from the distant past, affecting how we relate to that loved one, especially when there is stress, conflict, or when our needs are not being met. The toxic effects of the emerging wounds will interfere with our ability to be intimate, connected, and emotionally safe with our partner. Over time, the love we felt in the beginning will then become diminished and contaminated as our hearts begin to close.

Although it seems obvious, most people don't seem

to realize just how much childhood wounds affect their interactions with their partners. They can't see the correlation between their wounds and the recurring fights, unmet needs, misunderstandings, and unhappiness they've endured with the person they love. All they know is that moving in with a lover seems to make that person a touch crazy. With familiarity, partners might become jealous, overly sensitive, irritable, or defensive about little things that are said or done. And inevitably, there are those times when a partner's thoughts and ideas just don't make sense. And while we're experiencing these troubling things about our partners, they're usually experiencing similar things about us.

As if our wounds weren't enough to make relationships difficult, there is an unconscious defense system that keeps most of us from seeing how we contribute to the misery and suffering we go through. My personal and professional experiences have convinced me that in a huge majority of divorces and unhappy marriages each partner blames the other for the downfall of their relationship. It seems that we have the eyes of an eagle when looking at the flaws and shortcomings of a partner, and yet are blind as a bat when it comes to seeing our own. This selective seeing is one of the biggest impediments to self-awareness, emotional growth, and ultimately to love. If you can't see that you're sabotaging the very things you want and need from your partner, how will you ever change your own unhealthy attitudes and behavior?

Interestingly, because your partner can serve as a mirror, your love relationship may be the best place to discover your particular brand of craziness and the various impediments to love that *you* place between yourself and your partner. Harville Hendrix, in his best-selling book, *Getting the Love You Want*, states that committed love relationships can provide an excellent opportunity to heal psychological and emotional wounds. Some of his quotes include:

"Romantic Love delivers us into the passionate arms of someone who will ultimately trigger the same frustrations we had with our parents, but for the best possible reason! Doing so brings our childhood wounds to the surface so they can be healed."

"Nurturing relationships help us grow psychologically . . . in ways that are not possible in non-nurturing relationships. As adults, our most important opportunity for a nurturing relationship comes through a committed partnership. It's a breakthrough to realize that the purpose of committed-relationship is not to be happy, but to heal. And then you will be happy!"

"We are born in relationship, we are wounded in relationship, and we can be healed in relationship."

If you live in a cave, go to silent retreats, or mop floors in an ashram, your unhealthy, relational wounds will usually stay hidden and remain dormant. Even in therapy, it's difficult to get at those little landmines and sensitivities that love partners seem to step on without even trying. It may sound strange, but your partner and his or her toxic ways of relating will expose your wounds and the defenses that guard them.

Just think about it for a moment; your love relationship might provide the opportunity for you to achieve more self-mastery, more personal power, and even more enlightenment than you could get anywhere else. It's all right in front of you, just waiting for you to accept the challenge. And here's the really good news: your partner doesn't have to grow, change, or treat you in a more loving way. Of course, if your partner *does* change for the better, your life and your relationship should definitely improve. But do you really want your happiness and well-being to depend on your partner's moods, attitudes, and behavior?

What matters is whether or not you can transform your errant beliefs, your unhelpful thinking, and your reactive feelings into a wiser and more heart-infused way of being in the relationship. If you can do this, you can become the master of your own ship and everything about your life will change for the better. And that includes your relationship and maybe even your partner.

If you decide to embark on this hero's journey to find self-mastery, joy, happiness, and love, this book will help you achieve those things. With enough desire and the right information, you *can* become a force for change in your relationship and your life. Like adventure? You could climb Mount Everest or sail around the world. Or . . . you could decide to change your early programming and transform yourself into the incredible human being you were meant to be. And in the process, you might just create the amazing, loving relationship you've always wanted. If you choose the adventure of a lifetime, this book is for you.

Like countless other men and women, my wife, Jenny and I grew up with a fairy tale view of love relationships, honestly believing that once we fell in love with the right person, our lives would be so much better than they had ever been. We honestly believed that living with the love of our lives would fill the holes and heal the turmoil inside us, automatically bringing us the joy, happiness, and connection that had been largely missing in our childhoods. With the right person we could finally feel seen, appreciated, and truly loved.

When Jenny and I met eight years ago, we were both in long-term, committed relationships that, while pleasant enough, didn't challenge us in the right ways and didn't meet our needs for connection and emotional intimacy. After falling in love over a period of months, we were convinced that being together would bring us the things we'd always wanted in a relationship. The first few weeks of marriage gave us a peek at the amazing world love relationships could provide. Sadly, little by little, that world began to darken in the midst of arguments, disappointments, and unmet needs. Challenges seemed to come from everywhere. We began to blame each other for our unhappiness and distress. And because we were both outspoken, alpha-type personalities used to being the boss, we had so many fights and arguments we began to lose those wonderful feelings and the emotional safety we'd felt in the beginning. And as our hearts continued to close, our conflicts and arguments were just that much harder to tolerate.

Before we knew what was happening, we found ourselves in the middle of a relationship that challenged our ways of thinking, feeling, and behaving. Neither of us was able to be the kind of partner that the other wanted and needed. Although there were wonderful times of shared love between us, we increasingly held each other responsible for our disappointment and loneliness. After a year together, Jenny and I were faced with a choice that many couples have to make: we could either settle for a conflicted, unhappy marriage, get divorced, or roll up our sleeves and get to work.

Our marriage is not that different from countless others in this country. When partners don't meet each other's needs and wants, they naturally tend to take it personally, which often leads to complaining, criticizing, or silent withdrawal and a closing of hearts. These upsets can provide us with awareness that our way of loving and being with our partner might need improvement.

Our partners need us to be forgiving, attentive, empathic, understanding and validating. We need to be good listeners, to be in the present moment, to share honestly from our hearts, and to be emotionally intelligent. We need to be willing to extend ourselves, even occasionally when we don't feel like it. To be a good partner requires that we consistently treat our lover with dignity, respect, and kindness. When our loved one is in a bad mood, critical of us, or even angry at us, they need for us to stay present without becoming defensive, withdrawing into our shell, or attacking them back. As you might imagine, the ability to achieve these things requires that most of us do whatever work it takes to increase our emotional maturity, personal power, and relational wisdom. Of course, no matter how much you grow or change, you can't do this all the time. Just shoot for consistency, not constancy.

In this book, you'll learn not only what you need to do to give usable love to your partner, but also how to make the personal changes necessary to live more from your heart. Remember that a truly loving relationship requires more than just *doing* the right things; it requires *being* the right person. In other words, to love deeply and effectively, you'll probably need to grow and develop as a human being. What's wrong with that?

At this point, you might be thinking, "Hey, this is all fine and good about me becoming a better partner; but what about this person I'm living with? What about all the crap I have to put up with from my partner and all the baggage they brought with them into this relationship?" Understandably, we'd all love a book that would change our beloveds into great partners who would always meet our needs and continually treat us with thoughtful kindness. Unfortunately, that book has yet to be written. Until then, our best shot at changing them is to first make changes in ourselves. You will be amazed at what you can do for the relationship when you develop the skills, the awareness, the emotional intelligence, and the self-mastery that mature love requires.

A relationship is a system and if you change a *part* of that system, the entire system will change. If your partner doesn't change much after you've learned how to open your heart and give usable love as prescribed in this book, then you've done all you can do. At that point, it might be time to reconsider staying in the relationship. However, some men and women have found that as they get smarter, more forgiving, and more self-aware, they decide that living with their partner is at least more tolerable. In any case, becoming a better, more loving, more powerful person has to be a good thing, whether you stay or not and whether or not your partner changes.

Chapter 2:

A Little History

Like so many others, I've spent a lot of my life struggling to be happy and at peace with myself. Even as a teenager I believed that a love relationship with the right woman would fill the hole in my heart and heal my anxious mind. And sure enough, while I felt whole and healed with each new relationship, sadly, that feeling never lasted. My scars from a difficult childhood had become barriers to intimacy and connection. Looking back, I can see a frightened, lonely man reaching through the bars of an emotional prison, trying desperately to connect with someone who would love me and make everything OK. I didn't understand how my past had set me up for failure no matter how hard I tried.

I spent the formative years of my life in Fort Worth, Texas with a neurotic, extremely religious mother and an angry, punishing father. Unable to tolerate my dad's rage and physical abuse, I left home at sixteen and moved in with a friend and his mother.

Without realizing it, I had jumped from the frying pan into the fire. While my mother was merely neurotic, my friend's mom was dangerously psychotic. In fits of rage, she physically attacked me on more than one occasion. A couple of months after moving in, I moved out.

I finished high school while living with two young men who

worked at the same grocery store as me. I attended one year of college before falling in love and getting married. Just prior to my twentieth birthday, my wife and I were blessed with a daughter. Young and clueless about babies or raising children, I spent most of my time and energy trying to make a living. With no money, one year of college, and few job skills, I managed to start a small construction company by the time I was twenty-two. Although I became successful at an early age, inside I was a mess of anxiety and self-doubt. The pressure of work and the strain of attempting the roles of father and husband, plus the hell I'd been through as a child all combined to overwhelm me with a sense of inadequacy and a terror of failure. Bottling up all my feelings left me dealing with two frightening anxiety attacks, shattering what little self-confidence I had.

Working and making money distracted me from the inner mayhem I struggled with, so I buried myself even more in my business, leaving little time or energy for my wife, our sweet daughter, and a new son. As my anxiety diminished, I actually flirted with happiness for a while, but it was too late for the marriage. My wife and I had grown apart and were unable to put things back together again. Divorced shortly after my thirtieth birthday, I was lost. Not only was I saddled with sadness, disillusionment and confusion, I was afraid of being alone. I found some solace, pleasure, and an occasional bolstering of my injured self-esteem by dating and engaging in short-term relationships. But after a few years of that I noticed a growing feeling of emptiness that I just couldn't shake.

Hoping to find peace and change my life for the better, I enrolled at a university and spent the next four years managing my company and taking a full load of classes. After three additional years in graduate school, I received a master's degree in counseling psychology.

With degrees in hand, I was ready to change the world

one person at a time. I saw a lot of clients, and eventually taught classes and workshops around the country on love and intimacy. I even became a leader of a national movement designed to help men become more emotionally authentic. In the midst of all this, I got married again, hoping that all I'd learned might help me create a beautiful marriage that could heal my heart and soothe my soul. I had good intentions, but I just couldn't make it happen.

Intellectually, I understood the psychology of healing and romantic love but my heart remained out of reach most of the time. To love someone the way I wanted to, and to actually experience their love in return, I needed some kind of deep inner change, much like the Christian idea of being "born again." At the time, I had no idea what it might take to get there. I found out when I married Jenny.

Chapter 3:

Why We Do the Things We Do

ALTHOUGH THE HUMAN brain is arguably the most complex and least understood system on the planet, it *is* possible to understand with some degree of accuracy why we think, feel, and act in certain ways. If we are jealous, critical, judgmental, often angry, pessimistic, depressed, anxious, or shy, there are "logical" reasons for it based on our previous experiences. We didn't just decide to be that way. Genetics, early infant and childhood experiences, and culture combine to mold us into who we are. For most of us, the early experiences in our family of origin have the biggest influence on our psychological and emotional development.

If, as adults, we are unable to connect and love in meaningful, heartfelt ways, we were more than likely emotionally or psychologically wounded as children. If we continue to pick wounded, difficult partners, it is because we, ourselves, are wounded. Like water, we seek our own level. Make no mistake about it; if you are having trouble with love and intimacy in a committed relationship, your partner *and* you probably have emotional wounds that are getting in the way.

Because the wounds of most people are woven into their psyches and expressed through "normal" ways of thinking, feeling, and behaving, they don't realize they are wounded. In their mind, if they're critical, they either don't see it or believe that they're just trying to be helpful. If they're judgmental, they're just discerning between right and wrong, or good and bad. If they're unable to express their feelings, they're just being reasonably unemotional about things. If they withdraw their love when hurt, they're just teaching their partners not to hurt them in the future. If they get angry, it's because someone upset them and caused them to lose their cool. If they feel resentment or hold a grudge against a partner, it's because he or she was unkind and mean to them in the past. If they desire to fix a partner, it's just because he or she needs fixing. Men and women rarely see that these and other everyday mental and emotional "activities" are part of their wounded way of interacting with others.

The truth is that few of us want to believe that we are wounded to the extent that we are. Simply put, having a shadow side that sometimes makes us mean, insensitive, or defensive is not an easy thing to accept. And it's hard to even imagine that *our* closed heart and *our* way of relating interfere with the very intimacy and connection we've always wanted. For instance, Jenny and I fought for three years over who was more wounded and whose wounds were causing all our problems in the marriage.

It is essential to understand that wounded people develop unconscious strategies to protect them from being wounded again in the same way. Ironically, those strategies tend to wound others, especially in intimate relationships, thus sabotaging their chances for harmony and connection. To start the process of healing, it is often necessary to see the correlation between our early childhood experiences and our behavior as a grown-up. Everything that happens between you and your partner is the result of the actions of your brains, minds, and bodies, which were all impacted during your early years with your parents or primary caregivers. How you and your partner deal with intimacy, connection, and love were, to a significant extent, literally sculpted into your brains and minds as babies and children. Because the various strategies you both use to protect yourselves will determine the depth and quality of your relationship, understanding and addressing them will help you discover what is getting in the way of vulnerability, authentic connection, and the love you have both always wanted. To effectively deal with and change these unhealthy ways of relating, it's helpful to understand how the brain, the mind, and the body work together to keep us "safe."

Chapter 4:

Understanding the Brain

MANY EXPERTS BELIEVE that evolution has provided humans with what they call a triune brain composed of three somewhat-distinct layers piled on top of each other. Our first and oldest layer, the brain stem at the base of the skull, oversees autonomic functions like breathing, digestion, and sexual response. Like animals and reptiles, the reptilian brains of humans are also heavily involved in survival and territorial issues.

The second part of the brain is the limbic system or mammal brain, which, among other things, regulates the emotions and the creation of memories. For our purposes, we'll just call our brain stem and limbic system our survival brain. These more primitive parts of our brains contribute to our survival by scanning the environment for potential threats and dangers. In some ways, it's like the security settings on your computer; although you're not aware of it, it's always on the alert for whatever might threaten your safety. These security settings helped our distant ancestors avoid real dangers like saber-toothed cats, bears, and other critters that might do them harm.

For modern humans, however, the survival brain is more likely to be activated by "threats" like being late for work, realizing we forgot our partners' birthdays, being criticized, having a conflict with our mates, problems with recalcitrant children, and countless other interactions and situations that our survival brain perceives as potentially harmful to our well-being.

Filled with neural pathways and complex systems, our survival brain contains levers that are ready to flood the body with chemicals at a moment's notice. In a quarter of a second, this system can dump neurotransmitters into the bloodstream if it perceives that someone is attacking, criticizing, threatening, shaming, or taking love away. These chemicals course through our bodies, urging us to react by attacking, withdrawing, or shutting down and dissociating. Research has shown that survival brains are more sensitive to possible threats and are definitely more reactive if we've been wounded in infancy and childhood.

Early in our relationship, I couldn't keep from reacting each time Jenny became even a little irritated or disapproving of me. My survival brain perceived her less-than-positive reactions to me as disrespectful, unloving, critical, and most importantly as a threat to leave me. With this distorted perception, I immediately began to see this love of my life as an unsafe adversary who was hurtful and didn't have my best interests at heart. Hurt and offended, I would usually say something back to her that was defensive or ugly and certainly ill-advised. At other times, I just buried my anger and hurt, closed my heart, and acted as though I wasn't affected. With "safety" in mind, my survival brain caused me to either return the attack or retreat behind my protective wall, withdrawing the part of me that was necessary for intimate connection and goodwill.

Our protective reactions, whether attacking, retreating, or freezing, are strategies we develop in early childhood as a result of wounds like neglect, abuse, loss, or lack of attunement. As adults, those hidden wounds become invisible armor around the heart, making trust, intimacy, and connection difficult, if not impossible. Insidiously, when we close our hearts for protection, those hearts often remain closed later on when our partners are loving and kind to us. Like a man wearing four condoms when making love to his partner, defended hearts dampen, or even prevent, our ability to actually *feel* the good things happening to us. And without the feelings, we can't really benefit from connection and intimacy. We just go through the motions and think the few scraps of intimacy that get through to us are the real thing.

Defensive strategies not only get in the way of connection, they also cause us to unwittingly hurt our partners. Have you ever noticed how distant or angry you feel when someone has hurt your feelings? You might hurt the person back or withdraw your good feelings and positive regard. You didn't just consciously decide to take those actions or have those feelings; they came over you automatically as an unconscious defense against being hurt. Your distance or angry feelings are a strategy to protect you. And the more you are wounded, the more defensive strategies you develop to avoid being hurt. The point here is that you're not *choosing* to react or to "be that way." Your defensive strategies and actions are nothing more than preprogrammed reflexes your survival brain uses to protect you.

In many relationships, partners blame each other for being reactive or unavailable because it appears that they are "choosing" to be that way. But the truth is most partners are unwittingly acting out the scripts from their wounded programming. Being critical, aggressive, judgmental, or emotionally unavailable comes naturally to them; they don't choose to do it. Their unhealthy parts formed unconsciously without their awareness or permission; so in a certain way, it's not their fault. Blaming them for their reflexes is like blaming someone for their legs jumping when the doctor taps their knees. On the other hand, while it may not be their fault, once they become aware of what they're doing, it *is their responsibility to do something about it.* We'll address this conundrum later on.

After enduring the gauntlet of an abusive, neglectful, or frightening childhood, the survival brain learns to scan conversations and interactions with friends, family members, and especially mates. In these interactions, it scrutinizes faces, words and phrases, tone of voice, eyes, body language, and meanings for anything that might be offensive, indicate disapproval, or cause mental, emotional, or physical pain or injury. Of course, the majority of conversations will be just fine. However, if your partner says or does something that could be perceived as potentially harmful to you, your survival brain will likely get alerted and cause you to react in some sort of protective way.

The word *perceived* is essential to understand because this area of the brain, depending on your emotional scars, can misunderstand, misinterpret, or distort innocent things your partner might do or say. That's why your survival brain can be triggered while sitting on the couch with your loved one in the safety of your home. Or it might get activated at the Sunday morning breakfast table, in the middle of making love, or during a conversation about paying the bills. And when protective parts of the survival brain get triggered in any of these or dozens of other situations with your partner, there's likely to be some form of attacking, freezing, or retreating.

If your husband forgets something at the grocery store that you requested, your survival system may perceive him as disregarding you or not even caring about you. Another example could be the proverbial bedroom "headache" where the husband interprets his wife's lack of interest that evening as proof that she doesn't like sex with him and, furthermore, that she may have even stopped loving him (while those interpretations might be true in some relationships, in the large majority of cases the wife is simply not in the mood or actually has a headache).

While the limbic system is designed for survival, it also plays a positive role in what has been called "the social engagement system" by greasing relational tracks as it allows us to respond to others with empathy, understanding, and compassion. Best of all, because it is the seat of our emotions, the limbic system is largely responsible for producing our feelings of joy, exuberance, satisfaction, and love. These positive feelings give our lives richness and meaning and make our efforts in this world worthwhile. Unfortunately, when we have been traumatized or emotionally wounded as children, the wellspring of these positive emotions is partially blocked, limiting our ability to experience and express them.

Our most recently evolved brain is the neocortex, which is responsible for our conscious thinking, our awareness of self, and our ability to reason and solve problems. This executive human brain uses reason to make decisions based on the known facts. It understands cause and effect and can make predictions based on history and current information. Like the emotional or survival brain, the neocortex plays a significant part in the design and the operation of our social engagement systems. It can pave the way toward intimacy and connection with a partner, or it can become a major impediment to achieving those felt experiences of love.

Masculine gender conditioning, emotional wounds, culture, and even certain personality types can cause this executive part of the brain to over-function, minimizing the influence of the emotional parts. When influenced by one or more of these conditions, men and women tend to intellectualize their world, including their personal relationships, in much the same way as Mr. Spock from *Star Trek* would. Because his social engagement system was completely controlled by his neocortex, he and other Vulcans remained rational under all circumstances. They had no interference from the emotional parts of their brains. On the other hand, their social interactions lacked the depth and richness that feelings can deliver. I've had many clients and several friends who have buried their emotions so completely that comparisons to Mr. Spock are not all that outlandish.

A classic case of this is the "typical man" who, when confronted with a woman's tears or feelings, reacts by trying to fix her *circumstances* instead of understanding and attending to what's going on inside *her*. His social engagement system is not designed to empathize or understand the feelings of another because he's out of touch with his *own* emotions. From all appearances, he may be living a reasonable, normal life, but underneath his veneer, there's a certain hollowness that often shows up in his interactions with others, especially his loved ones. Ironically, his rationality causes him to actually be *irrational* because he's often unaware of and unable to effectively deal with the emotions of his loved ones.

Chapter 5:

Internal Family Systems Therapy

A BASIC AWARENESS OF the neocortex and the survival brain is a good step toward understanding why you and your partner relate to each other the way you do. To truly understand what makes the two of you tick, however, to end your loneliness, and to successfully deal with the wounds that actually cause you the most trouble and suffering, it will be helpful to know more about how your mind operates.

It has been suggested by a variety of neurological researchers and mental health care professionals that the human mind/personality is actually composed of various discrete parts that are largely responsible for our thoughts, behavior, and feelings. These parts comprise a *system* that is designed to keep us safe, avoid pain, seek pleasure, and create connection with other human beings. Although most of us have never heard much about it, the different parts that make up a personality have been talked about by scientists and psychologists for decades.

As early as 1890, the psychologist and researcher William James wrote: "It must be admitted that the total possible consciousness may be split into parts which coexist but mutually ignore each other" (*Principles of Psychology*, Chapter 4). Analyst Carl Jung wrote, "The natural state of the human psyche consists in a jostling together of its components and in their contradictory behavior" (*Civilization in Transition*, 1964).

Recent research in neuroscience has validated earlier ideas that the mind is composed of various parts that can dictate our thinking, feeling, and behavior. Michael Gazzaniga, a scientist in the field of split-brain research, has posited that the mind is composed of semi-autonomous modules that have separate roles. In his book *The Social Brain,* Gazzaniga writes, "From our studies, the new idea emerges that there are literally several selves and they do not necessarily converse with each other internally."

A well-known researcher in the field of artificial intelligence, MIT scientist Marvin Minsky suggested that "It can make sense to think there exists, inside your brain, a society of different minds. Like members of a family, the different minds can work together to help each other, each still having its own mental experiences that the others never know about" (A Theory of Memory, 1980).

It is essential to remember at this juncture that just because our personalities or minds are made up of various parts doesn't mean we're like Sybil, the movie character who was afflicted with multiple-personality disorder. Sybil was portrayed as having multiple *personalities*; the huge majority of us have one personality with multiple *parts* or sub-personalities. So not only is it normal to have several discrete parts to our minds or personalities, it's actually the way the human brain is designed. The parts of the mind/brain are a system much like our physical bodies. Although the heart, pancreas, liver, stomach, and every other organ in the body are connected in some way, they also operate independently from one another. The mind has various parts that sometimes act in concert with one another while at other times they might act independently. And quite often our parts are even in conflict with each other, causing us to feel that inner turmoil.

Without having read about it previously, Jenny and I dabbled with the notion that human personalities were made up of various parts that each had their own agendas and behavior patterns. When we had spats, we realized that both of us had unique, unhealthy, almost childlike ways of reacting. And we reacted to a particular stimulus in pretty much the exact same way every time. For instance, I just couldn't handle Jenny being mad, irritated, or disappointed with me. Her disapproval left me struggling with defensiveness, withdrawal, or even anger. I literally couldn't help being put out with her. It was as though I was "taken over" by a part of me that absolutely believed she was being mean to me, didn't love me, and was even my "enemy." And my unhealthy reactions happened for the first several years, even though I knew better and even though it drove her through the roof. Understandably, she wanted a little wiggle room to have her feelings and reactions, even if they weren't one hundred percent positive. Sometimes, with some effort, I could keep quiet, but my hostile silence wasn't much better. Even though it was in my best interest to just let her have her irritations without my defensiveness, I couldn't do it.

We both seemed to have parts of ourselves that acted out scripts that we weren't aware of writing. We looked for answers but were basically stumbling through the fog. Then, about three years ago, while reading Dr. Bessel Van Der Kolk's excellent book, *The Body Keeps the Score: Brain, Mind, and Body in the Healing of Trauma*, I came across a chapter in which Van Der Kolk was praising the work of psychologist Richard Schwartz and the Internal Family Systems Therapy that he developed. We read Schwartz's book and found some much-needed answers.

Validating our "discoveries," Schwartz believes that the human psyche is like a mosaic, a complex system composed of various parts that we are mostly unaware of. In other words, the mind has multiple compartments or sub-personalities with their own attitudes, beliefs, and memories. These different parts of our minds operate independently of each other and at times even have conflicting goals and strategies. For instance, imagine eyeing that cinnamon roll in Starbucks that you've been lusting after for the past three coffee visits. One part of you (we could call it the *Happy Pig*) says, "OK, we've waited three days and it's high time we treated ourselves to that roll. We've been working hard; we haven't had a dessert in a long time and we deserve it." Another part, however, says, "If you give in now, you won't know when to stop. Do you really need those extra calories? Let's at least wait one more day." Your frugal part might jump in the fray saying, "That roll is not worth five bucks. Let's just get some ice cream after work." Finally, your Self, or Captain, might listen to the chatter and decide to resolve the issue by purchasing a small cookie for two dollars. If the Captain isn't strong enough, however, you'll probably be munching on the cinnamon roll as you walk out the door. In situations like this, the Happy Pig part often wins.

In an argument with your husband, one of your parts might get angry while thinking, "He's just so stubborn and stupid about things." Another part might be quizzical, silently saying, "I have no idea why I married this man!" A more smiling, benevolent part could say," I love him, bless his heart, but sometimes I just don't understand where he's coming from." Each of these parts wants to express itself, but only the strongest one gets center stage. Created in our psyches to help us avoid pain and get pleasure, these sub-personalities "take over" and influence, or even determine how we feel, what we think, and what we do. Understanding this fascinating way that our minds work can make a huge difference in how we view healing, intimate relationships, and even love.

Chapter 6:

The Parts of Our Mind

BY BREAKING DOWN the mind or personality into its discrete parts, including an authentic Self or Captain, Schwartz's method helps us to explain our feelings and behavior in nonjudgmental and compassionate ways. Using the idea of parts allows us to explore the "negative" shadow sides of ourselves and our partners without blame or shame. This is huge because nonjudgmental understanding of what's behind our unhealthy behaviors allows us to look more clearly at ourselves and take the actions needed to change from the inside out. Employing a nonjudgmental approach also creates a healthier, more loving attitude toward our partners and the struggles they have with *their* parts.

Fortunately, a part of our psyche contains a true Self or Captain that can use reason and heart to guide us in the right direction. *Unfortunately,* many of us live out our lives without much guidance from our Captains. Instead, it is those lesser parts that seem to greatly influence our interactions with others, especially our loved ones. If you really think about it, it makes perfect sense that there are different parts of our minds that can cause our feelings and that vie for control of our thoughts and actions. For instance, surely you've been angry or hurt and lashed out with a cutting remark to a friend, coworker, or loved one, only to have a part of you regret it later, wondering how you could have said such a thing. You were momentarily taken over by a maladaptive, protective *part* of you that reacted with anger to something that was said or done to you. That angry *part* has a strategy that automatically punishes others for saying or doing hurtful things to you, believing this will protect you from future hurt.

I remember one evening many years ago taking a young woman I was terribly infatuated with to a dance. After dancing cheek to cheek a couple of times, I went to the restroom. When I happily strolled back to where I'd left her, she wasn't there. Looking out at the dance floor, I saw "my" girl slow dancing in the arms of a handsome guy. I noticed a panicky feeling in my stomach seconds before a wave of hot anger washed over me.

When the music stopped and the two of them walked toward me, I was livid. I stared at him with intense dislike and muttered in as sinister a way as I could, "Looked like the two of you were having a good time out there." Seeing that I was not in a happy frame of mind, the fellow left immediately. I quickly turned to my girlfriend and began to grill her about why she felt compelled to dance with another guy when she was supposed to be with me. I accused her of flirting and not being the kind of woman I thought she was.

Of course, the whole night was ruined, and the event proved to be the beginning of the end of our relationship. Although one part of me liked her and was even falling in love with her, another part of me disapproved of her and developed an immediate dislike for her because she had danced with another man. I acted like an irrational jerk and hurt her because a *part* of me felt threatened and jealous—not all of me, mind you, just a protective part. Another more rational part of me felt perfectly secure, knowing that she liked me and was probably just dancing with the guy because he talked her into it.

Because it involved my security, the part of me that was

jealous was stronger at that moment than the part that knew everything was OK. My reaction was unwise and made no sense, but as you will see very clearly, *our protective parts are seldom rational in terms of the present reality.* The quintessential question is what are the protector parts really protecting you from?

Chapter 7:

The Exiles

SCHWARTZ'S THEORY BREAKS down the parts of our minds into the Captain, the exiles, the manager parts, and the firefighter parts. The exiled parts are memories of events and feelings that happened to us that are so painful, shameful, or frightening that our minds never want us to recall them, and especially, never to experience them again. The wounding often happens in infancy or early childhood and can be one traumatizing event or a series of hurtful experiences like repeatedly being left alone, shamed, criticized, physically abused, neglected, and so forth.

Making these events even more traumatizing, there is often no one available to help us cope with or mitigate the overwhelming, terrible feelings that result from being hurt or frightened. Being a child alone with these intolerable feelings is so traumatizing that the incident and the emotions that come with it are frozen into our brains and bodies as memories/stories that we exile into the basements of our minds.

An exile is like the inner child we've read about in self-help books, except that most people have several "inner children." Each different traumatic wound could create yet another exile. For instance, someone could have an exile that developed because as a child he or she experienced an extremely shameful event or a series of shameful episodes. That same child could develop another exile because the mother was neglectful and unavailable when the child needed her the most. Yet another exile might be created if that child was frequently bullied and tormented by an older sibling. Having an exile is a little like having watched a horror-filled movie that we never, ever want to see again, only an exile is much worse because it actually happened *to us*. An exile is simply a painful, frightening memory/story lodged in our brain that is infused with emotions. Without our conscious awareness, our minds develop protective strategies to keep those emotion-laden exiles confined to the basement so we never have to remember or re-experience them or the horrible feelings of shame, terror, abandonment, neglect, or rage that resulted from them.

I can't emphasize enough that if you were born into a normal American family in this culture, you *will* have exiles and those exiles *will* have protector parts that *will* affect your personality and your committed love relationships. And without question, certain exiles and their parts can contribute to anxiety, depression, avoidance of vulnerability, lack of intimacy and connection, and often result in hearts being at least partially closed. Unless your exiles and their parts are effectively dealt with, they will continue to have a negative impact on you throughout your lifespan. This book is designed to help you understand and heal your exiles as well as re-educating and repurposing your protective parts.

Real-Life Examples of Exiles

When Jenny was an infant, her mother neglected her and failed to give her the physical contact and attunement she desperately needed. Jenny was left with an exile that was not only filled with an inexpressibly painful craving for attention and skin-to-skin touching, it was also enshrouded in terrifying emotions and excruciating body memories. Her little child exile was defined by fear, terrible neglect, a deep hunger for physical affection, and a distrust of anyone claiming to love her. That exile would be frozen in a state of not only extreme emotions but helplessness, innocence, and vulnerability until some kind of healing intervention could take place.

In addition to her "neglect" exile, Jenny also developed what she calls a "forcing" exile that was created under the thumb of a strong-willed mother who disregarded her feelings, needs, and desires while coercing her to work in the yard; do housework; and especially, to practice at the piano. Jenny was forced to do scales and lessons for up to an hour every day of the week while enduring critiques of her performance along the way. She grew to hate the piano and struggled through her lessons, while the helplessness to change her circumstances generated frustration and growing, silent rage.

Her mother seemed like a bully who pushed Jenny around and told her what to do, when to do it and how to do it, leaving little time for her to do what *she* wanted to do. As a consequence of those particular childhood experiences, Jenny's "forcing" exile became like a deeply embedded thorn that when bumped, caused her protective parts to surface. And when they surfaced, they were ready for battle. I've learned the hard way that when she perceives that you are telling her what to do or how to do it, those parts will make you regret saying whatever it was that you said.

It's important to note that the exiled part doesn't have access to ration or reason, and so it can't comprehend the passage of time. It has a story, and it is sticking to it throughout the lifespan unless it is somehow accessed and healed. Our exiles do not comprehend the passage of time or that circumstances have changed since we've grown up. They still see the world through the eyes of a baby or small child, not understanding that as we get older we're more capable of handling situations and feelings that were overwhelming to us as infants or toddlers.

For instance, Jenny's *forcing exile* doesn't understand that as a grown person, she has the power and resources to decide whether or not she is going to engage in a particular activity. As an adult, she has options that she didn't have as a child. No one is going to force her to do anything. But because her exile is stuck in time, it experiences everything as a helpless child and depends on protective parts to keep it safe. When that exile becomes activated by some threat, Jenny's parts react toward the offender with defensive strategies that might include attacking with anger or shutting out the threat by withdrawing into a shell.

I have a "don't fuck with me" exile that my psyche developed over several years when I was a child. Small as a boy, I was picked on by bullies in the schoolyard and in my neighborhood. The bullying at school and the whippings and slaps administered by my parents at home left me with a hurt, angry exile. Years ago, this was often referred to as having a chip on one's shoulder.

Frightened and hurt by the unfairness of it all, my exile was so filled with painful, overwhelming feelings that my psyche banned those experiences to the basement of my mind. That way, I wouldn't have to deal with them anymore. It may have solved one problem, but it created another. Although the exile was hidden away, the part created to protect it still had a powerful influence on my life and my love relationships. If a loved one criticized me, was disappointed or irritated, or "picked on me" in any way at all, my exile got activated and its protective part took center stage. So pretty much every time Jenny became irritated, disappointed in me, or angry with me, my protective part took over and reacted with defensiveness, anger, or hostile withdrawal.

Because the psychological mechanisms were invisible and hidden from my conscious mind, I had no way of understanding my unhealthy behavior. So, to avoid seeming irrational to myself, I blamed my unreasonable reactions on her, saying that she was too irritable, difficult to live with, and in need of help. This happened many times in our relationship and caused some of our worst fights.

Without our awareness, the psyche bans and basically disowns the exile because it is a painful and frightening problem that seemingly can't be fixed. It's a little like the proverbial family who hides the crazy uncle in the attic so he won't cause them trouble or embarrassment. While it's true that this banning and disowning of the exile helps to mitigate some of the discomfort it might cause us or others, it is also true that neglecting that vulnerable, wounded part of us makes it impossible to heal it.

As a frightened and hurt little boy, I didn't have a parent to comfort me and to understand what I was going through, so a neglected, scared, and lonely little exile was formed inside my mind. Years later, that neglected, frightened little boy was still being ignored, only this time by my adult self. My *don't fuck with me* part and its primitive, childlike strategies have, for a long time, been hurting friends, love partners, siblings, and anyone else who made the mistake of upsetting my feelings or offending me. As you will see, an important part of this work is to communicate with the exiles and to help them release their burdens so there will be no need for protective parts.

To further illustrate how exiles are formed, I'll share one more personal story about my mother and me. My mother developed a strong exile at fourteen years old when her best friend and beloved twelve-year-old sister, Martha, died suddenly from rheumatic fever. One day my mother was playing and laughing with her sister, and a few days later, Martha was dying in her arms. Unbelievably, my grandmother blamed my mother for Martha's death.

That terrible loss was so traumatic with such overwhelming feelings that my mother buried the experience and built a wall around it, creating a devastated exile that would affect her for the rest of her life. Her unhealed exile also affected me, causing me untold agony and concern about my physical well being.

As her "favorite" child, I was a frequent source of anxiety for my mother who worried excessively about my health. She bought me a back brace to straighten my spine, even though there was nothing wrong with it. She told me several times that she was concerned about me because I was too skinny and might have tuberculosis, which scared the hell out of me. One day, she fretfully stared into my face with her eyes narrowed and said that my eyes were crossed. They weren't. Another time, when I was twelve or so, she again stared at me and then, with a serious and anxious tone, said, "What's wrong with you?" Again, it scared me. I couldn't imagine what she was seeing. It was nothing.

After many episodes of mother's anxiety about my health, I developed a fear of my own, becoming somewhat of a hypochondriac. Thanks to her anxiety, I developed an exile that fearfully made a potential catastrophe out of virtually every bump I noticed or pain I felt. Fortunately, I didn't turn into a Howard Hughes or Woody Allen character, but I've suffered through many anxious days and nights over symptoms and minor ailments that were just a part of life in a physical body.

It's important at this juncture to understand that exiles are not only formed by some horrible event like forcible rape, witnessing a murder, or being locked in a closet. When an infant or small child is left alone too many times or for too long, an exile will likely be created. Being the butt of an ongoing joke in the family can be so painful that an exile might form. Being shamed during potty training can do it as well. Exiles can even be created in small children when their parents occasionally insinuate that they are fat, not smart, lazy, or selfish. In fact, there are an infinite number of ways a baby or child can be hurt, frightened, or shamed sufficiently to develop an exile. Most people have several exiles that have never been dealt with or attended to because they're hardly even aware that the exiles exist. It's incredible that these barely known parts of ourselves can have such a huge impact on how we live and how we love. Just like the organs of our bodies, our exiles and their protective parts will continue to operate without our awareness until we wake up.

Because an exiled part is in a virtual time warp, it continues to be frightened by situations that are perfectly harmless or that can be easily resolved by a thinking, rational adult. For example, many males have an exiled part that, when confronted with an angry wife, can't tell the difference between her and an unhappy, punishing mother from the distant past. The exiled parts of these husbands will often unconsciously experience a wife as their frightening, impossible-to-please mother, causing a protective part to react with defensiveness, anger, or withdrawal. This reactivity is often so overblown and irrational that it should be obvious that something is not right.

I've also seen wives whose exiles get stirred up at a husband's irritation or mild anger because they were traumatized as little girls by their fathers' out-of-control anger or rage. An anxious wife in the presence of her husband's anger might regress back to an exiled, childlike state and try to mitigate his angry feelings by excessively soothing or placating him. Other wives, triggered by a husband's anger, might react with anger of their own. Without realizing it, in stressful situations with their husbands, many wives unconsciously experience their dads instead of their husbands. Their protective part doesn't realize that a partner's anger is only a temporary feeling that will pass and that no harm will come to them (unless he's prone to violence).

Of course, it's understandable and can even be healthy for

a wife to help her husband regulate his angry feelings; but it's often counterproductive when her exile causes her to feel such disproportionate anxiety that she feels *compelled* to calm him down to avoid harm. In this case, her calming behaviors could easily escalate her husband's anger.

A good example of this happened to a middle-aged male client of mine whose wife grew up with an angry and punitive father. Her vulnerable, frightened exile would get triggered in the car every time he yelled with frustration at another driver. Her exile's protector would respond with something like, "There's no reason to be upset. I've seen you do the same thing he just did." Or, "He's not a son of a bitch; he just made a mistake."

These "calming" attempts might be acceptable and even helpful at the right time, but *not* when my client was flooded with angry chemicals. Her anxious exile activated a protective part in her that used an unnecessary strategy to calm him down. That got him a lot more riled up with *her* than with the errant driver because *his* protective part felt like he couldn't express a feeling without her trying to shut it down.

As I mentioned above, there are a host of experiences that can cause an exile to form in one's psyche. The most common exiles, however, are created when infants/children have inadequate or unhealthy relationships with their mothers or primary caregivers. As detailed in an upcoming attachment chapter, important parts of babies' brains develop according to their relationship with their mother.

When mothers are dependably affectionate, nurturing, attuning, and supportive to their babies and provide consistent physical contact, infants will feel securely attached and emotionally safe. If, however, the mothers are unable to fill these essential developmental needs, the babies' survival systems will experience overwhelming feelings of need, fear, and even rage.

These traumatizing experiences with the mother cause injuries to the psyche that become deeply wounded exiles. And until those exiles are successfully dealt with, all future committed love relationships will struggle with intimacy and connection, and neither partner will understand why.

Chapter 8:

The Protectors

HAVE YOU EVER spent the morning loving and snuggling with your partner and then by noon you're so angry at him that you don't want to speak to him? How can something as powerful as love be turned off like a faucet by an argument or hurt feelings? And once it's turned off, why would someone choose to keep it that way by angrily sulking for hours or days? If you were in your right mind, why would you consciously choose to stay with the hurt, angry, and disconnected feelings over the warmth of understanding, forgiveness, and empathy? It's essential at this point to understand that when you choose to stay angry and hurt, you're not in your right mind. *Your normal adult mind has been taken over by a protective part.*

To avoid being traumatized again and again by overwhelming feelings from past wounds, the human brain evolved to create what Freud called defenses. Internal Family Systems theory calls those defenses *protective parts.* These parts have only one job: to keep our exiles from getting triggered and coming to the surface of our conscious minds. In other words, the protectors are there to keep us from re-experiencing childhood trauma and the painful memories, thoughts, and feelings that go with it. Unfortunately, protective parts don't worry about the feelings or well-being of one's partner; they are only concerned with keeping the exiles safe.

The protectors do this in two ways: managing our environment so that we don't get triggered and if that strategy doesn't work, a different part of us uses attacking, retreating, or freezing to prevent us from having to deal with overwhelming feelings of abandonment, terror, shame, or rage. Dr. Schwartz calls these parts proactive managers and reactive firefighters.

Proactive Managers

These protectors are designed to manage our environments, ourselves, and even other people so that our exiles don't get triggered. Their strategies might include compulsive caretaking and pleasing to make sure no one is ever displeased with us. These caretaking behaviors are also designed to take our minds off our own frozen needs that were never met in childhood. Another managing strategy is designed to control the world around us in an effort to reassure and assuage a frightened and anxious exile traumatized as a toddler by chaos and unpredictability.

Excessive pride can mask a painful memory/story of shame and humiliation experienced as a child. Exiles created by fighting, screaming parents will often create protective managers who go to great lengths to avoid upsetting loved ones, because conflict brings up memories of those past traumatic episodes.

One of my managing protectors created a pattern of pleasing people because I needed approval, appreciation, and love. I also tried to please everyone around me because I couldn't handle *anyone* being mad at me. Since my exiled part believed that anger at me was a sign that I would be punished or abandoned, I tried especially hard to please my partners. If a partner became angry or upset with me, I apologized profusely to stop her angry feelings. If that didn't work, my reactive firefighter attacked her right back to keep me from feeling threatened, frightened, or ashamed.

Like everyone, I came by my exiles and firefighters honestly. When I was a young boy, my dad's frustration turned into out-of-control anger, which often led to a beating with his belt. It wasn't just the pain of his belt; it was also the look of rage and hatred on his face that terrified me. And because he was six feet tall to my three feet, he must have seemed like a giant to me. I can only imagine how I would feel today if a twelve-foot man grabbed me and jerked me around in a fit of rage while he prepared to whip me with his belt.

When she was stressed or anxious, the love my mother felt for me seemed to vanish, often replaced by a wave of anger that left her shaming and blaming me. Most of the time, she was a pretty good mom, but those times when she came after me were hurtful and frightening. I desperately needed her to soothe me and assure me that everything was going to be all right, but she had trouble expressing tenderness and caring. When her frustration and anger caused her heart to close, I'm sure I must have felt alone and abandoned, with no one to turn to and nowhere to go.

As a little boy with few defenses, I had to face overwhelming emotions of fear, abandonment, and rage and had no way to deal with them. Those early experiences left memories emblazoned in my psyche that were filled with terror, shame, and a rage for vengeance that comes from being treated harshly and unfairly.

These are not the emotions I want rushing out at Jenny because she complained that I forgot to buy cream for her coffee. My managing protectors not only try to keep my extreme feelings at bay, but they also work overtime in our relationship to keep her happy and pleased. If my pleasing efforts failed and she became irritated or upset with me, my manager part would then immediately start with a mea culpa and a string of apologies. When that didn't assuage her upset, my firefighter came on the scene yelling, defending, and trying everything it knew to shut her down. Unfortunately for me, there was nothing my parts could do to accomplish that task.

One of Jenny's protective managers is a reflection of her avoidant attachment style. Because of the neglect and emotional deprivation she suffered as a baby and small child, she developed a protective strategy that essentially closed off a part of her heart. She couldn't risk being vulnerable in relationships because she might get hurt again, which would open up the Pandora's box of terrifying and painful feelings she'd endured before.

Jenny told me shortly after we met that she had trouble letting love in. She said that she felt it when she hugged her spouse, children, and friends, but felt no warmth or positive feelings when they hugged her or expressed love. Her protective manager was making sure she never let down her guard, lest she fall victim to those horrible feelings from her past. If she never opened the door to her deepest self, no one could ever come in and break her heart again.

I've had several clients who were witty and if I let them, would spend much of our sessions trying to entertain me with vignettes and humorous stories about themselves and their families. When I attempted to guide them toward their emotions and the issues they brought into therapy, their protective managers often caused them to get sleepy or to veer off the subject to avoid opening up and being vulnerable.

Others intellectualized everything we talked about. They reported painful and even traumatic events from their childhoods with no emotion, as though they were reading them from a newspaper. Their managing protectors made sure they wouldn't be dealing with the overwhelming emotions of their exiles. Mental health professionals often call this phenomenon *resistance*.

An extreme case of this took place in my early twenties while I was in therapy following my anxiety attacks. I began each session smoking a cigar, drinking a Coke, and chewing gum, using every prop and distraction I could to avoid dealing with what felt like overwhelming emotions hidden just below the surface of my conscious mind. My protective manager was hard at work, trying to protect an exiled part that was terrified of feeling anything powerful because it might result in another horrible attack of emotions.

My fear at the time kept me from realizing that expressing all my feelings was *exactly* what I needed to do. It had been my *unexpressed* emotions that caused the anxiety attacks in the first place.

Protectors can take many different forms, but they are always there to help us avoid painful or frightening feelings. A protector might drive us to succeed so that we don't have to face the pain and shame of being the failure we've always been afraid of. Even shopping, television, or porn can be protective strategies to distract us from inner pain and anxiety. The human psyche is resourceful and has no limits when it comes to creating protectors and strategies to help us avoid the psychological and emotional agony of our past hurts and wounds.

One of the more common and powerful protective managers is anxiety, which tries to control certain situations around us so that we can avoid the frightful or even terrifying feelings beneath. This anxiety plagues love relationships because it shows up in areas like money, attachment, sex, and self-esteem.

Partners who are anxious about money, for instance, will likely try to control their loved ones' reasonable spending habits by showing disapproval when they buy something new, spend "too much" on groceries or the kids, or give too much to charity. A strategy to control a partner's spending might include shaming, blaming, angry intimidation, or temporary withdrawal of love and positive regard. In extreme cases, it could involve taking away checkbooks or credit cards. These anxious partners think they're trying to keep from going broke, but the real truth might be that they have a desperate, frozen need for security and believe that money will fill that need. Every time their loved ones spend "too much" money, their needy, frightened exiles get stirred up, and their protective manager part starts its controlling strategy.

I'm familiar with this real and problematic type of anxiety. As a boy, I witnessed the intense worry about bills and finances that my mom and dad dealt with on a regular basis. Sometimes they fought and argued during breakfast about who spent the most money on unnecessary things. Then they would leave for work to spend eight hours of their lives at soul-killing, repetitive jobs. They were stuck in a financial purgatory with no apparent way out.

Their painful plight had a tremendous effect on me, leaving me to vow that I would never, ever allow myself to be in that position. Terrified of being trapped in an unhappy relationship or enslaved in a boring, meaningless job, I developed a belief that money was a get-out-of-jail-free card that could protect me from the angst-filled, unhappy life my parents endured.

What I never realized as a boy was that my parents were deeply wounded emotionally and that most of their fighting and arguing was a reflection of those wounds, not a lack of money. But once that exile was created in me, I was stuck with it for most of my life. No matter how well I did financially, it was never enough for me to feel secure.

As an example of how insidious and toxic anxiety can be, I'll share an experience Jenny and I had while vacationing in Santa Fe. We decided to have dinner at a fun pizza place with an upstairs veranda that overlooked the city. It was a beautiful, romantic evening with a sky full of stars above and twinkling city lights below.

We each ordered a slice of pizza, and she wanted a glass of wine as well. The wine was expensive, and I felt myself shifting in my seat with some nervous energy. Then she decided to get her pizza with truffle oil sprinkled on it, which cost an extra five bucks. Suddenly our fifteen dollar meal was going to run upwards of thirty dollars.

With my anxious part in charge, I gave Jenny a look of disapproval and talked about how ridiculous it was for the restaurant to charge us almost as much for the truffle oil as it did for the pizza. I then continued with a few remarks about how restaurants exploit customers by overcharging for drinks and extras.

Jenny tried to laugh it off, but she was hurt because it seemed to her that she wasn't important enough for me to spend a little extra money on her preferences. She had an exile that was activated because her parents rarely let her choose meals at restaurants, claiming they were "too expensive." With my managing part and her offended protector part triggered, our nice, romantic evening had abruptly ended.

It's important to note that if someone had asked me if I'd risk hurting Jenny's feelings over fifteen dollars, I'd have said, "No, of course not!" But I did. And I had done it several times on our trip, unwittingly activating an exile in her that felt disregarded, unimportant, and unloved.

Of course, I loved her deeply. It's just that at certain times and in certain situations, my anxious exile, terrified of going broke, became upset. When that happened, my protective part took over, making it impossible to *see* Jenny, and certainly unable to be in touch with her wants, needs, or desires. It took some time to realize it, but I finally got it that my anxious "money part" didn't care at all about Jenny; it only cared about "squandering" money that I might need someday. It's essential to understand that our various protective parts do not care about the well-being or happiness of others; their only purpose is to protect us from the extreme feelings and memories of the exiles.

At least I'm not alone with my fears around money. Recently, while having breakfast with two friends, Jenny and I witnessed an anxious exile and its protective part in action. We were all happy and having a great time until "Mary's" anxiety over money came out of the closet. "Bill," her husband ordered pancakes and specifically asked for real maple syrup, even though it cost an extra three dollars for a very small container. When he ordered a second container of syrup, Mary chastised him, saying that he already had plenty of syrup and spending the extra three dollars was wasteful.

Her reaction brought an air of tension to the table. The happy, carefree atmosphere was gone. Then it got much worse. Bill, seeing that I was out of syrup, ordered yet another container. Mary was livid. As soon as the new syrup arrived on the table, she was overwhelmed by an angry firefighter part and proceeded to grab the container and dump the whole thing on his plate, drowning his remaining pancake. As she dumped the syrup, she yelled out, "There! Do you think that's going to be enough? Or should we order another one?"

Jenny and I were shocked as a momentary silence took over the meal. Mary, a lovely person (and independently wealthy), regained her senses and apologized for her behavior. Unless a protective part is triggered, she would never knowingly hurt someone else's feelings. Although she loved her husband very much, her irrational anxiety about money caused her to react in a way that hurt him and put a big damper on what would have been a fun breakfast.

Whether it's about money, sex, self-esteem, or attachment,

anxiety can play havoc in a relationship. In the grasp of anxiety, a partner will say or do most anything to quell those scary feelings underneath. That includes attacking an innocent mate or shutting them out.

Jenny used to get anxious every time we were getting ready to leave on a trip and most of the time, I paid a price. Edgy and easily irritated, she often became critical, pointing out how I didn't pack this or that or didn't plan far enough in advance. It wasn't a fun way to start a trip.

As you continue to work on yourself and your relationship, it will pay big dividends to become aware of the various ways anxiety affects you and your partner. If people are anxious or insecure about their competence or intelligence, they might argue intensely or even get ugly to their partners in an attempt to prove that they're right. If they have attachment anxiety, they might try to control their spouses' behavior so that they won't feel jealous or fearful of abandonment. If they are anxious about their sexual prowess, they might not tolerate any feedback about their sexual performance.

Make no mistake about it: anxiety can wreck a love relationship. Anais Nin, an influential author and philosopher said, "Anxiety is love's greatest killer…" As you explore this toxic phenomenon, you'll more than likely understand that Nin was not exaggerating. Underneath the anxiety is always a frightened and vulnerable exile with a wound.

In committed love relationships, an anxious partner's protective manager will often sabotage a loved one's attempts at closeness, intimacy, and connection. If the anxious partner's beloved gets too close for comfort, his or her manager part will often use strategies like shutting down emotionally, changing the subject with a distraction, or even starting a fight.

If you can become aware of how your protective parts operate to keep you "safe" with your partner, you will have made an important first step toward changing yourself and the relationship.

Chapter 9:

Reactive Firefighters

WHEN THE MANAGING protectors' strategy breaks down and an exile is triggered and threatens to surface, alarm bells go off and a *firefighter* part gets activated. The strategies of the firefighters are more drastic and usually cause more damage than the managers because there's a psychological or emotional "fire" in the psyche that feels menacing to our well-being. That fire needs to be put out before it gets out of hand. My friend's syrup episode is a good example of the mess a firefighter can make.

Firefighters use reptilian approaches to defend exiles from perceived threats or harm. Those approaches are primitive and usually involve some form of attacking, retreating, or freezing. When firefighter parts get involved in interpersonal relationships, there will usually be a mess of hurt feelings, anger, and resentment.

Firefighter attacks include lashing out at the offending party with name-calling, biting criticism, defensiveness, blame, and threats. In extreme cases, firefighters might even use physical violence to protect an exile. Someone with a different personality might have firefighters that retreat by quickly raising the white flag while apologizing profusely to soothe the offending person and assuage their anger or threatening behavior. If that strategy doesn't work, the retreating part may abruptly leave the threatening person or situation. Men and women who abhor conflicts might have firefighter parts that withdraw and shut out a "threatening" partner to lessen whatever hurt might be coming their way. This freezing strategy uses withdrawal as a way of protecting the exile and its emotions. By withdrawing into one's protective shell, the heart and mind can be closed, effectively cutting off connection and any kind of meaningful interaction.

Notice that the three strategies of the firefighters are reflective of the reptilian/survival brain. Our rational, thinking selves are not consulted by the firefighters and are basically MIA during their reign. When the firefighters take control of our normal selves in a relationship, there will usually be a fight or conflict of some kind. It's especially tough when the firefighters of both partners are activated and in attack mode at the same time. In this case, there is no rational Self or Captain available to bring reason and calm to a messy situation. Instead, the childlike firefighters are trying to put out the fire by spraying gasoline on it.

Earlier I mentioned that I can't tolerate someone being mad at me, especially a love partner. When Jenny is angry at me, my exiles get activated, and those feelings of fear, shame, and rage start roiling around in my psyche, threatening to surface. When my repeated apologies and repair efforts don't placate Jenny's anger, my firefighter switches strategies, using the attack mode to spew angry, hurtful words and hostile looks.

This particular firefighter showed up one evening years ago when a woman I was living with came home from work and, picking up a dish sponge on the counter, made a modest complaint about it being left wet. She said I'd left it that way before, and the next day it was slimy and had a mildew smell, which really turned her off.

Immediately taken over by an attacking firefighter part, I

exploded. "How can you bitch about a fucking sponge after all I do for you? I pay the mortgage, do the cooking, take care of the yard, and do a lot of the cleaning up around here. Would it really be *that hard* to just rinse it out? Are you the fucking princess around here, bitching about a sponge?" And so it went.

My firefighter took over my normal self because my managing protector hadn't done its job perfectly. Although I'd tried to support and please her as best as I could, I screwed up with the sponge, leaving her momentarily unhappy with me. To my frightened exile underneath it all, her discontent meant she didn't love me. While it seems incredible that her comments about the sponge could bring about such a torrent of anger and upset in a normally rational person, it's not that strange if you look at what her reaction meant to that insecure part of me.

To that irrational, little boy exile, it seemed like she was using me; wasn't grateful for anything I'd done for her; wasn't happy with me; didn't love me; and, most importantly, might even decide to leave me. Thinking those things could easily bring up feelings of righteous indignation and worse, the terror of abandonment and being alone and unloved. The prospect of feeling all those things lit up my firefighter part. My regrettable overreaction demonstrated why my protective manager had worked so hard to keep my exile buried in the basement.

If we dug into my psyche a little further, I'm sure we'd find another part that deeply resented having to go out of my way to please a woman just to get her to love me. Why should I have to try so hard? Why couldn't she just love me for who I am and not for what I do for her? So beneath all that nice behavior is another opposing part that doesn't buy into that pleasing stuff at all. Thus, not only do we have various parts to our personality, those parts can sometimes have conflicting agendas. Whether they are conflicting with one another or not, there is one thing you can be sure with respect to extreme parts:

they continue making messes as they try to protect exiles that no longer need protection.

There is a true story about Japanese soldiers in the 1960s that is an excellent analogy for the protector parts of our psyches. The soldiers were shooting at American tourists who happened to sail their boats too close to certain tiny islands in the South Pacific. Incredibly, these soldiers, stranded on the islands by the Japanese military at the end of World War II, still believed the war was going on twenty years later. The soldiers had survived and kept their weapons in good working order while maintaining a readiness to fight whatever American enemies might show up. They were still fighting a war that had ended two decades earlier!

Our protector parts, like the well-intentioned but misguided soldiers, fight against enemies and situations that no longer exist. Created from painful and frightening experiences in infancy and early childhood, our parts have been kept alive and in a state of readiness in the memory systems of the reptilian/survival brain. In many cases, we don't even know what the memories are because they reflect hurts and trauma that happened before conscious memory was possible.

This is why the protectors can be so perplexing at first glance. It's impossible to know why they react in such apparently bizarre and destructive ways. It's natural for us to try to rationalize and explain the behavior of our protectors, but we may not have a clue as to what is going on. This is a major reason why therapy or other kinds of detective work are often necessary to get to the bottom of our unresolved emotional and psychological wounds.

An example of an extreme reaction due to a firefighter took place while Jenny and I were making the three-hour drive from Austin back to our ranch. After an hour or so, I became too sleepy to drive and asked Jenny if she minded taking over for a while so that I could lie across the back seat and catch a little sleep. I asked her not to speed because without a seatbelt I'd be vulnerable. I'd been in a horrible head-on collision that killed one person and put five others in the hospital. At the time of the accident, I was sleeping in the passenger seat while a friend was driving *and* speeding.

On this particular trip with Jenny driving and me lying in the back seat, I noticed that the van seemed to be going faster than usual. Happily listening to some of her favorite songs on the MP3 player, she was apparently unaware that the van was whizzing along at eighty miles per hour. I leaned up, saw the speedometer, and kind of playfully said, "Hey, you're speeding." She nodded her head and slowed down.

After about ten minutes I again noticed that the car was going fast, and, once more, I leaned up, looked at the speedometer and said, "You're speeding." She didn't respond in any way, so I decided to sit up and put my seatbelt on.

Shortly thereafter, I saw Jenny jerk off the earphones and slam them down on the seat beside her. When I asked her if everything was OK, she stared straight ahead, saying nothing. I asked her again and still nothing.

Finally, in a curt voice she spewed out, "I don't like to be corrected."

Struggling with disbelief, I said, "But all I said was, 'you're speeding.' I was getting a little scared back here and just wanted you to slow down a bit." I reminded her that she'd agreed not to speed while I was lying down in the back.

Completely taken over by a protective firefighter part, she loudly continued, "If you were so worried about your safety, why in the hell didn't you just sit up and put your seatbelt on? Here I am, taking over so you can relax in the back and you're nitpicking about my driving. You want to lie in the back and control me and tell me what to do and how to do it, and I don't like it."

I thought, "Oh my God, she's lost it and gone over the edge." Although her anger scared and confused me, I tried to stay as calm as I could. "Jenny, I wasn't trying to control you. It had nothing to do with that. I was nervous. You were doing eighty, and if we had a wreck at that speed with me in the back, I'd end up dead or crippled for life." I tried to reason with her, but she was so flooded with angry chemicals, she couldn't hear a word I said.

"Everybody wants to tell me what to do, and I'm sick of it. You're not my parent, and you're sure as hell not my boss, and you don't get to control me or push me around."

In those few moments, it seemed as though she was possessed. And, in fact, she was. She was possessed by the forcing part that we mentioned earlier in the exile section. When her protective firefighter took over her normal self, she was unable to hear me or relate to me in her usual way. The fact that she loved me and wouldn't want to hurt my feelings, and certainly wouldn't want to have me seriously injured or killed, was completely irrelevant at that moment. None of that mattered to a firefighter part that was only concerned with protecting that little, vulnerable girl or exile, whose fear and rage at being controlled was stirring and pushing toward the surface.

I want to emphasize again that the primitive protectors were formed early in life under stressful and even traumatic conditions and didn't have the luxury of being vetted or thought through. Our parts and their strategies have been embedded into the psyche and frozen in time; they are unaware that we've grown up and now have more resources than we did when the traumatic events happened.

As adults, we don't need the outdated and mostly unhelpful protective strategies to deal with life's slings and arrows. Jenny didn't need a firefighter to protect her little girl exile from being forced. My pointing out that she was speeding was in no way a threat to her, but because of the pre-existing condition of her wounded exile, her firefighter part caused her to overreact. As adults, the huge majority of us could easily handle slights, criticisms, and various hurt feelings without overreacting and getting all worked up. Unfortunately, our protective parts, believing we can't deal with uncomfortable feelings, jump in and make a mess.

The truth is, we *can* handle distressing situations reasonably, and not only that, most of us can safely and effectively deal with those traumatic memories and experiences from the distant past. We don't really need to be protected from them anymore. As adults, we can experience the frightening emotions and move through them, especially in the presence of a good therapist or a wise, compassionate friend. And by doing this, we can begin the process of healing our exiles once and for all.

To change ourselves and our circumstances, we need to address the wounded and vulnerable inner child parts of ourselves. Once those exiles have been tended to with compassion, empathy, and understanding, we can help our protective parts learn new strategies that actually get us what we want. True safety, trust, confidence, self-empowerment, intimacy, and love are waiting for us to solve the riddle of our wounds. Fortunately, there's a way to accomplish that, and it's inside you right now.

Chapter 10:

The True Self or Captain

PROTECTIVE PARTS HAVE many tools and strategies to achieve their goals. Deceit, judging, accusing, blaming, defending, withdrawing, stonewalling, attacking, denying, righteous indignation, closing the heart, and threatening are some of the more common ways protectors use to keep the exiles "safe" when they are "threatened" by a love partner's behavior, attitudes, body language, or words. Thankfully, there is a special part in each of us that has the potential to stay calm and act like an adult in the midst of the turmoil, while it sorts out the truth in the moment and makes a decision to act in a healthy and wise way. Dr. Schwartz calls this special part of our mind the True Self.

Jenny and I prefer to use the term Captain to describe this amazing resource that, when used wisely, can help you change your life and your relationships. You might call it your Real Self, your Essence, your God Within, or whatever suits you. The important thing is that you understand that this is a very special part of you that can work wonders in your life if you develop it and allow it to lead you. This special part of you can deal with, reeducate, and repurpose your unhealthy protective parts. And when developed, it can intervene when your parts are triggered. When trained and strengthened, this marvelous essence can also detect your more subtle parts when they are making sneaky little pokes and prods that seem well-intentioned but are compromised and contaminated by surreptitious agendas.

Jenny and I like to use Captain to describe that special part of ourselves because we created a particular analogy that helps us understand the dynamics between the parts, exiles, and Captain. We think of our True Selves as captains of our ships of life and the protective parts as stowaways on the ship. The exiles are the treasures hidden away in the lower deck. When faced with threatening weather, the fearful stowaways, afraid of losing the treasure, rush to the wheel on the top deck and wrest it away from the Captain even though they know nothing about operating the vessel.

If the Captain is weak and underdeveloped, the stowaways can easily knock him or her from the wheel and take over. Given their ignorance about ships and navigation, the stowaways (parts) get off course, run sideways into waves, and may even end up ripping the sails, making a big mess. Then, fatigued from all their activity, they retire to their hiding places, leaving the Captain to return and clean up the mess. Many times the stowaways rush to the deck and push the Captain out of the way when the slightest breeze ruffles the waves or innocuous clouds drift across the horizon. In other words, the stowaways might get activated and make a mess when there is not even a threat of harm coming from anywhere. Like protective parts, the stowaways often see and react to problems when there are none.

Continuing with the ship analogy, our Captains are wise, capable, and always have a destination for the ship. For instance, Jenny and I have as destinations intimacy, connection, safety, fun, peace, joy, and contentment. As long as our Captains are in charge of our "ships of life," we are headed in that direction. However, when our stowaways or parts take over or share the wheel with our Captains, we get off course and occasionally get temporarily lost. Only when our Captains are in charge of the wheel of our ship (or in charge of our conscious minds) can we get back on track toward our destination.

For the sake of simplicity, the remainder of the book will continue to use protective manager, firefighter, and exile to describe the various wounded parts of the psyche. We will use Captain instead of the Self, however, to refer to that special essence or god-like quality within because it feels right to us.

With the Captain in control as the centerpiece of our personality, we are more able to make good decisions and set life-affirming priorities. It is not our parts, but our enlightened Captain that should be the keeper of our moral compass, distinguishing right from wrong and choosing the best course of action in any given circumstance. It is our Captain who can reach out to our partner with heartfelt apologies and repair efforts.

According to Dr. Schwartz, our Self or Captain is curious, wanting to understand others instead of judging them. This beacon of light is also compassionate, genuinely cares about other people, and is capable of loving and feeling loved. Open and vulnerable, our Captain is ready to connect with the Captains of others.

There are many reasons to aspire to live a Captain-led life, but for the purposes of this book, it is the Captain's ability to therapeutically interact with our wounded exiles and protective parts that will get most of our attention. According to IFS theory, the Captain can be an "agent of psychological healing," not only for yourself but for your partner as well.

It's amazing that each of us has this wonderful, awesome Captain that could transform our lives into something we've only dreamed of, and yet we're pretty much unaware of it.

Based on my experiences and observations, I believe that the huge majority of people are living out their lives in what might be called their "normal selves." They're busy earning a living, raising kids, negotiating relationships, and dealing with their inner turmoil. Because we think, feel, and act from this normal self, we're convinced that it is who we are. We don't understand that our everyday selves are mostly just a composite of parts dedicated to getting through another week while protecting our egos and keeping our traumatized exiles in the basement. To experience the inner leadership that can change our lives, we need to find a way to bring the Captain on board.

One way I've learned to find my Captain is to get very quiet, take some deep breaths, and focus on relaxing my arms, legs, torso, neck, and face. Once I feel calm and relaxed, I think about how much I care for my wife, one of my children, or even the planet I live on. I quietly continue deep breathing, thinking heartfelt, loving thoughts of gratitude and appreciation until I notice a peaceful, contented, and grounded feeling. Continuing to relax, I then let my loving thoughts settle onto at least one other person for a couple of minutes. I am now in my Captain.

The challenge is *staying* in my Captain. If I begin to worry or get anxious, think negative thoughts, or become reactive to some perceived threat, I'm probably not in my Captain. For most of us, learning to live a Captain-led life will take training, intention, effort, and even courage. To do this, we must break out of our ego shell and jettison our prideful, righteous indignation. Of course, our protective parts, used to running the show, will resist changes that are counter to their protective agendas. Because of that resistance, Jenny and I began this journey by trying to be in our Captains for only a minute at a time. Gradually, we worked our way up to a few hours a day and the difference in our levels of intimacy and connection was amazing.

Today, although we may not be in our Captains even most of the time, our "normal selves" are much less anxious and reactive. When we have conflicts, we rarely defend, attack, or withdraw as strongly as before. Because of the influence of our respective Captains, we have become different people. I'm not one to talk about miracles, but to feel like we do after all we've been through, it's not all that outlandish.

Chapter 11:

Parts Blending With the Captain

IN IFS TERMINOLOGY, when our Captain is being influenced by a protective part, it is *blended*. When this happens, we cannot be completely present in the moment and our ability to be fair, compassionate, and rational is compromised. Blending occurs on a continuum and could be likened to stirring a small amount of mud into a glass of clear water. Less than a quarter of a teaspoon of mud might not cloud the water much at all, while a tablespoon might turn the water opaque. The more blended we are, the less we can see and understand what's going on around us. Instead of perceiving the current reality, we're reacting to the stories our parts are telling us about it. Although blended people believe they're seeing and thinking clearly, they're only experiencing their own distorted versions of reality at that moment.

Using our analogy about being the Captain of our ships, Jenny and I believe that when blending takes place, the "stowaway" has hold of the steering wheel along with the Captain and is negatively affecting the course of the vessel. When this happens there is a *shift* that has taken place which limits and compromises the Captain's ability to function in a positive way. These shifts are common in love relationships and play a huge role in conflicts, misunderstandings, and the deterioration of trust.

Sometimes a shift takes place without either partner realizing what is happening. For instance, in robust discussions about things like national politics, religion, money, or sex, the stowaway or protective part will grab the wheel and steer the ship in a negative direction. In this case, it looks and sounds like the Captain speaking, but it's actually a Captain compromised by a part.

This often happens when, in the middle of the dialogue, one of us makes an insensitive remark or uses an inflammatory word that offends the other. Without either of us realizing it, the offended partner becomes blended and then, with emotions gradually surfacing, starts raising his or her voice, getting more intense, and finally saying something personally offensive. Then a full-blown argument often ensues, with both of our protective parts leading us into a very unhappy evening.

It's important at this juncture to know that blending happens without our awareness and without our permission. Shifting into a part is an unconscious reflex that our survival brain uses to protect us, nothing more and nothing less. It's critical to understand this because there are times when your partner becomes blended without even realizing it. Because it is a mental/emotional reflex, he or she is literally taken over by a part and cannot help it. Although it seems counter-intuitive, in an important way, it's not your partner's fault for behaving in an irrational or unpleasant way. And it's not your fault either when you get blended.

I've found an analogy that really helped me understand blending in a way that fosters compassion and even forgiveness. In the story of Dr. Jekyll and Mr. Hyde, the doctor is a socially graceful gentleman with a good heart and a caring attitude. But when he takes a particular potion he developed, he turns into someone who still looks like the good doctor but has now morphed into a sinister ogre who is capable of cruel and malevolent behavior.

When we get taken over by an exile or protective part, it's very much like someone has slipped a potion in our drink that causes us to think, feel, and behave in a way that is contrary to our normal selves. We look like the same person we were before the shift took place, but we're not. Although it is true that the potion came from us, it is also true that it was administered without our consent or knowledge. And once we've consumed it, we think we're still in our normal selves and that we're just upset. We don't realize that, in an important way, we've become someone who thinks, feels, and behaves differently than our normal selves. Understanding this helps a person develop a little compassion for their blended partner.

Sometimes, if only our managing protectors are involved, we might be just a little blended and can still mostly think and act from the perspective of our usual selves. In other words, we're just a little bit contaminated. This partial blending has happened many times with Jenny and me. For instance, she might suggest that we fly up to Minnesota to visit her dad. Since I'm not a big fan of flying (OK, I'm a fearful flier), I'm going to have a managing protector get in on the conversation.

If she doesn't push me, my response will be influenced by my protector, but I'll still manage to mostly talk and listen as my usual self. I'll make excuses about money, the inconvenience of airports, and all the chores I should be doing rather than taking off for a couple of weeks. So I'm just partially blended.

But if she pushes me, my firefighter might get involved, completely usurping my Captain. I'm now angry and ready to attack, retreat, or freeze. In that case, my firefighter would probably start with an attack of some kind, blaming her for wanting to waste money on a whim. Of course, that's ridiculous because I like to do things on a whim and I don't mind spending money either. It's just that when my firefighter part gets activated and takes over, I usually react like an idiot.

Because it's important, we'll remind you throughout the book that it's not your fault your protective parts take over, but it *is* your responsibility to learn strategies to minimize the hurt and damage caused by them. It's also your responsibility to make permanent changes to your exiles and parts so as to minimize or even eliminate the harm you do to your partner and your relationship. Later chapters are designed to help you do both.

Chapter 12:

Summary of the Captain and the Parts

LIKE OUR PHYSICAL bodies, our psyches are systems made up of different parts that can interact with each other or function separately, depending on the situation. These parts are designed to protect us from overwhelming emotions like terror, shame and humiliation, abandonment anxiety, and rage.

Exiles are the hidden parts of our minds that contain the traumatic memories or stories of what happened in our pasts. Although our protector parts don't realize it, they are created by our psyches to protect us from the pain and terror that the exiles have stored within them.

Managing protectors are proactive and strive to control the environment to prevent exiles from being triggered and releasing their frightening and painful emotions into the conscious mind. Reactive firefighters are designed to take immediate action when managing protectors' strategies don't work. If the exiles are triggered and nearing the surface, the firefighters employ strategies like attacking, retreating, or freezing to keep them at bay.

The Captains are the true centers of our beings and are curious, confident, capable, creative, courageous, and compassionate. The wisdom of this inner Self can guide us toward priorities and decisions that are best for us, for others, and for our planet. This sacred Self is our essence and is always there beneath the chatter, the hurts, the disappointments, and the anxieties we've accumulated over the years. Connection, intimacy, and authentic love happen naturally when we're in the Self or Captain. The Captain can also be a powerful agent for healing our emotional wounds and reeducating our protective parts. As we do the necessary work, we will be able to develop and access the Captain more often and for longer periods of time.

Please keep this paragraph in mind as you and your partner begin this work of transformation. The shell around our hearts and minds is made of our defenses (exiles and protective parts) that were created to protect us from pain and fear. When that shell is confronted by our well- or not-so-well-intentioned partners, it feels like *we* are being attacked. But the attack is almost always against the shell and our unhealthy attitudes and behaviors, not against us. Remember that we are *not* our shells or defenses. We are wonderful human beings with a shell of protection around us. It is that *shell* that causes trouble in love relationships. This is essential to understand when you and your partner start getting real with each other. *In a huge majority of cases, your partner's problem is not with you, it's with your defensive parts and their unhealthy strategies.*

Adults who experienced excessive pain or trauma as infants or very young children can't remember the events because their cortexes weren't developed enough to store those types of memories in the brain. Instead, these memories are stored in the emotional body as feelings and are often called *implicit* memories. They could be positive feelings like being loved, soothed, mirrored, and safe. Or they could be feelings like abandonment anxiety or the inexpressible pain of a neglected infant. These implicit memories of hurt and trauma are obviously much harder to access and successfully deal with.

Other painful or traumatic episodes that happen to us later on as small children, or even adults can create *explicit* memories, with remembered images and details that go with the overwhelming feelings of terror, shame, or humiliation. Although these memories are easier to get at than the implicit ones, they are still difficult to access because the protector parts are working to keep us from re-experiencing them. Extreme examples of this are violent rape, witnessing a murder, and experiencing combat in a war. Of course, a parent beating a small child, an unexpected death of a loved one, a traumatic divorce, the loss of a job, and many other experiences that happen in the normal lives of average people can create exiles that will need to be dealt with.

It's important to remember that you and your partner are doing the best you can, considering your life experiences since birth, your genetic makeup, and the cultural and familial environment you grew up in. Give yourselves a break. Neither you nor your partner is perfect and you never will be. Negative thoughts and feelings about yourself or your loved one are never helpful. I'm not suggesting a Pollyanna approach, just one that is honest, realistic, and non-shaming. As we mentioned earlier, it's not your fault that you are the way you are, but it *is* your responsibility to make whatever changes you can to become more self-aware, more compassionate, and more loving. The fact that you are reading this book is an indication that you're looking for answers to improve yourself and your circumstances.

Never forget that there are two essential ways to look at yourself, your partner, and even the world around you. One is through the prism of your defensive-part-infused "normal" self that sees things with a careful, jaundiced eye while maintaining a protective tension "just in case." The other way of seeing is with a Captain-infused heart and reason. With these compassionate eyes, you see the beauty, the potential, and the love that lives within you, your partner, and the whole human race. Yes, everyone has flaws, but focusing on them will not bring you joy, happiness, or a sense of well-being.

    Life is short; learn to see the bigger picture with heart-infused reason rather than focusing on the narrow, fearful view that leaves you feeling small and bereft of joy.

Chapter 13:

Parts and Captains in Action

Over the years, Jenny and I have had many arguments and fights where our protective parts were mostly in charge. With the hope that it will be helpful, I'll demonstrate how our protective parts get involved in a typical fight between us and then illustrate how those fights could have been handled by our Captains.

Jenny loves to have long phone conversations of up to three hours with her siblings, two of her sons, and several friends. Sometimes those long chats involve just talking, while other times she gives the person a sort of therapy/coaching session. These episodes happen fairly frequently, and occasionally, I resent them, especially if they interfere with plans we've made. Other times (especially in the past), I feel disregarded and that the phone calls are more important to her than spending time with me.

We've had several "discussions" about this that didn't go well at all because, at the time, our parts were stronger than our Captains. One of these went something like this:

Jenny's Captain: "I've made a phone date with Margaret for five o'clock."

Marvin's part, with whiny voice: "So does that mean we're not going to have dinner together this evening?"

Jenny's Captain: "Well, I might be through by seven, if you want to wait."

Marvin's part: "You *might* be through at seven? How will I know when to start dinner? Besides, I don't like to eat that late; you know that."

Jenny's faltering Captain: "OK, suit yourself; I'll just eat later."

Marvin's part, getting sneaky: "I know I'm asking a lot, but it *would* be nice to have a sit-down meal together once in a while. You know, like lots of other people do? I can't understand why you have to take calls at mealtimes."

Jenny's annoyed part: "Look, you really don't have to understand. People have lives going on and call me when they can talk. And besides, it's not actually any of your business when I talk on the phone."

Marvin's whiny part shifts into an indignant and angry part: "That was a shitty thing to say. It's none of my business? I'm your husband, and I live with you, and it just seems like I should have a little say about you being on the goddamn phone all the time. You don't think it affects me? Well, it does. And if it affects me, doesn't that mean it might be a little bit my business?"

Jenny's angry part: "Yeah, well it only affects you because you can't stand for me to enjoy myself with anybody else. You need to get over it. Grow up and give me some space. I don't bitch about you playing golf, do I? What if I whined and complained every time you wanted to go play golf? How would you like that?"

Marvin's angry part: "Why do you have to bring up my golf every fucking time we have a fight?"

Jenny's angry part: "Oh, is this a fight? I thought we were just having an intense discussion. I bring up golf to try to get you to understand how it feels to have the person who's supposed to love you always giving you shit about doing the things you want to do. You know, I think you forget that there are two people in this relationship. Why can't you give me the same latitude and freedom I give you?"

Marvin's angry part: "Freedom? Jesus Christ, you don't work, you don't cook, and you don't really do that much around the house. You travel around the country to see your sons, your sisters, and your dad, sometimes staying over two weeks. You do pretty much whatever you want, and you talk about freedom? You just can't stand it when I ask you to change anything about yourself or your behavior."

Jenny's furiously indignant part: "That's it. I'm done talking to you. We're done."

When I say something else, she puts her fingers in her ears while she marches into her bedroom and closes the door behind her.

I scream out, "That's right, you bitch. Just walk off and leave me standing here. That's a great way to end a so-called discussion."

Needless to say, the evenings after such "discussions" rarely went well. When Jenny shuts her door like that, she's closing me out. Then my anxiously attached, exiled little boy feels the threat of abandonment. And when *that* happens, my firefighter part comes out with guns blazing. Interestingly, my protectors never realize that their behavior is driving her further away, creating the very situation that terrifies my little boy exile.

After such an intense fight, my angry, frightened part would usually start a blaming inner dialogue that went ·something like this: "That fucking bitch. She's a spoiled brat. She wants everything her way or no way. All those people she talks to are more important than I am. How did I ever end up with somebody who spends all her time on the goddamn phone? She is the most stubborn woman I've ever known. I'm sick of her!"

If it weren't so tragic, my part's reaction was so far off the mark it would be funny. My angry part gave her grief and then silently castigated and blamed this woman that I usually loved and respected. I skewered her because she talked on the phone more than I would prefer? Yes, hard to believe, but it's happened more than once.

Meanwhile, once in her room, Jenny's parts are talking to her as well.

"What the hell? Why is this *still* going on? He obviously doesn't care about me. Is this ever going to change? He refuses to see my point about golf. What's the use? To hell with him then."

At least in this scenario, Jenny's parts are not as blaming and punitive as mine. Interestingly, we couldn't talk about the phone situation without getting riled up because the issue was charged and the parts were just too close to the surface. More about that later.

The Compromised Captain

Now let's look at the same situation, except with a Captain partially involved.

Jenny's Captain: "I have a phone date with Margaret at five o'clock today."

Marvin's Captain: "Hmm . . . I was planning to have dinner ready at about six-fifteen this evening. Do you think you'll be through with your call by then?"

Jenny's Captain: "Well, I don't know. You know how long some of my calls can take."

Marvin's Captain is getting compromised by a sneaky part's agenda: "Yes, I do. But you *do* have control of how long a phone conversation will take. You can always say you have to go."

Jenny is struggling but still in her Captain: "Marvin, she's a client and she might need more time. I've told you that I let my clients decide how long the session is going to be. It takes as long as it takes."

Marvin's manager part is now posing as the Captain: "Jenny, clients shouldn't have control of the time. You, the therapist, should set boundaries. A session should go on no longer than an hour. A client can't absorb more than that anyway. They teach you that in graduate school."

Feeling pushed, Jenny is shifting into her defensive part: "Just because I'm new at counseling doesn't mean I don't know what I'm doing. And I don't care what they teach in graduate school. I know what I want to do and what works for me and my clients. I've told you that I don't believe in all those rules and guidelines."

Marvin's part is still posing as his Captain: "There are reasons for those guidelines, and if you're going to be a professional, you need to know what they are. Jenny, it's OK to take input from others. That way you don't have to reinvent the wheel every time you start something."

Jenny's part is triggered: "Look, I've told you that you don't need to be involved in this part of my life if it's upsetting to you. You know, it's not really any of your business."

Marvin's Captain is out of patience and, offended by her last statement, shifts completely into his protective part: "You're so fucking arrogant. You know it all. It's got to be your way. You won't take input from anybody because that means you might not know everything."

Jenny's forcing part is activated: "Yeah, well, I especially don't want to take input from you! Your input is always contaminated by your own self-interested agenda. You're not going to boss me around and tell me what to do. You don't care about me or my friends or my clients. All you care about is yourself. Why don't you just mind your own business for a change?"

Notice in the above exchange how we started the interaction with our Captains but were quickly overtaken by our protective parts. These sorts of "conversations" take place quite frequently in many relationships. They start out just fine but end up in a fight because one or both partners shift into a protective part that got triggered by an inflammatory word or phrase, or by a loss of patience at not getting any agreement after several attempts.

Notice too, that while my manager part was posing as a Captain telling Jenny about the guidelines and so forth, he was actually trying to protect my exiled little boy, who felt threatened by Jenny's unpredictable, long phone calls.

My mom told me that when I was a baby and toddler she had to frequently and abruptly leave me alone while she tended to other demands on her attention. Apparently some of the time she was gone long enough for me to experience the terror of abandonment. It's hard to imagine, but this terrified, exiled little boy of mine was likely getting stirred up by Jenny's seemingly random and open-ended calls that left her inaccessible.

Although my adult self or Captain doesn't care that much how long she talks to friends or clients, those extended conversations leave my exile feeling alone and threatened, causing my protective parts to take over. Of course, my manager part doesn't want to be embarrassed by coming clean about the part of me that's irrationally fearful, so it poses as my Captain and tries the ruse of suggesting professionalism and other straw dogs to convince Jenny to cut down on the length of her calls.

Jenny, who has a "forcing issue" that was mentioned earlier, hates for anyone to tell her what to do, especially if it's me. It's no wonder our parts got involved. This is just an example of how couples with protective parts can get into a serious argument about "nothing."

A Captain-Led Discussion

Now let's look at the exact same scenario when both Captains remain in charge.

Jenny's Captain: "Honey, I've got a phone call with Margaret at five today."

Marvin's Captain: "Okay. What are your thoughts about dinner? I was going to have something ready about six-fifteen."

Jenny's Captain: "Well, you know my calls sometimes take quite a while to get through. I might not be finished by then."

Marvin's Captain: "Hmm . . . I've got to think about that. I prefer to eat early and I kind of had plans for us to eat together."

Jenny's Captain: "Why don't you go ahead without me, and I can just eat later?"

Marvin's Captain: "I know it's not true, but a part of me feels disregarded and is thinking that the folks you talk to on the phone are more important than me."

Jenny's Captain: "Marvin, you *know* that's not true. You are more important to me than anyone else I know. It's just that I really care about my clients' happiness and personal growth. I feel the same about my sons and siblings. I'm committed to helping them get better. Maybe after dinner, it might be helpful if we did a session and let you have a chance to be heard. There's got to be something behind that agitation. What do you think?"

Marvin's Captain: "Yeah, I guess you're right. I'm tired of having to deal with all these feelings every time you get on the phone. I'll save you something to eat."

In this scenario, I was able to stay in my Captain even though I experienced some agitation from my parts and anxious feelings from my exile. In other words, I was able to regulate my feelings instead of letting them push me into blaming and saying inflammatory bullshit that wasn't really true. And, significantly, because I could finally come clean and become vulnerable about my feelings of abandonment anxiety, Jenny no longer needed to defend herself from my attacking. Instead, her heart-infused Captain could tell me with feeling that I was the most important person in her life. That is a wonderful way to end what could have been a painful, angry fight.

Millions of couples let their negative feelings dictate hurtful words and actions toward partners they are trying to love. How many times have you said something hurtful to the one you love simply because you were angry, hurt, frustrated, or anxious? Because it's crucial to personal growth and healthy relationships, learning to stay in your Captain and regulate your feelings will be addressed in several of the remaining chapters.

Sessions Using the Captain

When you hear about therapy sessions, chances are you think of a patient and a therapist or "shrink" sitting across from each other in an office. In this safe, supportive, and confidential environment, the therapist invites the patient to not only talk about issues and problems, but also often encourages the expression of whatever emotions come to the surface. You've probably heard that for most therapy methods, the unresolved, painful, and traumatic experiences from the patient's past are considered fertile grounds for doing healing work. Before patients can get beneath their protective defenses to the real, emotion-laden issues, however, they must trust that they and their therapist can handle whatever comes up.

In the IFS model, your compassionate Captain is the therapist, and your protective parts and exiles are the "patients." Like patients with a conventional therapist, exiles and protective parts must trust their Captain enough to risk sharing their thoughts and feelings. Once the parts feel safe and understood, a powerful healing dynamic with the Captain is possible. *This* is the jewel and centerpiece of the IFS method of transformation. Incredibly, the ability to heal from old traumas and wounds is within you.

Using the Captain and the IFS theory to work with ourselves

and each other has been one of the more exciting discoveries Jenny and I have made in our journey toward love and intimacy. By employing this model, we have each made more meaningful changes in the past year than in the previous five.

Chapter 14:

A Therapeutic Session with a Captain and Parts

THERE ARE MANY benefits to participating in a session between your Captain and your protective parts and exiles. First of all, sessions allow your parts to express themselves, thus releasing the anger, frustration, fear, or other difficult feelings that make clear thinking almost impossible. And trust me, if you give them the opportunity, parts *will* let it be known what they are thinking and feeling. Offloading these "negative" thoughts and emotions also helps to avoid an accumulation that could lead to resentment and grievances. (I've found that when I'm unable make myself let go of my angry feelings, a session will usually do the trick.)

When parts express their thoughts and feelings, you also get a chance to witness their exposed unhealthy beliefs and strategies. And by reasoning with parts and pointing out the real truth, your Captain can reeducate and eventually train them to use healthy, life-affirming strategies to get what they want so that protective parts can actually become assets rather than liabilities.

Having the Captain work with the parts and exiles is also an excellent way to heal the grievances between partners that so often become major impediments to intimacy, trust, and emotional safety. And most importantly, sessions create opportunities for the Captain to befriend the exiles while helping them to unburden themselves from traumatic memories and feelings.

It might sound a little weird at first, but your protective parts can "talk" and "listen" to your Captain, or even others for that matter. Remember that much of your thinking is simply your various parts talking to you. Let's look at some common examples of different parts talking and Captains answering them.

You look into the mirror after taking a shower and a part says, "Look at you; you're fat. You ate all those desserts last week and now just look at you. Don't let John see you without something covering those thighs."

The Captain might reply with, "You're not fat and those three desserts didn't do that much. That's a nice body for fifty and with the right clothes, I still look pretty sexy. Besides, looks aren't everything and John loves me for who I am and not just how I look."

You walk past your boss and she looks at you stiffly and doesn't answer your hello. Your part says, "Oh my God, she hated my report. She's going to demote me or maybe even fire me! What am I going to do? I'll never get another job this good."

Your Captain answers, "Calm down; she's probably had a rough morning and this has nothing to do with you. You worked hard on that report and it's very good. And even if she fired you, which she won't, you found this job and you can find another one."

Some examples of a critical part talking to another part:

"What's wrong with you? Why do you sit there and argue with her when you know it's going to lead to a fight? Why can't you just say, 'Yes, dear,' and let it go?"

"Why did you scream at Mandy this morning? She's a little kid, for God's sake! Just because *you* overslept doesn't mean she should have to put up with your crap."

"I can't believe that, out of all your clothes, you picked this outfit to wear. Look at everybody else. You wanted to look sexy and every woman here looks like she's dressed for Sunday school."

"Why did you drink that fourth margarita last night? Now, this morning you've got a headache, you look like hell, and it's time to go to work. And you got so wasted you slept with someone you never want to see again. What's wrong with you?"

"Why in the hell do you keep swinging your golf club like you're trying to kill a rattlesnake? You said you were going to swing smoothly today and just now you hacked at the ball and knocked it into the lake."

In a session, we're merely talking to those parts of ourselves that keep hurting us or others. Except that in a session, our Captains don't blame or get angry with these different parts. Instead, they are curious and want to learn why the parts keep doing the things they do.

By talking to a part in a compassionate and nonjudgmental manner, the Captain can gain its trust enough for it to share why it thinks, feels, and behaves the way it does. Once this is accomplished, the Captain can point out the flaws in the part's "logic" and thinking. Once this is accomplished, the Captain can begin enlightening that part with the truth and a new, more accurate way of seeing reality. It's a little like teaching a child how to successfully function in the world. As the parts begin to accept and integrate the new information, the Captain can then begin working with the underlying source of the problem: the exile.

Fortunately, because the brain's plasticity allows it to actually change its structure, the protective parts of our mind (which, of course, are rooted in our brain) can be transformed into something less hurtful, less rigid, and less reactive. Our protective parts *can* be taught to be more relaxed and less defensive.

A session is most effective when we begin with a protective part that is already "up" or triggered. Because that part will usually be anxious, angry, or withdrawn, it will likely be primed and ready to express its thoughts and feelings to the Captain. Notice that when doing a session with a love partner, the protective part talks to the Captain, NOT to the partner. The part *does not* address him or her with its complaints, blame, or anger. Your partner should feel safe in this process so that he or she can remain a curious, caring, and mostly silent witness. Also, it must be clear that this entire process is not a dump session, but an opportunity for the part to express itself within certain restraints. If a part is filled with rage or contempt for the partner, it should discharge those feelings with someone else.

The following is an example of a real-life session I had about Jenny's phone calls. Jenny witnessed and was available as a "therapist" if I needed some assistance. Note: when the circumstances warrant, Jenny and I often switch chairs when we talk from different parts. In other words, the Captain sits in the Captain's chair and the protective part sits in a different chair. Sometimes we even sit in a third chair when we're in our exile. This is not necessary but often helps to "get into" the role we're playing and also allows us to more easily differentiate from our parts. It is vital to realize that we are not our parts; a part is simply a misguided amalgam of beliefs and strategies designed to protect us from harm.

It didn't take much for me to "get into" the part that resents Jenny's phone calls. Talking to my Captain, the frustrated part began.

Part, angrily: "I'm just sick and tired of her incessant phone calls. Every time I look up, she's texting, talking on the phone, or emailing somebody. My God, how that woman keeps up with everybody and all their problems is beyond me. She schedules 'phone dates' with her brother, her sisters, her friends, and her clients, and then might talk with one of them for hours. She has no boundaries. She'll let whoever it is talk until the cows come home. It really pisses me off. Doesn't she ever get tired of yakking on the phone? We never have any time together anymore."

Captain: "I hear that Jenny's long phone calls and all the texting and emailing piss you off and that you're sick of it. There's way too much of that going on and, because of it, you don't get to spend time together anymore. Is that it?"

Part, feeling understood: "Yes, that's right. I mean, who spends hours on the phone every day, anyway? I never spend more than ten minutes on a phone call. How can a person spend two hours just yakking on the phone? She even does it on the weekends, for God's sake. She knows Saturday evenings are special to me but she even takes calls then. She says her work and her clients are a priority. That tells me how *I* fit into her scheme of things."

Captain: "So, she won't even promise you a Saturday evening without calls or texting, and that leads you to believe that her clients are more important to her than you. You used to think you were special to her, but not anymore."

Part: "Yeah, how could she love me and want to spend time with me when she's always texting, talking on the phone, or sending somebody an email?"

Captain: "It must be hard on you to believe that you're no longer special and maybe even not loved the way you used to be. You obviously have some feelings that go along with that belief."

Part, feeling even more understood: "Oh yeah, I have lots of feelings. I especially don't like it when she takes a call right in the middle of our conversation. I get angry and give her a look, but I don't say anything. And when she gets a text, I get nervous because I never know who it is or what they're going to want from her. I just feel anxious, stressed, disregarded, and mad about this whole thing. When I feel like that, I don't feel close to her at all. In fact, I don't even like her and don't want to be around her."

Captain: "Okay, I got it. All her calls, texting, and emails upset you because they interfere with your relationship and, even worse, make you feel unimportant to her. When that happens, all your good feelings for her are gone, including your love. I can understand how you could feel that way, believing the things you do. But what if your beliefs are not based on reality? What if they are simply not true?

"You said that you *'never'* have any time together anymore.' Since you live in the same house and spend most of your days and nights together, it seems unlikely that you *never* have any time together. There are probably sixteen hours a day when the two of you are not sleeping. Would it be accurate to say that on a typical day, Jenny probably spends no more than three or four of those hours texting or talking on the phone?

Part, reluctantly: "Well, it sure as hell *feels* like she's on the phone a lot more than that, but I guess you're right.

Captain: "Even if she spends four hours a day on the phone, there are still twelve hours she could be spending with you every day. Do you even *want* to be spending twelve hours a day just talking and hanging around with her? Don't you like to have time for yourself to do things on your own? Don't you like to write, practice golf, work on your projects, exercise, and watch a little TV? Isn't it true that her phone calls give you the chance to do whatever it is you want to do without having to please her or interact with her every minute of the day?'

Part, with a little puzzlement: "Well, if you put it like that, it *is* pretty strange that I get so upset with her calls and texting. I do enjoy time to myself and have lots of things I like to do every day that doesn't involve Jenny. If I look at it that way, I guess it's kind of weird that I get so nervous or mad when she's doing her thing."

Captain: "Is it possible that your frustration and anger is a way to distract from something that is going on deep within? Could it be that you're protecting an inner part of us that is threatened or hurt in some way by her phone calls?"

Part, with a growing awareness: "I don't know. All I know is that I've always gotten upset and nervous and wanted her to stop doing all that. I guess there's got to be a reason for it. Maybe I could be protecting something. Otherwise, why do I get so upset?"

Captain: "You *are* a protective part, after all. That's what you do. That's your job, to protect. I'm thinking there's a part of Marvin that you're protecting, maybe a scared, little inner boy that keeps feeling abandoned and unloved."

Part: "OK. That makes sense. So you're saying that's why I get so upset? I'm protecting that little boy part who is scared when Jenny gets on the phone and leaves him alone?"

Captain: "That's right. It doesn't take much for the little boy to get frightened or even panicky. Every time Jenny gets mad or takes phone calls, ignores us, or treats us badly, he gets upset. That's why you've learned long ago to protect him by getting angry, withdrawing, or closing our heart. You've actually learned to punish whoever seems to be threatening the little boy."

Part, trying to take it all in: "Wow. So I've been doing that from the beginning. And I just thought I was getting upset all this time because people were being mean to me or they weren't being rational. So I've really been protecting that little boy? That's amazing."

Captain: "Yes. I think that's true. Your protecting was

probably helpful when we were an infant and toddler, but I don't believe it's helpful at all now that we're adults. You are still using methods and strategies you developed back then and they no longer work. In fact, the 'protections' you're using today are unhealthy and undermine our attempts to get intimacy, connection, and love.

"Think about it. What does it do to Jenny when you get angry, criticize, withdraw your love, or close your heart to her because she talked too long on the phone? Do you think those reactions make her want to be close to you or love you more? Probably not.

Part, feeling sheepish: "'I never thought about it like that, but I guess you're right. I'm supposed to be protecting the little boy and making sure he won't be abandoned or unloved and all I'm doing is driving Jenny away. But I don't know how to do anything else. It's what I've always done and it's always caused trouble. I don't know why I keep doing it. To tell the truth, I'm tired of doing all this reacting every time Jenny does the slightest thing wrong. I've done this in other relationships as well. I've been doing it all my life and I'm just plain tired of it all. I'm tired of always reacting and tired of being on the alert all the time too. I put out all this effort and it only hurts people and makes them mad at us."

Captain: "I know it's hard to accept, but I'm glad you can see that. Maybe it's time you traded in your methods and unhealthy reactions for something new and different—something that wouldn't interfere with the little boy getting what he wants and needs. I'd like to help you with that a little later. But for now, there's one other thing you said that I'd like us to look at. You indicated that Jenny said that her clients and career were a higher priority than you. Let's ask her if that's true."

Jenny: "Marvin is the love of my life and is always my highest priority. I've said on a couple of occasions that my clients are a high priority and that, if needed, I would skip a meal or alter my plans if they were in distress and need me right then. I've never said, and would never say, that my calls are a higher priority than Marvin."

Part, feeling reassured: "Well, that's good to know. I've always wanted us to be special to her."

Captain: "Yes, it feels good to know we're special and loved. Now that you're feeling more relaxed and secure at this moment, I'd like to invite you to stand by and listen to me as I try to contact that scared inner boy you've been protecting all these years."

Captain to exiled little boy: "Judging from the strength of your protective parts, I can only imagine that you've been frightened and alone since you came into this world. I'd like to hear what it's been like for you all these years."

(It is often difficult to communicate with exiles because they are primarily emotional memories stored in the body and are not used to "talking" or being exposed to the conscious mind. For that reason, they may not express themselves in words. Communication can also be tricky because exiles have usually been hurt by people who were supposed to love and nurture them, and so, they have trouble trusting anyone. There are times when accessing the exile is not easy. It can be helpful if the Captain takes some deep breaths, invites the exile to come out of the "basement," and then silently senses the feelings rising up from the unconscious. At those times the Captain can interpret the emotions and put them into words for the exile.)

Exile: Deep feelings of sadness are rising to the surface, followed by loneliness and longing. There are flashes of panic and a vague sense of abandonment mixed in.

Captain giving words to the exile's emotions: "It's been so hard for you all these years to be frightened and alone with nobody there for you. And it must have been so terrible to be a baby and little boy when your mother left you alone all those times. It seemed like she would never come back. I'm guessing you went through some terrifying feelings with no one to turn to or comfort you. You were so scared and overwhelmed. It was way too much for a little one to deal with. I'm so very sorry you had to go through that."

Exile: Feeling an even deeper sadness, mixed with a sense of relief after finally being acknowledged and even partially understood by the Captain, the exile is moved to tears.

Captain: Understanding and compassionate, the Captain speaks again to the exile. "I deeply regret ignoring you all these years. I'm so sorry. I should have been there for you long ago. Someday soon, when I've proven myself to be dependable and caring for you, I hope that you can trust and believe in me. You no longer need the protective parts to defend you from all those hurts and horrible feelings; I will protect you from now on. No longer will those parts alienate the people you depend on for love and security. I know that I will have to prove myself to you, so I want you to observe and notice that your Captain will be looking out for you.

"I want you to know that when Jenny is on the phone or with other people, she's not abandoning you. She loves us and will come back to us when she's able or ready. It's going to be hard to accept, but her love is not always going to be there for you. She has other interests and obligations, and her love is less than perfect anyway. She has wounds that keep her from loving at times, just like we do. And she's not your mother and never will be. Your mom is never coming back for you. She's gone forever, and you'll never have that kind of love again. I can't be your mom, but I want you to know that *I*, your Captain, will always be there for you. I will love you unconditionally and will never desert you or disregard you again."

Exile: The exile hears the Captain but has only a slight

comprehension of what he is saying because the message that a loving, ever-present mother is never coming is too devastating to take in all at once. Because of this, it usually takes several sessions before the exiled little boy can let go of the fantasy that someday a mom-like figure will come to take care of him. Over time, he will learn to rely instead on the Captain, who will offer support and protection until he can mature and grow up. (Remember that because of trauma and or developmental deficits from the mother, the exiled little boy was arrested in his emotional and psychological growth and has remained in that helpless, childlike state for years.)

Captain: Sensing that the exile has heard him and has begun the process of understanding the situation, the Captain turns back to the protective part. "Please pay close attention to me because what I'm going to say is important. We've agreed that your methods of protection are hurtful to you and others and are not effective at getting what we want. It's time to stop with the anger, the blaming, the criticizing, the withdrawal, and the defensiveness. It's time we all grew up and acted like adults."

Part: "I hear you. I'm tired of the reacting and all the fighting and trouble that are part of it. I'm ready for something new."

Captain: "Good. I'd like to start by inviting you to change your attitude and beliefs about Jenny's phone calls. Instead of criticizing and judging her, I'd like you to join me in supporting and encouraging her in her new career. And I would like for you to realize that her calls have nothing to do with whether or not she loves us or wants to spend time with us. I want you to understand that she is a separate person from us and has her own wants, needs, and desires, many of which have nothing to do with us. In other words, she has a life with us, but she also has a life that doesn't include us. Just like our golf and fishing don't really have anything to do with her. I want you to join me in being glad that she's doing something she enjoys and gives her meaning. And if we can do all this, if we really can support Jenny to do the things she wants to do, she might just love us more and be even more available to us. Would you be willing to change your beliefs and attitude about the phone calls?"

Part: "Yes. It might take a while, but I'll do my best."

Captain: "Perfect. I appreciate you listening and really hearing me. I know it's a different way of looking at things, but I assure you, it's not only a healthier and more loving way of relating to Jenny, it's the best way I know to get what we want and need from this relationship."

After the session, I took some deep breaths and let everything settle into my being. Then, when I could really feel it, I sincerely apologized for the times I'd given her so much grief about the phone calls. Smiling, she accepted my apology before giving me a big hug. This session started me on a road to understanding what was going on beneath my protective part. It was hard to admit that the vulnerable little boy part of me was feeling alone and neglected when Jenny spent hours on the phone or with a client. Transforming the beliefs and attitudes of my exile and its protective part took several sessions spread out over four or five months, but it was worth the effort to finally end the hassle that part caused Jenny and me. Protective parts from an early wound are deeply embedded in our minds and can be resistant, requiring multiple sessions and lots of time to change the way they operate and see the world. Educating and re-purposing parts are not easy, but it can make such a huge difference in how we feel about ourselves and our loved one. It's worth the effort.

In the above example, I've purposefully chosen a dialogue between the Captain and *one* part for simplicity. Sometimes sessions involve several parts who may even have conflicting agendas. The first couple of sessions might feel a bit awkward as you become familiar with the process, but they should become easier and more effective as you go along. It might be hard to believe at first, but sessions similar to this one really do work to increase our self-awareness, lower our reactivity, and open our hearts.

Chapter 15:

Anatomy of Arguments and Fights

A NY TIME YOU'RE in an argument or fight with your lover or spouse, you can be sure that both of you have been taken over by protective parts. Have you ever called your spouse a name like bitch or bastard (or worse) and then later said that you didn't really mean it? Well... *you* might not have meant it, but your part certainly did. Parts can be ugly, mean, and hateful and can say or do things that your normal self would never do.

This is critical for you and your loved one to understand. If your partner, in a fit of anger, ever says he hates you and wants a divorce, his outburst is but the thoughts and feelings of a triggered part. While it's true that the part may indeed hate you and want to leave, you must remember that it's only a protective part that's in upset mode. That part is just one piece or component of your husband's mind and doesn't represent his Captain or even his "normal self." More than likely, your husband, in this case, loves you very much and wouldn't dream of leaving you. For this reason, you should never take to heart what a spouse says in a fit of anger. Now, if he's calm and relaxed and tells you he hates you and wants to leave, then yes, there's trouble in River City.

Of course, both partners need to reeducate and re-purpose their protective parts so that they don't go off and cause so much pain and fear, but until that happens, it's good to know that your lover's part is just blowing off steam and using survival strategies that are thoughtless and childlike. Whenever possible, it is best to not take your partner's angry words and behavior personally. He or she is just acting out with a misguided survival brain in charge.

When this happens, respective parts are doing the talking and causing the mischief. And if both of your parts are upset and expressing thoughts and feelings, the two of you are destined for increasing anger and frustration and neither of you will get your needs met. Let's look at a typical argument/fight and see what those needs are and how they get sabotaged.

A year or so after we married, Jenny and I visited the house she and her ex had lived in for nearly twenty years. They'd spent thirteen of those years remodeling and adding a second story, doing all of the work themselves. Having built several houses in my younger years as a general contractor, I felt compelled (stupidly, insensitively, and unwisely) to make a couple of unflattering comments about the color scheme and the choice of certain building materials. Although most of my observations were somewhat complimentary and congratulatory, my stupid comments were understandably all Jenny's protective part seemed to hear.

Jenny's Part, angrily: "You know, that really hurt my feelings. Those were shitty things to say. You have no idea how hard we worked on that house. You can be so damn mean and thoughtless sometimes."

Her anger alerted my protective part, who immediately jumped into the fray.

My Part: "Hey! For Christ's sake, here we go again. I didn't do anything and now you're pissed at me. All I did was to give you a little feedback and now you're ready to bite my head off.

You're so freaking sensitive about every little thing. If I hurt your feelings, I'm sorry, OK?"

Jenny's very angry Part: "Oh, this is perfect. It's like every other time when you want it both ways. You want to be able to say something shitty that hurts me and then you don't want me to have any feelings about it because my feelings upset you. Well, you better get ready for some feelings, Buster, because I'm tired of holding them in."

My Part: "Oh, so you've been holding them in? Is that a joke? All those times you yelled at me and lectured me like I was a little boy and you've been holding them in? No, your problem is that you keep getting irritated and bent out of shape over nothing and then blame me for your crappy feelings."

Jenny's furious Part: "That does it! I'm through talking to you. You can be such an asshole!"

My furious Part: "Go ahead. That's what you always do: just turn your back on me. What a bitch!"

This was a mercifully quick fight because something in Jenny told her that it was going to get even uglier if we pursued matters much further. Not everyone's parts are as "enthusiastic" as ours; some protective parts just stuff feelings, leaving them roiling around inside. Some other partners are actually able to pretend that nothing is wrong; they just block out anything that might be upsetting or cause a conflict. Unfortunately, these types of partners also inadvertently block out virtually all feelings, including kind, loving ones. Although they don't show it, the hurt affects them deep inside where it festers and leaks out in passive-aggressive ways. Despite the various ways fighting partners respond on the surface, they all have exiles that are upset and needing something. And interestingly, no matter what the fight is about, the exiles of both partners need similar things.

In this particular fight with Jenny, I had an exile that wanted to feel acknowledged and appreciated for my expertise in home building. (Most of us have a pretty strong need to be recognized for our knowledge or experience in certain areas) Unfortunately, my protector part chose the unwise and hurtful strategy of critiquing Jenny's house as a way to get her to see that I was an expert in that field. On the other hand, Jenny probably had an exile that needed to be recognized for all the hard work and effort she put into that house. After all, she raised three kids, worked full-time, engaged in a relationship with her spouse, *and* worked on the house for thirteen years! It had been a major accomplishment and my comments completely ignored all of that. My negative feedback and disregard for her achievement hurt and activated Jenny's exile, which aroused her protective part.

Her protective part activated an exile in me that was afraid of her anger and potential abandonment, which aroused *my* protective part. Without our Captains to mediate or repair the rift, we were stuck with angry parts determined to get in the last blow. If I could have been present and accessed my Captain, I could have recognized immediately that Jenny's exile had been hurt by my comment. With that awareness, I could have genuinely apologized and given her validation for all she had done to get the remodeling finished.

You can be sure that in the midst of a fight, both you and your partner need something. At that moment, you may need to be heard, understood, or validated. Or maybe it's empathy you need, or feeling loved, appreciated, or forgiven. It's possible you just want to feel emotionally safe. Fights continue because neither of you is in any shape to give those kinds of things to each other. Protective parts are designed to attack or retreat, not to be nurturing, curious, generous, or forgiving. In fact, in a fight, your protective part sees your partner as an enemy. Sadly, when parts are activated, there is no room for the Captain to even notice a distressed partner's needs, much less attend to them. When one partner's part is triggered, there will be a little turbulence; when both partners are in their parts, there's usually going to be a full-fledged fight.

In the chapter on anger, there will be more on fighting and how you can stop it in its tracks. For now, it's imperative to understand that one of you needs to take some deep breaths, settle into your body, realize that you are in the grip of your childlike part, and then summon your Captain to return to the helm. This often works for me in the middle of an escalating conflict and allows me to actually think about what I'm saying and what's going on between us.

Chapter 16:

Attachment in Love Relationships

UNDERSTANDING OURSELVES AND Our Partners
Ever since boyhood, my fantasy woman has been soft, demure, kind, understanding, and loyal to a fault. After those essential traits came qualities like attractive, sexy, smart, lively, interesting, and a good sense of humor. Although I seemed to end up with women who were either wounded and angry or wounded and withdrawn, I always intended to be with a "nice, easy-going gal."

It took me a while to understand that my criteria for a mate were hugely influenced by my unconscious anxiety about something called attachment. In truth, I wanted someone sweet and kind so that she wouldn't fight with me or be upset by my occasionally prickly behavior. My unconscious had a belief that if a mate were to get mad at me, then maybe she would stop loving me or, even worse, leave me. And if she left me, the abandonment anxiety might overwhelm me to the point that I might lose it or even die. Yeah, that's a radical belief, but then again, protective parts have some pretty crazy ideas.

Although I wasn't aware of it and would never have admitted it, I needed to be with a nonassertive, dependent woman so that I could feel emotionally safe and secure in a relationship. To that hidden, insecure little boy inside me, emotional security and safety trumped everything else, including true connection, intellectual compatibility, intimacy, fun, or even authentic love. If it's between safety and love, the insecurely attached person's unconscious will always choose safety. It's all about survival.

This preference for security in a relationship is due to what is called attachment anxiety. Although most couples are probably not familiar with the psychological meaning of the term attachment, it is intricately woven into the fabric of every committed love relationship. If you and your partner are securely bonded together, then the phenomenon of attachment will simply make your relationship stronger and more stable. But if like millions of other couples, you and your partner are insecurely attached, the two of you will likely suffer some or all of the following consequences:

You feel insecure in your relationship, needing frequent reassurances from your partner that you are loved and OK.

One or both of you will unconsciously give up your sense of self so that your partner will love you.

Jealousy and possessiveness may plague your relationship.

One of you seeks more warmth, intimacy and time together, while the other remains "cool," needing "space" and independence.

To create inner safety, the two of you have settled into an emotionally and intellectually deadened "couch potato" relationship, where the threat of challenges and conflict are minimized.

While intimacy and connection are what you seek, something seems to keep it just out of reach.

Attachment between two adults is a biological and psychological process that happens automatically without any effort, skill, maturity, or awareness. It is a natural *result* of falling in love, but it is not to be confused with love itself. Attachment is an unconscious process that doesn't necessarily involve the heart at all.

I've had many insecure clients who were deeply attached and needed their partners desperately, but didn't seem to love or even like them all that much. Their fear of being alone was reason enough to stay with their partners and whatever efforts they expended on pleasing them was mostly to keep them from leaving. Authentic love, intimacy, and meaningful connection often play a minor role in this type of marriage. Unfortunately, these hollow relationships seem to be widespread in American culture, leaving millions of couples wondering why they feel lonely, empty, and wishing for something more.

Although attachment isn't love, it *is* very powerful. The pain, fear, and trauma associated with most breakups and divorces often have as much to do with the loss of an attachment figure as the loss of love or the partner. An extreme example of the power of attachment occurs when people fall into a debilitating depression or even kill themselves or their partners when they are threatened with abandonment. Jealous people who abuse their mates emotionally or physically mistakenly believe they do such things because they "love them so much."

Insecure attachment creates a powerful fear that feels to an inner child that losing one's partner and facing abandonment is like death itself. Because of this, a partner who is not securely attached will need frequent reassurances that the relationship is solid and that he or she is loved.

It is important at this juncture to understand that needing your partner doesn't mean you have an insecure attachment. Needing your partner to love you, "be there" for you, give you emotional support, care about you, and think you're special are healthy qualities of secure attachments. This kind of "dependency" is natural and healthy and plays a critical role in establishing intimacy and connection. Humans have a natural, biological need to connect with a particular person. It's that simple. We need to be held and soothed, validated and appreciated, and to feel special to someone. We also need to feel a deep sense of connection to another. We need shoulders to cry on and arms to hold us tightly. We need someone to snuggle with intellectually, emotionally, and physically. We *need* each other, period. It's the way we're wired.

While insecure partners need the same things, being in a committed relationship often feels to them like skating on thin ice. They never feel secure and are unable to hang on to the reassurances, appreciation, soothing, and love from their partners. Their mates may keep putting "money" into the insecure partners' bank accounts, but the balance is always near zero. With nothing to fall back on, insecure partners need a regular stream of assurances to feel loved and safely attached. Simply put, on the deepest of levels, anxiously attached partners seldom feel lovable or loved for any length of time.

Anxious partners in love relationships often avoid risk-taking behaviors like emotional honesty because being truthful could threaten the relationship. That lack of honesty makes it impossible for partners to become self-aware or to grow as individuals in relationships. Unable to connect in a felt, meaningful way, they tend to flounder in a world of unspoken thoughts, unexpressed feelings, and empty, deadened lives.

The Roots of Attachment

Unhappy couples are seldom aware that hidden, insecure attachment issues are often behind repeated misunderstandings, arguments, and even fights. Nor do couples realize that emotional states like numbness, anxiety, perpetual longing and loneliness, dissatisfaction, and anger can be caused by attachment difficulties with each other. As mentioned earlier, in that deep, inner place, too many of us have an exile with a persistent belief that we are not loved. That painful belief negatively affects our feelings, our attitudes, and our behavior toward our partners and the relationship.

Insecure attachment can be hard to fathom, however, because in so many cases, it seems to make no sense. For instance, how can a six-foot, physically powerful man who is also a wealthy and successful leader of his own company be insecurely attached to his wife, while an unremarkable janitor working for him has no trouble with it at all? Why are movie stars, politicians, preachers, and doctors just as likely to be plagued with insecure attachment as are plumbers, school teachers, and bus drivers? Interestingly, some of the most securely attached individuals I've known were poor immigrants from Mexico who grew up in traditional, loving families.

It's helpful to understand that being insecurely attached is not a reflection of one's successes, character, inner strength, or spiritual qualities. It is simply a natural result of not being sufficiently held, cared for, and loved as a baby and toddler. Attachment insecurity can result in what appears to be normal "loving" families. I've had many clients tell me that they believed they were loved by at least one parent and that they were treated well as children. But upon closer examination, they admitted that their parents weren't that interested in them and made few efforts to understand their feelings or actions.

Children aren't stupid; they know when their caregivers don't care enough about them to connect, validate, or empathize with them and their feelings. Countless children feel alone and unknown in their "normal" families. This lack of interest in the inner world of children just adds to the attachment wounds of babies and toddlers. Feeding, clothing, and providing shelter and schooling aren't nearly enough to produce securely attached, emotionally healthy children. Parents who are unhappy, overly stressed, anxious, or insecurely attached themselves are rarely able to raise securely attached children.

The ability to be securely attached to another person starts with an emotionally present and available mother who gives her infant plenty of skin-to-skin contact, feeds him or her in a loving and timely manner, and is sufficiently attuned to provide the right attention, mirroring, and nurturance. The influential psychiatrist W. D. Winnicott called this a healthy "holding environment," which comes from "good enough mothering." He believed that the relationship between mother and baby creates the basis for good mental health and secure *attachment*: "The foundations of health are laid down by the ordinary mother in her ordinary loving care of her own baby."

Since a baby's brain is adding more than seven hundred neural connections per second from birth to age three, it's no exaggeration to state that mothers are actually sculpting their infants' brains during this unique and irreplaceable window of opportunity. It is largely in this all-important phase that attachments, either secure or insecure, are formed.

With the right kind of mothering, the conditions are favorable for a baby to develop a positive sense of self, an inherent belief that the world is a safe place, a feeling of belonging, and an ability to trust and depend on an attachment figure. These attributes will become a part of that baby's personality and social engagement system for the rest of its life.

Unfortunately, in modern Western cultures, the importance of early attachment is not sufficiently taught or understood. Even with the best of intentions, overly stressed, depressed, or busy mothers are compromised when it comes to giving their babies a "good enough" holding environment. This often results in infants with unmet developmental needs and insecure attachment issues.

The pain and anguish of neglect, the loss of security, and the trauma that occurs with a compromised mother-infant relationship leave the baby trying unsuccessfully to cope with overwhelming feelings of terror, abandonment, and even rage. In this milieu, *an exile is created and protective parts are developed* in the survival brain to cope with the traumatizing emotions and to defend the wounded baby from experiencing those emotions in the future.

Why is this so important to you and your love relationship? If you or your partner didn't develop a natural, healthy attachment to your respective mothers, protective parts will play a significant role in your interactions and attempts at intimacy. These parts will complicate your relationship by using strategies like personal attacks, withholding, criticism, distrust, anxiety, or closing the heart when they are activated by even the *perception* of too much closeness, too much distance, or doubts about being loved.

Chapter 17:

Four Types of Attachment

CHILDREN WHO GROW into anxiously attached adults often become romantics with a strong need for closeness and connection. They tend to be overly invested in the relationship, worry about it, and are hyper-vigilant to changes in their partner's moods and behavior. They seek frequent reassurances not only that their partners love them, but that they are committed to staying in the relationship. When they perceive threats to their relationship, anxiously attached adults can be jealous, controlling, blaming, or clinging. They place so much emphasis on their relationship that they tend to feel as though they are nothing without their partner.

No matter how many reassurances or "I love you" statements they receive, they rarely feel securely loved. Anxious partners are likely to react strongly to cues that signal a threat to their attachment. Feeling threatened by conflicts and their partner's displeasure, they are usually the first to apologize and attempt to repair a broken connection. These are the typical pursuers of closeness in relationships. Avoidant partners of anxiously preoccupied mates often feel smothered by *too much* closeness.

For the most part, anxiously attached men and women may seem just fine and may function very well in relationships. Their problems show up in two areas that deeply affect their attempts at love and intimacy. In one of those areas, a lack of confidence in a partner's love and commitment to the relationship causes them to feel that their loved one is somehow not safe. This leads to an often hidden belief that this extremely important person could fall out of love with them at any time or leave because of a minor upset. Because of this irrational belief, anxiously attached persons can rarely let down their guard or truly open their hearts for fear of upsetting the apple cart. In other words, it's difficult for them to be real. Interestingly, in most cases, anxious persons are not even aware that they are guarding their hearts and making real intimacy and connection virtually impossible.

Another problem created by insecure attachment happens when the anxious partner distorts or exaggerates a loved one's innocent words or behavior as threatening to the relationship. The anxious partner will then unwittingly withdraw into their shell of defenses or start attacking with grilling questions or criticisms. These behaviors will usually end up hurting or offending loved ones, which causes them to react by defending, withdrawing or attacking in return. The anxious partner then ends up feeling even more insecure, alone, and unloved.

I know from experience that being anxious about your partner's love and commitment can be excruciating. A part of you knows that everything is OK, but another part feels like you are always skating on thin ice and may at any moment fall into the freezing abyss. Dealing with this worry and anxiety over the years cost me an enormous amount of mental and even physical energy and needlessly inflicted pain on my partners.

Dismissive-Avoidant Style

Dismissive-avoidant types appear to take relationships for granted and rarely pursue intimacy and connection with the same enthusiasm as anxiously attached partners. They usually regard themselves more positively than they do their partners. Uncomfortable showing vulnerability when they're hurt or stressed, they often isolate themselves and lick their wounds in private, leaving their anxious partners to fret about their inaccessibility. Because of this strategy, they don't apologize easily and are in no hurry to repair rifts or conflicts, which also drives their anxiously attached mates crazy. Avoidant persons see themselves as emotionally healthier than their anxiously preoccupied partners because they're not as "emotional" and don't demonstrate clinging behaviors.

It's important to understand that these avoidant behaviors were usually learned at an early age as a protection from overwhelmingly frightening and painful emotions. On a deep level, they want intimacy and closeness just as much as their anxious partners, but their defense systems are designed to avoid it. They may act like islands, but somewhere inside they are just like the rest of us. This doesn't mean, however, that you can expect to change an avoidant into a soft, emotionally accessible partner overnight. It takes a lot of work and some corrective emotional experiences before they can feel safe enough to let down their walls.

A recent conversation between Jenny and a late middle-aged acquaintance demonstrates a corrective emotional experience. Jenny's friend, who's never married, presents herself as extremely self-reliant and tough. Although unaware of it, she's prickly to the point of making those around her uncomfortable. She doesn't like hugging or all the incidental touching that goes with being close to someone. "Joan" is the epitome of the *dismissive-avoidant* type and yet she broke down and sobbed from someplace deep within after telling Jenny about a hurtful incident that happened with her mother. Underneath all her protection is a soft, vulnerable woman who wants and needs to be held and loved. Sadly, her parts make that all but impossible.

Fearful-Avoidant Styles

Fearful-avoidant personalities will vacillate between the

dismissive and preoccupied types. They want close relationships but usually retreat into the safety of their shells when presented with the opportunity for actual closeness and intimacy. They often seek reassurances and may use clinging behaviors, but, if rebuffed or unsatisfied with a partner's response, they usually employ attacking or withdrawing, avoidant behaviors.

It's important to note here that insecurely attached people all have frightened exiles that were wounded during the critical mother-infant relationship. Their protector parts, however, may have very different strategies to protect them. As we've seen, some protectors use the John Wayne approach, the "I'm cool, tough and don't really care all that much anyway" strategy, while other protectors use the vulnerable Woody Allen style of "I need you so much, I can't live without you. You do love me, don't you?" Underneath both strategies are exiles that are hurt, scared, often enraged, and don't feel securely loved. These terrified inner selves need lots of protection to keep them from surfacing and causing havoc.

In contrast, the securely attached adult usually has a strong sense of self, is confident, desires connection and intimacy, and is able to maintain a healthy balance between closeness and independence in a romantic relationship. Because these adults believe their bonds with their partners are safe and secure, they are not preoccupied with their attachment and do not anxiously react to minor issues regarding spouses or intimate relationships.

Our Attachment Styles

It's important to understand that we all were raised in unique circumstances and that, although your early experiences may very well be different from Jenny's or mine, you could still have issues with insecure attachment. There are hundreds of ways between birth and adolescence that a child can develop problems with attachment. Like so many other couples in the world, Jenny and I started out insecurely attached to each other and have been through a lot of hell because of it. Jenny's *dismissive-avoidant* style and my *anxious-avoidant* way of being in the relationship have created a pageant of misunderstandings, arguments, hurt feelings, and fights that have been performed many times on the stage of our marriage.

At first, we just blindly played out our parts and danced our futile dance without realizing what was going on beneath the surface. Like puppets on a string, we acted and reacted in lockstep with the dictates of our attachment styles.

When Jenny's avoidant-attachment fear was activated, she often abruptly ended our discussion and, with lips tight as piano wire, marched into her room, closing the door and leaving my stirred-up parts crazy with abandonment anxiety. That's when I usually shifted into my avoidant part and screamed out, "You bitch," as I stormed out of the house, slamming the front door behind me. Like I said, we went through hell when our insecure exiles got triggered and protective parts took charge.

While studying and researching attachment theory, I quickly learned that I was an anxious-avoidant kind of guy. I didn't want to accept that label because it sounded unhealthy, needy, and I don't know... kind of weak. I don't like to think of myself that way. I'm a psychotherapist for God's sake and shouldn't have problems like that. I resisted mightily but finally let go of my pride and accepted that I'd been damaged as a child and had let my baggage leak into my relationships ever since.

My first several hours on this planet were not spent securely attaching to my mother. As Mom liked to tell me, she nearly died while giving birth to me. Her serious condition required a blood transfusion, leaving her unavailable to a baby who desperately needed his mother. Apparently, I spent much of the first twenty-four hours of my life alone in a crib having to deal with the frightening new world by myself. I can only imagine that I endured powerful, overwhelming feelings of fear, panic, and even the rage that comes from being helpless and deprived of the essential warmth and skin-to-skin contact that every baby needs.

By toddlerhood, my traumatic beginning had been exacerbated by an anxious dad who was jealous of me and, according to Mother and some of her relatives, became angry if she "spent too much time" with me.

By the time I was four years old, I had a frightened, wounded exile and had already developed a managing protector part that tried to please Mother so she would love me and be nice to me. Her caring attention helped my little exile to temporarily feel comforted and safe. I remember trying to sweep an area around the front door of our house with a broom that was way too big for me. Struggling to hold on to the broom, I was delighted when I managed to make a little pile of dirt by the door and couldn't wait for Mom to see what I'd done. When she came into the room and saw the little dirt pile, she happily exclaimed that I was a good little helper and told me how proud she felt. She knelt down and hugged me, gave me a sweet kiss, and told me she loved me more than all the stars in all the sky. I still remember the flush of delicious feelings that went through me and how right everything felt in that moment. My efforts to please Mother were rewarded with her love and appreciation. It was a lesson that my manager part would never forget.

Although I had what would appear from the outside to be a "normal" childhood, the real truth was that without sufficient love and attention from my mom, I must have been terribly lonely and needy. She was a deeply wounded woman who was mildly depressed, worked outside the home, had problems with my dad, and was heavily involved in the local Baptist church. I know now that her ability to love was compromised by her own traumatic childhood and that her attempts to show me love just scratched the surface, leaving me needing so much more. To make matters worse, her occasional anger and the way she shut me out when she was displeased left me feeling even more insecure and anxious. It's no wonder I developed a strong motivation to please her and make her happy.

That experience with the broom and several more like it created a *pleaser part* in my personality that is with me to this day. I've always tried to anticipate and meet my partners' needs and wants so that they would appreciate and, especially, love me. I bought flowers, took them out to dinners, cleaned the house, cooked, and worked hard in my business so that we could have the things we wanted. I expended a great deal of energy and effort to make sure my mate was happy. This was my proactive manager part doing all it could to ensure I would be loved and not abandoned.

From a distance, it might seem to an outsider that I was filled with love for my partners, but a closer look would reveal that I was only playing a role dictated by my pleasing part. I pleased automatically without thinking or feeling. My unseen motivation was to be loved and appreciated, as well as to make myself indispensable so that no one would ever leave me.

Jenny, an outspoken alpha female, tends to let you know it if you've upset her. And, much like my mother did, when she is overtaken by her dismissive-avoidant parts, she can take her love away and cut you off like a gangrenous foot. So it's not surprising that my protective parts had a tendency to get activated when she became mad, irritated, or even displeased with me. When she became upset, I typically began a series of defensive apologies intended to appease and assuage her so that she would "get over it." In other words, I tried desperately to shut down her upset feelings so I could feel safe again. Of course, in those moments, my protective part didn't care if I had hurt or offended her, nor did it care *why* she was hurt or offended. All it cared about was stopping her anger and getting back in her good graces.

If my groveling "Woody Allen" apologies didn't work, my avoidant "John Wayne" part took over, withdrawing into an angry silence filled with self-talk about not needing her and finding a woman who was nice and caring. A different, judgmental part cursed her hypersensitivity, inflexibility, and inaccessibility. Unfortunately, there were times when my attacking part took over and let her have it with criticism and put-downs. If she wasn't happy with *me*, I wasn't happy with *her*; and my attacking part let her know it. This made matters much worse because Jenny absolutely hated it when I overreacted to her minor irritations and disappointments. It made her furious that I couldn't give her a little wiggle room to have her feelings.

Jenny's avoidant-attachment style began in her infancy with a mother who was unable to give her enough of what she desperately needed. The loving touch, mirroring, joyful feeding, and skin-to-skin contact Jenny needed were in short supply. Tough and largely unresponsive, her mother wasn't the sort of nurturing, present, available mom that every baby needs. This kind of injurious neglect must have caused traumatic feelings of abandonment, deprivation, terror, and even panic that overwhelmed baby Jenny. Her traumatized exile needed powerful protective parts to make sure she never again had to experience the hell she went through as a baby and toddler.

Her avoidant parts developed a story that vulnerability and neediness were dangerous and could cause severe disappointment, pain, and even trauma. Thus, for her, it was safer to be *protected* from a love partner than to be *dependent* on him.

Avoidant partners seldom complain about a lack of intimacy or connection because they are actually more comfortable when those things are left on the back burner. I've seen many cases where the anxiously attached partners are desperately pushing for more intimacy, while their avoidant mates say that everything is just ducky, thinking all the while that something is wrong with their "needy" partners. In this instance, it would be easy to imagine that the anxious partners have a problem, while the calm avoidant ones are reasonable and healthy. In fact, pursuing partners might actually be healthier because they are at least trying to meet their natural needs for intimacy, connection, and love.

Although some avoidant personalities are standoffish and even a bit prickly, many of them are people-pleasing, caretaker types who can be quite social. It's just that when their hearts are on the line and vulnerability is required, they tend to be protective and overly careful. When stressed, avoidant men and women often "go inside" for safety rather than reaching out to others for help. Their sanctuary is a solo affair where they can lick their wounds by themselves like they did as infants and toddlers. Jenny learned early to soothe herself by sucking her thumb, which remained a comforting habit until she was fourteen years old.

Avoidant personalities seldom offer up repairs or apologies during rifts with their significant others. Because it requires them to open up to their soft and tender, hurt feelings, avoidant mates also tend to reject offers of repair from their partners. Uncomfortable with vulnerability, they feel safer playing their cards close to their vests and waiting until the whole thing blows over. You may have heard that in love relationships, one partner often pursues connection and intimacy, while the other tries to maintain a comfortable distance from the pursuer. Of course, it is the avoidant partners who need distance because connection and intimacy require a certain kind of softness and surrender, which they fear and tend to shy away from.

Jealousy

Jealousy, born of insecure attachment, can play havoc with a love relationship. I once counseled a couple where this form of attachment anxiety played a major role in their lives. In this case, Martha, a middle-aged woman with a vivacious personality, was plagued by her insecure attachment to Bill, her new husband. He was an electronics engineer whose specialty required frequent overseas travel, which kept her anxious parts activated with suspicion. She couldn't keep herself from checking his e-mails, his telephone, his hotel records, and his coat pockets for any evidence that he'd been with another woman. She called him at all hours and grilled him when he got home from a trip. Her anxiety and suspicion took up all the air and energy in the room, making intimacy, closeness, and connection virtually impossible to achieve. Tired of defending himself and feeling alone in the relationship, Bill made an appointment with me for couples counseling.

In therapy, Martha focused on Bill's infidelity in his past marriage, his trips that took more time than they should have, and the fact that he was a good-looking guy who had women "falling all over him." She brought up a charge in Australia on a credit card he couldn't remember making. Of course, any one of those things could arouse the suspicions of a jealous mate. A securely attached mate, however, probably wouldn't have given them a second thought.

Because jealousy is so intricately connected with the survival brain, the affected exile and its protective parts are difficult to deal with. It's almost like they are hard-wired into the brain. It took three months of weekly sessions before Martha began to show some real progress. Finally, she began to develop a sense of inner value and personal strength as her exile learned to trust and connect with her Captain. Believing that she was worthy of being loved, Martha could accept that Bill actually loved her and wasn't going to leave her for some woman he might run into while on one of his trips. As her anxiety relaxed, there was more mental and emotional energy available for intimate, caring talks and connection. Martha was thrilled to experience the empowerment that came with a stronger Captain and the liberation she felt with a little freedom from her jealous parts.

Early in our honeymoon phase, Jenny casually mentioned a past lover in a story she was telling. I'd met him once, didn't like him, and couldn't imagine the love of my life being with him. Totally ignoring her story, I said, with a definite edge in my voice, "What'd you see in that guy anyway? I can't believe you'd sneak around just to be with somebody like that. I'm not sure I even know you."

Like a couple of times before, my reaction surprised Jenny and left her in a bit of shock. "What? What are you talking about? That guy was ten years ago, for Christ's sake. What's going on with you?" she fired back as she held up her hands in exasperation.

Now you could say that I reacted the way I did because I was jealous, shallow, and insecure, and that would be one way to describe me. Another, more helpful and more realistic way to explain what happened is to point out that an insecure part of me, an exile, felt threatened when it heard the man's name. Once the name was spoken, an immediate shift took place in me that I didn't even notice. One moment I was talking to Jenny from my normal self and the next second, I was grilling her from a part of me that perceived a threat to an insecure exile. Without me even realizing what took place, I was "gone."

Jealousy is hard to treat because it often results from an insecure attachment that happened early in a child's life.

Sometimes there isn't even a memory or image of the neglect or other hurtful interactions with our primary caregivers that left us feeling abandoned or alone. These ancient wounds are *emotional* memories that can be locked inside the body and emotional brain. Those who don't understand the origin of their jealousy will naturally blame their partners and accuse them of flirting or sneaking around behind their backs. Their lack of self-awareness leads them to irrationally believe that their partners' attitude and behavior are "causing" their upset.

Even when it is pointed out that he or she had jealousy issues with several different partners, the protective parts of a jealous person will often continue to react to "signs" that their current loved one might be interested in another. Because jealousy activates the survival brain and its powerful emotions, it is difficult to treat with cognitive solutions or talk therapy. It is often necessary to work with the frightened, abandoned exile to root out the real cause of this tragic wound.

Chapter 18:

Attachment Cues

Activated protective parts often perceive a loved one's anger, disappointment, or even annoyance as a cue that the relationship is in peril. A partner's roll of the eyes, a sigh, or a look of frustration can set off the parts of an insecurely attached mate. This reminds me of the fearful flyer grasping the seat with white knuckles every time the aircraft encounters the slightest turbulence. Neither the plane nor the frightened passenger is in any danger whatsoever, but the anxious parts of the passenger are activated by *cues* like unfamiliar sounds, bumps, or even a worried look on a flight attendant's face.

To an insecurely attached lover, there could be an endless number of cues that seemingly reveal that a partner is losing interest. To make matters even worse, the anxious partner will often exaggerate, misinterpret, or even imagine cues out of whole cloth. For instance, just looking at an attractive person of the opposite sex could get your insecurely attached partner's jealous parts firing.

If you're not as bubbly, affectionate, or emotionally present to your insecure partner as you usually are, he or she might see your change in behavior as threatening, never imagining that your actions might be caused by a headache, work stress, or a physical ailment.

Anxiously attached mates react to a perceived threat to their relationships in a variety of ways that include compulsive pleasing and seeking reassurance, withdrawing and emotionally shutting down, or attacking with criticism or other verbal abuse. I have reacted in each of these ways at various times when it seemed to my parts that Jenny's love for me was weakening. There were occasions when all it took from her was a sigh of irritation, an angry look, or a minor criticism. My insecure attachment parts have been very sensitive.

Earlier in our relationship, that sensitivity was unmistakably evident. My brother and I had planned to spend several days at the coast fishing. We would stay in our RVs, and our wives, who weren't into fishing, would stay home. When the trip was canceled at the last minute, Jenny seemed disappointed and said that she had been looking forward to spending a few days by herself. Misinterpreting her response, my anxious insecure parts heard that she wanted to get rid of me because she didn't enjoy my company. In their "infinite wisdom," they then deduced that if she didn't enjoy my company, she would probably prefer to live without me. With a mixture of anxiety and anger, I sought answers.

Bereft of my Captain and in my "sad sack part," I started out with, "You know, it doesn't feel very good to hear you say that you'd rather be alone than to be with me. For one thing, I'd never say that to you. And for another, I had no idea you felt that way. What is it? Are you just sick of me being around?"

Jenny answered in a flat, monotone voice, "You're taking this all out of context. I just said that I was looking forward to getting some time to myself. You know, we're together all the time, and I just wanted to relax and do my own thing."

"Well, if being with me gets challenging for you, all you have to do is say the word, and I'll take off for as long as you want." My sad sack part was getting the best of my Captain and was more than happy to steer the conversation in a negative, subtly threatening direction. "I can stay with friends for as long as you want. There are a lot of places I could go to give you relief." Then, hoping for a little reassurance, I continued, "I just had no idea you felt that way. I always thought that you *liked* being with me."

As a dismissive avoidant, Jenny wasn't inclined to give my parts what they needed, "Marvin, you're making a mountain out of a molehill. Why are you doing this? Why are you asking me questions that you should already know the answer to? I tried to tell you that this has nothing to do with you. I just wanted some time to piddle around, play my music, and finish this project I started without having to worry about you and your needs and wants."

My sad sack was hitting full stride. "I wasn't aware that my needs and wants were such a great burden for you. Wow, I'm learning all kinds of things today. Anything else you need to bring to my attention?"

Tired of being pressed by my anxious parts, Jenny's protective part joined in the fray. "Look, when you're like this, it's no use talking to you. I've said all I want to say on this matter. If you haven't gotten over it in a couple of hours, we can try again."

"No, I don't want to go over it later. I want to know what's going on."

I waited for an answer, but it didn't come. My sad sack gave way to an angry part as my quest for empathy, soothing, and resolution turned into despairing, helpless anger. I left the room and took a walk before things got out of hand.

This simple incident illustrates several things about attachment issues. Because I was an anxious-insecure partner, I misinterpreted Jenny's desire to have some self-time. Then, taken over by my activated parts, I presented an offending series of comments and questions meant to get me reassurance and a declaration of love. Not surprisingly, that didn't come from an avoidant Jenny, leaving me upping the ante and getting even sillier and more irrational.

Now, out of patience and taken over by *her* frustrated part, Jenny was even further from offering a repair or any kind of reassurance. She continued in an edgy voice, speaking rationally and without feeling. I was rigid in my anxious reaction, and she was rigid in her emotionless, Mr. Spock-like response to my reaction.

If I could have shared my actual emotions of hurt and fear instead of grilling her with an edge in my voice, Jenny might have responded with caring and empathy. It would have been so much easier for her to hear my truth if, in a heartfelt way, I'd said something like, "Honey, a part of me heard you saying that you didn't want me around, and just for a moment I had this terrible feeling that you didn't love me. That left me feeling scared and rejected."

If I could have been vulnerable and emotionally honest, Jenny's protective part would probably not have been activated. In that case, she might have said something like, "It hurts me to see you feeling this way. It's so sad that after all this time you still don't know how much I love you. I might have looked forward to spending a couple of days just doing my own thing, but that in no way means I don't like being with my best friend."

Unfortunately, a triggered protective part overtook my Captain and tried to make Jenny wrong for wanting to spend a couple of days by herself. And according to that part, it was Jenny who "made" me feel hurt, rejected, and unloved. Protective parts are so sneaky. In this case, my part took the focus away from my real feelings of hurt and abandonment anxiety and turned it toward Jenny's "insensitivity" and desire to "get away from me." My complaining and accusing words were coming from my anxious, insecurely attached self and felt hollow, inauthentic, and offending to Jenny. Given my less-than-healthy approach, and her aloof avoidant style, Jenny was unable to soften and respond to my underlying need with heartfelt reassurance.

In this scenario, Jenny and I both had a need that wasn't being addressed or taken care of. She needed some time and space to be in her own little world so that she could do exactly what she wanted all day. She could play her music and turn the volume up, eat when she wanted to, work on her project when she wanted to, and basically just kick back without worrying about anyone else. She wanted me to understand and accept her perfectly healthy and legitimate needs. Instead, I made it something personal about *me* because my insecure parts had taken over, making it impossible to hear her side of the story or to be empathic to her needs and feelings.

I, on the other hand, needed Jenny's reassurance and understanding. A part of me was anxious and fearful that she didn't love or value me, and I needed her to assuage and help soothe that part. Although that part and those feelings didn't come from a healthy or rational place, her assurance of love could have subdued my part so that I could calm down enough to talk to her like an adult. Doing that and validating my feelings wouldn't have meant that she condoned my part or its irrational fears and strategies. It would just give me the message that I was seen, supported, and valued, even though I was flawed. Then, hopefully, I could have engaged in a healthy discussion about Jenny's need for some self-time.

Because attachment anxiety begins in infancy and toddlerhood, it is wired into the survival brain and cannot be diminished without intention, effort, and the right strategies. In the last part of the book, we'll demonstrate how to employ a compassionate Captain to help the exiles feel understood, safe, and loved. This can be an excellent way to lower attachment anxiety and, in many cases, even heal an exile's terrible wounds. We haven't completely healed our attachment exiles, but we've made a lot of progress and are on the right track. Jenny and I are less reactive, more vulnerable and emotionally honest. And because we are in our protective strategies less often, there's more room for us to *see* and empathize with each other. It hasn't been easy to break through our protective ego shells, but we are well on our way. Doing the processes and sessions with our parts and exiles has worked so much better than we could've imagined.

Chapter 19:

Anger in Relationships

Anybody can become angry —that is easy, but to be angry with the right person and to the right degree and at the right time and for the right purpose, and in the right way; that is not within everybody's power and is not easy.

— Aristotle

Anger as a Cover

KYLE BENSON, A writer for the Gottman Institute for relationships suggested that anger is like an iceberg. We can see the anger being expressed, but beneath it are feelings and needs that that are not apparent. Most adults are unaware that they have a pattern of using anger as a way to get their needs met. They are also unaware that they use anger to avoid underlying feelings of guilt, humiliation, shame, rejection, fear, or abandonment anxiety. For instance, Cherie might express anger at Henry because he commented that her dress was too tight in the stomach area. What she's really feeling, however, is probably shame or embarrassment about her weight. John expresses anger at his wife because she didn't want to have sex on a particular evening. His anger is covering up feelings of rejection. Jason is angry at his wife because she spent so much money on a new outfit. Jason's anger is covering up his long-standing fear of going broke and being poor. In each of these cases, anger is a secondary emotion that is being used to avoid feeling the more painful primary emotions.

Authentic intimacy and connection require emotional honesty and vulnerability and cannot happen in the midst of secondary emotions. If you're feeling ashamed and you're expressing anger at your partner, he can't empathize or connect with you because he doesn't know what's really going on inside you. And if he has to deal with your anger, it will be more difficult for him to stay present and available for you. Emotional honesty is the foundation of intimacy, connection, and love.

It is ultimately your responsibility to do whatever work is required to discover and express the primary feelings under your anger. Of course, this will require increased awareness and the courage to be vulnerable enough to express those tender, often uncomfortable emotions you've avoided for so long. Sharing those feelings instead of your anger can fundamentally change your relationship.

Hostile Anger

There are two common but unhealthy ways that many couples use to express anger. Some partners express their anger by criticizing, shaming, threatening, name-calling, contempt/mocking, lecturing, hateful looks, and angry gesturing. Other partners express their anger indirectly through passive aggressiveness, stonewalling, withdrawal of their love, having "headaches" in the bedroom, and avoiding a partner by spending more time with television, work, friends, or the bottle. Whether it's passive or aggressive, hostile anger contaminates relationships. It is hard to feel loved when someone is yelling at you, criticizing you, purposefully ignoring you, or threatening to leave. Never underestimate the power of toxic anger to sabotage loving feelings and committed relationships.

Hostile Aggressive Expressions of Anger

It's not uncommon for angry partners in love relationships to use controlling, frightening, punishing, threatening, or shaming behavior on their beloveds to get their needs and wants met. I'm sad to say that my anger pattern included all of these hostile, aggressive expressions at various times. My parents modeled reactive, hostile anger for me on a regular basis and turned that anger on me from time to time, creating three distinct exiled parts of my survival brain. One was terrified at their anger and another was filled with rage at being helpless to do anything about their abuse. Still another exile was overwhelmed with shame from the whippings and humiliating comments. Each of those exiles developed protective parts that became the foundation upon which my anger pattern was built.

Although research has shown that a certain amount of temperament can be inherited, the fact remains that if your partner regularly uses hostile, aggressive expressions of anger, the chances are very high that he suffered some kind of abuse as a child. Happy, emotionally safe, and well-adjusted children don't start out deciding one day to become a grouchy, angry, emotionally abusive person. If you are an angry, aggressive person, it's not your fault. And if your partner is a hostile, angry person, it's not his fault. Angry, hostile people shouldn't be shamed or demonized; they came by it honestly. They need help, not retribution. Underneath their anger is a need that is not being met and they have no healthy tools to achieve it. Of course, it is always the responsibility of hostile, aggressive persons to change the way they express anger.

Hostile Non-Aggressive Expressions of Anger

"Jackie," a friend of mine, is afraid of her husband "Larry's" anger because her father repeatedly frightened her as a child by roughly grabbing her arm, yelling and threatening her, or verbally abusing her. Whenever Larry raises his voice, Jackie retreats into her protective shell just as she did as a child. When he disappoints her, hurts her feelings, or treats her unkindly, Jackie rarely expresses anger directly at him for fear of making him mad. She has found other ways to retaliate, by ignoring him when he comes home from work and acting as if he's not there. When he walks through the door and says "Hi," she might make a grunting noise but continues with whatever she's doing, taking no notice of him at all. Because Larry is insecurely attached, her ignoring behavior makes him feel unloved, which drives him crazy.

After an argument or conflict, Jackie's protective parts will also punish Larry by sullenly retreating to her room and closing the door behind her. With her defeated body language and an angry tear or two, she makes sure he knows how much he's hurt her. At other times, she manages to suppress her anger and interact with him as though nothing has happened. But something has happened; her protective parts have completely closed off her heart and her positive feelings for him. If she consents to sex while still upset with him, she just goes through the motions, making sure he knows that she's not really there for him or with him. During those times, she can be polite and civil but remains indifferent and without a shred of warmth or interest in him. After unsuccessfully trying to get Jackie to talk or "work it out," Larry finally loses it and reacts to her indifference by yelling that she's frigid or a cold bitch. This scares her into giving him a couple of insincere, meaningless apologies, leaving him so frustrated he could pull his hair out.

Jackie's brand of non-aggressive anger also comes from a childhood scarred by parents who used anger in inappropriate, dysfunctional ways. Like with aggressive partners, it is never helpful to make a partner wrong because he or she is passive-aggressive. Criticizing a partner for being passive is never helpful. It is important to note, however, that withdrawal, stonewalling, and passive-aggressiveness can be more destructive to a relationship than yelling and making a big scene because they seem to say to the receiving partner, "I don't love you anymore and I'm not interested in you at all." If someone you love looks at you with those cold, dead eyes and acts as if you don't exist, it's hard to believe he or she loves you or wants to continue living with you. And that can be really scary.

Changing Your Anger Patterns

It's pretty hard to change or transform something if you are unaware of what it is you're trying to change. Let me share an example. On a trip to Europe with my wife, my sister, my two grown children, and my ex-wife, I became grumpy shortly after arriving. Jet-lagged and deprived of sleep, I gave in to my darker self and complained about the food, the accommodations, and the weather. It was my daughter's birthday and there I was, raining on her parade. By the end of the next day, a couple of my traveling companions had taken me aside and gently let it be known that I had acted like a jerk. My sister even suggested that I look back over the course of my life and see how my way of dealing with irritation, annoyance, and yes, anger, had either hurt, scared, or offended others.

Needless to say, I didn't want to hear any of it. I defended myself by saying that I was basically a nice, gentle guy who rarely became upset, and when I did my behavior wasn't that far out of line. Like millions of others, I literally didn't realize the hurtful impact my anger had on the people I loved. Apparently, my impatience, small irritations, and especially my anger, had made those around me uncomfortable. Even though they loved and respected me, my occasional behavior had affected their feelings for me. Because they didn't quite feel emotionally safe with me, it was hard for them to be vulnerable enough to truly connect with me.

Admitting to myself and my family that I had hurt them

and caused them to be uncomfortable for years was one of the hardest things I've ever done. Fortunately, my "teachers" persisted over the next few days, even though I resisted mightily, actually becoming angry on a couple of occasions. After hearing virtually the same thing from every one of my traveling companions, I finally stopped defending. Those three weeks became an eye-opening experience for me, as I learned things about myself that I didn't want to know.

Changing the Way You Handle Your Partner's Anger

An important first step in becoming an expert at handling your partner's anger is simply awareness. Start by noticing your feelings and reactions when your partner gets upset with you. Are you afraid, shocked, ashamed, or angry? And what do you do with those feelings? Do you get angry and attack back? Do you belittle or minimize his reason for being angry? Do you try to shush him and curtail his feelings like you would an angry child? Maybe you get quiet and steel yourself as you nurture an inner dislike for him. Or is it possible that you go emotionally and intellectually numb, or even dissociate? Whatever your reaction, it's helpful to be very clear about how your partner's anger affects you and what you do as a result.

The next step is to notice how your partner acts in very similar ways every time she gets angry. Observing this is important because you can begin to see that her anger is an automatic dance she does with a few details changed for each episode. For instance, during our first years together, every time Jenny became upset with me I responded in nearly identical ways. If my insincere apologies didn't work, I became defensive. If my defensiveness didn't work (it never does), I withdrew my love and goodwill and gave her the silent treatment. And if she was still angry, which was usually the case, I would lose it and scream out, "you fucking bitch" before walking out the door. I never varied because my protective part had no other tools or options available.

When your partner is very angry, he is probably not in his right mind because he's been taken over by a protective part that is unthinking, rigid, and regimented. If you know that your partner is just running his automatic dance of anger with a virtually clueless, childlike protective part, it's easier to not take it personally. Think about it: if a five-year-old child were angry with you, you probably wouldn't go into shock or overreact. In the same way, there's no need to get all bent out of shape and overreact to your partner's anger.

During our first few years together, Jenny usually expressed her irritation or anger by giving me a punishing lecture that pointed out all the ways she'd been hurt by my words or actions. Without cursing or calling me names, she let me know how I could've or should've said or done it differently. She reminded me over and over how she'd tried to help me be a better person. She asked me questions like, "Why can't you see that your behavior hurts and disappoints me?" Or, "It's been years and you still haven't changed." And if she didn't get a satisfactory response, she repeated everything all over again.

After enduring years of lecturing and verbal abuse as a child, I had an increasingly hard time handling Jenny's anger and brow-beating. Her lengthy lectures stirred up long-buried feelings of shame and humiliation in my little boy exile. Those feelings triggered a protective part that reacted with disingenuous apologies, defensiveness, and various verbal attacks on her. Because none of my reactions provided Jenny with what she needed in her moment of upset, she kept pushing and "lecturing" at me. Finally, in the midst of these overwhelming feelings of shame, helplessness, hopelessness, and rage, I would blow up. This scenario happened more times than I care to think about, with both of us stuck in repetitive patterns we couldn't stop.

I've read several books on anger in love relationships and each of them provided good advice about handling another's anger. Although I totally accepted the advice, it never worked that well for me. In the heat of the moment, with the fight-or-flight parts of my brain lit up, all those wise sayings and ideas just flew out the window. All the advice and all the willpower I could muster didn't seem to help because I reacted immediately and reflexively to my partner's anger.

When someone is angrily reading us the riot act about something wrong that we did or said, it's not unusual for us to be in a state of mini-shock, or even dissociation. In that split second when our fight-or-flight chemicals flood our bodies, our protective parts take over, defending, retreating, or attacking back. Because we've been expressing our anger in much the same way since childhood, our angry tactics and strategies feel natural to us. To change this "natural" programming won't be easy. I know, because I worked on it for months without much success.

Reacting to your partner's anger by defending, saying they do the same thing, minimizing, defusing, telling them they shouldn't be angry for such a minor offense, stonewalling, withdrawing, or attacking them with your own anger will rarely get either of you what you want. *Responding* to their anger with curiosity, openness, and open-hearted listening will create a much better outcome for both of you. Responding to your partner's anger with a mature, caring Captain sounds nice, but it is difficult to do without some real work and effort. Remember that your reaction to a partner's anger is likely an involuntary pattern that is hard as hell to break.

For two years I tried to use others' advice and my will to stop that automatic reaction with very little improvement. I had every incentive to change because my reactions *always* made Jenny even angrier. And yet, I just couldn't do it. Each time she became irritated with me, my thoughts came without my prompting: "Oh, God, here she goes again. What is it now? I can't believe she's upset at that! What a difficult woman to live with. Is she so mad that she's going to leave me?" Immediately following my thoughts came the obligatory apologies: "Look, Jenny, I'm sorry, OK? I won't do that anymore. You're right; I was wrong to say that, OK? Can you just let it go?"

When she wouldn't drop it after my insincere apologies, I usually upped the ante, saying things like: "Look, I said I'm sorry; what you want from me? What's it going to take for you to just let it go? I can't do a damn thing that pleases you. For Christ's sake, Jenny, let it go. What do you want me to do, cut my wrists? Why do you have to be so fucking irritable all the time? I'm sick of it." And all the while she continues to hound me about whatever I did or said that upset her. My reactive words only exacerbated her anger. She wanted me to understand why she was angry and she wanted me to empathize with her feelings. And all I could give her was my defensiveness and anger.

I wanted to change how I reacted, but using my will just wouldn't work; her anger triggered the flight-or-fight chemicals in my survival brain, immediately unleashing a reflexive emotional pattern. Incredibly, after all my life experiences and twenty years of formal education, my little boy exile and its protective part had never changed their view or attitude about anger. I had to find a way to get through to them and change their beliefs about anger in general and Jenny's anger in particular.

Finally, after too many fights and ruined evenings, I was ready to try something different; I decided to use a dialogue between my Captain and that irrational part of me that believed her anger was dangerous. Over the span of a year, I did several dialogues and began to notice a real change.

Remember that in these dialogues, the Captain acts as a caring therapist to the protective part and the exile. At first, the Captain earns the trust of the part by sincerely acknowledging and appreciating the part for all its hard work of protecting and defending. Carefully and compassionately, the Captain helps the part see that its beliefs and attitudes and its ways of handling anger were developed in infancy and childhood. The Captain shares the truth that those behavior patterns and beliefs are out of step with the new reality of adulthood with all the power and resources currently available. Hopefully, the Captain persuades the part that neither its beliefs nor its methods of protection are needed anymore.

As I mentioned, this session with my part is a brief version of my dialogues, but hopefully, you get the idea. Your dialogue may be very different, and that's okay. In fact, you may not feel comfortable having sessions with your "protective part," and that's OK too. However you do it, it is critical to convince the survival part of your brain that reacting to your partner's anger with hostile anger of your own is rarely going to be helpful or productive. In fact, your unhealthy reactions will continue doing harm to you, your partner, and your relationship. Repetition here is critical. You're trying to break a reflexive habit you've had for years so you have to keep reminding that reactive part of you about the new way of doing things.

I mentioned before that it may seem a bit strange to have the Captain communicate to a part or exile, but I can assure you that it works. I have changed over the past few years from the inside out and I attribute it to the dialogues and a lot of honest, constructive conversations with Jenny.

If your partner supports your growth and is willing to witness your dialogue, then, by all means, do your dialogues with him or her. It will help them understand and empathize with you. You can also do these sessions by yourself, or if there is an IFS therapist in your area, that would be a great idea as well. The important thing is to just do it. You can't get fit by reading about the gym and its exercise machines; you've got to use them. In the same way, you can't heal and grow without doing some work.

It is often more effective to use different chairs for the Captain and the part. Doing this will help to differentiate between the two by making it clear which one is talking. Sometimes, for convenience, I just sit on the couch and move over a foot or so when changing from the Captain to the part or exile. One further note: before starting the dialogue, it is imperative that you "get into" your Captain. Sitting quietly, taking deep breaths, and focusing on something positive will usually bring your Captain into the present moment.

In the hopes that it might be of value to you, I'll share a shortened version of one of the session/dialogues I did to help me change the way I responded to Jenny's anger.

Captain to the part: "I've noticed that every time Jenny gets mad or irritated at me, you immediately react in ways that make her even more upset. And your reactions never change; you throw her the same fake apologies, the same defensiveness, and then, when those don't work, you get angry right back at her."

Part: "She gets mad or irritated at us way too often. She an irritable person and she'd brow-beat us into the ground if I let her. It's my job to protect you from her and her anger and I don't know how to do it any other way."

Captain: "But, what are you protecting me from? I'm a big boy and can take care of myself. I don't want to be afraid of her anger."

Part: "Look, I don't care how big you are, I'm not letting anybody talk to you that way. I tried hard to protect you when

Dad was screaming at you and jerking you around while he whipped you with his belt. I was there when he shamed and humiliated you. I tried to protect you when your mother slapped you and withdrew her love whenever you displeased her. You don't need anybody else giving you grief."

Captain: "You're right; Mom and Dad hurt me and scared the hell out of me as a boy. I haven't forgotten that and I appreciate you for trying to protect me from that sort of thing for all these years. I think the way you used silent rage and hate at my parents may have blocked the overwhelming terror and shame I must have been feeling. You kept me from falling into the abyss and I'll always be grateful to you for that. But think about it; that was long ago when I was just a helpless little boy. I'm all grown up now and don't need a protector. When you take over and immediately fill me with reactive anger, I do or say hurtful things that are unnecessary and even irrational."

Part: "It's the only way I know. I just do what comes naturally to me. I can't help it if Jenny doesn't like it. Besides, she shouldn't have upset us in the first place."

Captain: "I'm not blaming you for the way you act; like you said, it's the only way you know. That's why I want to teach you a much more powerful and effective way to be angry without hurting other people and making things even worse. Would you be open to learning something new?"

Part: "Well, since you put it that way, I guess I'd be interested."

Captain: "OK, here it is in a nutshell. When Jenny is upset with us, she has some kind of underlying need that's she's not expressing and may not even be aware of. Like maybe she needs to feel loved or appreciated and she gets mad at us because our comments or actions seem to say to her that we don't care. If you react with defensiveness and anger, she will definitely not feel loved or appreciated. Instead, with your tactics, she'll get even angrier and we don't want that. To help her meet her need, we'll have to be curious, concerned, and compassionate, even though she's upset with us. For us to be upset because she's upset just won't work. We've tried that enough times, right?"

Part: "Yeah, I have to admit it; my way doesn't work very well. I'm not programmed to meet other people's needs. I'm programmed to protect you and that's it. What you're saying sounds reasonable, but I have no idea how to do it."

Captain: "OK. I totally understand, so here's what I'd like for you to do. When Jenny gets mad at us, please just stand back and don't do anything. Let me, the Captain, have a chance to respond to her in ways that might meet her needs and help her to feel understood."

Part: "But what about that part of you that's scared of her anger? She's mean and harsh and doesn't care about your needs. Why should you care about hers? It's not about meeting her needs; it's about protecting you from her anger and shaming lectures."

Captain: "Jenny might seem mean when she's upset with us, but she's not mean at all. She's not my mom or dad. She's just a good, but wounded woman reacting from her protective part. Her part is trying to protect her just like you try to protect us. I need you to hear this: there's no danger to us and there's no need for your reactive protection."

Part: "You mean that, after all these years, you suddenly don't need me? Just like that? How are you going to deal with that angry woman? Without me, she'll turn you every which way but loose. You need a defense against her, just like you needed a defense against your angry parents."

Captain: "Please hear me. Jenny is not my mom or dad! It is extremely important that you understand that. She's a good woman and I am perfectly capable of handling that good woman's anger. She's not going to hurt me, shame me, or beat me with a belt. She doesn't even call me names when she's angry. And she's not going to divorce me because I forgot to buy her cream at the store. Her anger is just a momentary feeling that is not going to harm us in any way."

Part: "Hey, are we talking about the same person here? I've never seen her as a good woman since that first nasty fight years ago. She yelled at you, made contemptuous gestures, and hammered you with an angry lecture. That's all I needed to know about her. I've always seen her as irritable, hard to get along with, and someone who gives you crap every time you turn around."

Captain: "Yes, there were times when Jenny was so upset she just lost it. Have you ever wondered why she got so angry at us? Could it be that we said or did something really hurtful to her? Could it be that she's wounded just like us and that even though she loves us, once in a while she gets overwhelmed with angry feelings? You're not giving her room to be a human being."

Part: "Maybe that's true, but it doesn't give her the right to mistreat you. My job is to protect you from her, not to sing her praises."

Captain: "Think about this for a moment: your job is to protect me so you're only activated and aware of what's going on when she is angry at us. The rest of the time, you never notice what Jenny does or doesn't do. If she's not angry, you're not needed and are not around."

Part: "Hmm . . . you've got a point there. I guess I'm not aware of those times when she's good to us because they don't concern me. So, you're saying that all this time I thought that she's a difficult, angry woman who's out to hurt you, and she's really not like that at all? She's just a good woman who sometimes gets angry? Damn, that's hard to believe that I could be so wrong about her, but you're making a good case."

Captain: "Yes, you *have* been that wrong. And thank you for having the courage to see it. Now you understand why we don't need you to use your tactics against her every time she gets upset at us. She's a good woman who doesn't want to hurt us. She just wants us to hear her and understand why she's upset with us. Sometimes she becomes over-stimulated and just gets a little carried away. That's all. She doesn't deserve to be treated with hostility and anger just because she's upset."

Part: "Well, this is a lot to take in for me. It's like everything is upside down and all this time I've been wrong. I don't like it but what you've said does make sense to me. It's weird, but I'm feeling a little sad that maybe I've been hurting her all this time when it wasn't even necessary. OK, I'm ready to back off and give you time to respond to her in a different way. But you've got to understand that I'm reflexive and go off in less than a second when I'm triggered. It might take a little time for me to learn how to be still in the face of her anger. I hear you and I believe that you can handle things, but what am I going to do from now on?"

Captain: "Good question. I think you can put your sword away and learn to relax. It would also be really nice if you could learn to be not only my cheerleader, but Jenny's as well. Just think; instead of hurting people and making messes, you could actually be helpful and contribute to our well-being!"

Part: "I'll do my best."

Captain: "Thank you."

On a recent trip with Jenny, after a couple of dialogues with my protective part, I had the chance to respond to her anger in a different way.

Hungry and tired of being on the road, Jenny and I stopped at a restaurant for dinner. The ribs I ordered were tough, leaving me irritated and disappointed. After expressing my frustration to the waitress in a terse, but civil way, Jenny became upset with me. With an angry look on her face, she spewed out something like, "What is it with you? Do you always have to let everyone in the restaurant know you're not happy with your food? And it's not the waitress's fault the ribs are tough. She didn't cook them and she shouldn't have to listen to your complaints. Can't you just keep it to yourself when you don't like the food?"

This was especially hard for me to hear because I wasn't allowed to express my feelings as a child, and as an adult I damn sure didn't want anybody trying to shut me down. But instead of immediately reacting, I took some deep breaths and created a little space to try something different.

"OK, I can see you're angry with me and I'm wondering what's going on."

Jenny, still upset but less angry, responded, "I used to be a waitress and had to put up with rude, unhappy customers all the time. You shouldn't make the waitstaff pay for your disgruntlement; they don't get paid enough for that."

I replied, "Oh, OK. I can see why my complaining could upset you."

Jenny, in a calmer voice, "It's not just about that. As a kid, I had to sit at the table listening to my dad loudly whining to Mother about how this or that wasn't cooked the way he liked it. His criticisms and irritation would usually end up ruining the meal for me, my mother, and my brothers and sisters. He even gave her grief about the way she ironed his shirts and the way she kept house. I just got tired of his bitching and how he treated my mother. She busted her ass for him and he never appreciated it. Instead, he hurt her feelings over and over. It makes me mad just to think about it."

I listened to her for once. "I've always had an issue with poorly cooked food, and although it has upset you several times, I never really got it that my issue caused you pain or discomfort. I'm sorry it's taken me so long to hear you and to understand. If I'm really honest, the truth is that I actually don't like myself when I get grumpy. I'm ready to really look at this and make some changes for both our sakes."

Jenny smiled and thanked me for listening without getting upset at her. There had been several times in the past where the same scenario around my disappointment over a meal resulted in a major fight and a ruined evening. I was thrilled to be able to handle Jenny's anger with me in a healthier way. I felt empowered because I wasn't taken over by an angry part that wanted to attack Jenny. My efforts and dialogues between my Captain and the part had actually worked!

Because I didn't react to her anger, we could talk calmly about an "elegant solution" that we could employ in the future. We decided that if I didn't like my food, I could get up and find the manager and very politely tell him about my problem with the meal. That way, Jenny wouldn't have to see it or hear it. The important thing was that Jenny felt that I cared enough to listen, to understand her needs, and to agree to a solution that worked for her. It was a win/win situation instead of the lose/lose deals we'd endured so many times before.

Drawing the Line

While it's certainly important to respond to your partner's anger in a healthy, supportive way, it's also important to draw the line if their anger is expressed in a toxic, punishing manner. Like so many couples I've worked with, Liz and Fred tended to abuse each other with their anger. When angry, Liz would frequently spew shaming words at Fred, such as, "I'm tired of being married to a little boy. Why don't you grow up! All you do is whine and mope around like a five-year-old." Fred would then punish her by not speaking to her for 24 hours or more.

In therapy, Liz learned that her angry attacks on Fred were not acceptable, but her protective parts were determined to get their licks in whenever she became irritated or frustrated with

Fred's way of doing things. After a few sessions, Liz dropped out of therapy, leaving the growing and changing up to Fred. Over several months, Fred strengthened his Captain and re-educated his protective parts. He was finally able to stand up to Liz and her anger. If she started with her abusive language, he stopped her immediately, saying something like, "That doesn't work for me. I can see that you're upset and that's OK, but calling me names or shaming me is not. Let's take a time out until you've calmed down enough to treat me like a human being."

Interestingly, at first Liz didn't like it when Fred "acted like a man" because it forced her to change the way she treated him. She didn't like taking timeouts; she wanted to continue giving him a piece of her mind, but Fred stood firm. He was determined to be treated with respect and dignity, even when Liz was angry with him. Over time, and somewhat reluctantly, Liz got on board and learned to express her anger without abusing Fred, whose inner strength and self-esteem had improved simply by standing up for himself in a healthy way.

Hostility and Grievances

Sadly, in their efforts to protect us, our parts do more than just express anger outwards; they also tend to hold on to some of that anger in the form of hostility or bitterness. Hostility and bitterness against a partner often develop when hurt feelings or conflict are not resolved. Leftover anger, in the form of hostility, causes us to exaggerate, misinterpret, and overreact to perceived offenses. If I'm already hostile toward my wife and she does something to upset me, I'll probably make a bigger deal of it because of my hostility. In other words, if my wife's offense is a two on a scale of ten, my bitterness or hostility will cause me to react as though her offense were something like an eight.

Another problem with hostility has to do with labeling. If

I'm hostile or bitter at my partner, a part of me will likely label her as difficult, unsafe, unloving, thoughtless, or in some cases, a bitch or an enemy. If a part of me sees her in such a negative light, you can be sure I'll have some feelings reflecting that view of her. Those negative feelings will contaminate my good feelings and my attempts at intimacy and connection with her. So my hostility toward her is getting in the way and taking some of the joy and pleasure out of my relationship with someone I love. It's actually hurting me as much or more than it is hurting my partner. Hanging on to hostility is like carrying around a bottle of poison that leaks on you as well as your partner.

Listening to your inner voices or protective parts will often give you a clue as to whether or not you're bitter, such as when they are saying things like, "God, he's difficult to live with," or "Who does she think she is, a fucking princess?" Other bitter thoughts might be, "She's impossible to please; no matter what I do, she's never satisfied," or "He's the most selfish person I've ever met;" or "He never listens to me; I'm just invisible to him." These and countless other negative comments coming from our inner dialogue tell us that we are harboring leftover anger that is poisoning our feelings for our loved ones.

I had a client once tell me that he knows he's still angry with his wife hours after a fight because he reflexively gives her the finger every time she's not looking. He does this even though they've been talking, being civil, and are apparently over the conflict. Unfortunately, it's not as obvious to many of us that we're still angry after a dust-up with our partner. It's always a good idea to check with our parts to see if there's any residual anger hanging around in the recesses of our mind. When you're alone, you might loudly proclaim something very positive about your partner. For instance, "Terri is such a lovely person and I like her so much." If a statement like this feels inauthentic or leaves a bad taste in your mind, then you're probably not over whatever he or she said or did to you. Remember, it is your Captain's responsibility to clean up the mess your parts made, and that includes the mess inside your mind.

My Grievance Toward Jenny

Since her days as a teenager, Jenny has always wanted to help others with their emotional issues and suffering. Occasionally, however, this noble penchant of hers can get out of hand. Many times in our relationship, she has expended great energy trying to convince me that certain beliefs and behaviors of mine were in error. And if one of those behaviors happened to hurt her feelings or offend her, Jenny, without realizing it, would let me have it until I felt like a humiliated little boy huddled in the corner of a classroom.

During those painful times, as I've mentioned earlier, the only defense I knew was to apologize profusely, withdraw in angry silence, or to scream back at her with impotent rage. Because those reactions never accomplished anything, I was "forced" to listen to her for what seemed like hours (it was really only a few minutes) while she went over in detail what I had done, why I had done it, and how much it had hurt her. She was on a mission to *make sure* I got it. Nothing I could say would slow her down until I gave her exactly what she wanted.

I felt ashamed at whatever I had done, furious at her for lecturing me, and totally confused as to why I kept upsetting her. I heard what she was saying, but because of the way she said it, I couldn't let much of anything in. My heart was closed and my Captain was nowhere in sight. By the time she finished, I would be a mess of roiled emotions and negative thoughts.

So, needless to say, over time I developed a *major* resentment over Jenny's lecturing and treating me like an errant student of hers. This grievance toward her created a powerful protective part that was infuriated and actually hated her for what she'd put me through. My little boy exile was frightened of her and how she could make me feel just like I did with my shaming parents.

One day a couple of years ago, we had yet another argument over something I'd said. Sure enough, Jenny got in her teaching mode and let me have it. It was difficult for both of us but like so many times before, we got through it. Later that evening when we sat down to talk about it, Jenny revealed that for some time she had sensed that a part of me hated and resented her. She said my negative, hateful part that surfaced from time to time left her feeling unloved and unsafe. We agreed that it was time for me to do something about it.

After my talk with Jenny, I was determined to get over my anger and resentment against this person I loved. I didn't want to admit it, but I knew that a part of me actually hated her and wanted me to leave her for someone who would be easier to get along with. That protective part took over pretty much every time Jenny was upset with me and I just couldn't allow that anymore. I decided to do some work with the part and exile that had been so affected by her irritation and lecturing.

The following is a session/dialogue between my Captain and the part that had such a strong grievance against Jenny. Of course, I don't remember word for word how my session went, but this is pretty much how it happened. I hope this can be a helpful example of how you might get over a grievance toward your loved one. Although it may take several sessions to completely end the grievance, going through this process can also be a major step in healing a deeper childhood wound.

I started the process by going into my room, closing the door, and taking some deep breaths. After making sure that I was in my Captain, I invited the angry, hurt part of me to have his say. Sitting in a chair designated for the part, I closed my eyes and waited for the part to rise up and take over. It didn't take long. The part quickly began to surface with feelings of anger and bitterness.

Speaking out loud with a vengeance, the part began. "She has hurt us over and over with her goddamn lecturing. I hate it when she points that finger at us. Her fucking arrogance and know-it-all attitude drive me crazy. We knew more about psychology thirty years ago than she'll ever know. Who the hell does she think she is? We're not her damn student and we're sure as hell not her whipping boy who she can sit down in the corner and humiliate and shame."

Yelling, with lots of anger and rage, my part continued, "She's not some fucking guru. Screw that! She's ruined our self-confidence with her goddamn lecturing and making us wrong all the time. She won't accept an apology. She won't let us explain. She just starts on us and goes on and on and on until we're ready to explode. I hate her for what she's done to us. We'll never be the same again. Fucking bitch! We do *not* deserve to be treated this way. *I'm sick of it!*"

My part then furiously hit a pillow with a plastic bat I had handy just in case. After nearly a minute of raging, the part dropped the bat and calmed down into a docile, almost defeated state.

After a momentary pause, my Captain began in a sedate, supportive voice. "Wow. You're really upset by what Jenny's done to us. Every time she gets mad, we end up feeling small, hurt and humiliated. When she's irritated, it's like it's our fault and we've got to be in the wrong. And it seems like we've lost whatever self-esteem we might have had. It's been so hard for you to protect us because nothing you do or say seems to stop her, or even slow her down. It must drive you crazy to be so impotent against her anger."

Part, in a quiet, beaten-down voice: "I hate to admit it, but I can't handle her. All I do just makes her even angrier. I keep trying because there's nothing else we can do. I don't want us to just sit there while she tears us down into a little puddle."

Captain: "It seems like there's a part of us that's been broken by all of Jenny's angry lecturing and blaming. Is it possible that this woman we loved so much broke a little piece of our heart?"

Saddened, my part paused and then nodded, "Yes, I think that's what happened. She's done something to us. She's broken our little boy's heart."

Captain: "I'm wondering if you could take a moment and see if you can remember this sort of thing ever happening to us before we met Jenny."

Part, thinking for a moment: "Well, it's never really happened with other women we've lived with; I can tell you that!"

Captain: "How about when Marvin was a little boy with his mom and dad?"

Part, getting stirred up as it remembered some painful history: "Yes, they lectured, screamed, blamed, and almost scared that little boy to death. And they beat him hard with a belt and hurt him till he screamed for them to stop. I hated them for what they did to him."

Captain, compassionately: "That makes me really sad to think of an innocent little boy being so hurt and frightened by a mom and dad who were supposed to love him."

Part: "He was so scared and had nobody to turn to or protect him. Those times were just horrible. I couldn't protect him, but I could close his heart and fill him with rage against them. They might hurt his body and scare him and shame him, but they weren't going to break his heart over and over. At least I stopped that."

Captain: "Do you think some of your hate for them has gotten mixed up with your feelings toward Jenny? Is your hatred toward her left over from your hate of that little boy's mom and dad?"

Part, puzzled but interested: "Well . . . it could be. She's supposed to love us but she makes me feel just like they did: ashamed, scared, and unlovable. So yeah, I can see that my angry, hateful feelings towards Mom and Dad could be directed at Jenny. In a way, she's just like them, always hurting, scaring, and shaming us. She's become an enemy just like them."

Captain: I can see how easy it would be to mistake Jenny for an enemy like the parents were. But the truth is she's not anything like them. Let's look at a recent event that might help you change your mind about her."

Part: "She's hurt us a lot and she's been mean, but I'll listen to what you have to say."

Captain, in a soft voice: "Thank you. OK, let's just look at a situation the other day when Jenny got mad and started lecturing. Remember I asked Jenny to help me fix dinner that evening, and she sighed heavily and made an unhappy face at me. You got offended and immediately jerked the reins from Marvin and took charge.

"You then reacted to Jenny's sigh with, 'God, I can't believe it. You're not even willing to *help* with dinner? I've cooked the last three meals, and it *bothers* you that I just wanted ten minutes of your help? Jesus Christ!' You attacked her without waiting for her to explain the reason for her sigh or momentary irritation. You had no idea what was going on inside her at that moment. You just tried to make her feel guilty with your comment and your tone of voice. And she became angry. What'd you expect, a smile?"

Part, still confused, but a little interested: "So you're saying that *I* caused her to go from a minor irritation to getting angry and giving us a lecture."

Captain: "Yes. I'm saying that your combative comments created a mountain out of a molehill. If you hadn't reacted so strongly to her sigh, none of this would have happened."

Part: "Well, she didn't have to get upset and go on and on about how we never give her any room to have a feeling. We didn't say that much and then we even apologized. We told her, 'OK, OK. I'm sorry I said anything. Can you just let it go? I'll fix dinner by myself.' Remember?"

Captain: "Those were *your* comments, not mine. In an effort to protect us, *you* reacted and made Jenny angry. And it was you who aroused her protective parts. She kept repeating herself because she could see that (because of you) no one over here was listening or letting in a single thing she was saying. You got involved and tried to defend us by shutting her up because her words and her emotions were making you uncomfortable. Your anger and defensiveness kept us from really *hearing* anything she was saying. That's why she kept repeating the same things over and over.

"Jenny was not upset with us because we asked her to help with dinner. She was angry because *you* took over and reacted with anger to her slight frustration. It was your *reaction* that led to her anger; it wasn't the request for help that got her so riled up. Can you hear that?"

Part: "OK. Yes, I can see that. She didn't really get mad until I made a fuss over her sigh."

Captain: "Good. Now let's look at the real reason she got angry at us. *Your* angry comments were hurtful and were intended to make her feel guilty for not wanting to help at that moment. *That's* why she became angry. She was reacting to what you said and how you immediately blocked our love for her. You were hostile to her. Can you see that? You hurt her with your reaction."

Part: "Well . . . yes, I can see I was ugly to her. I treated her unfairly and I got all of us in trouble to boot. She didn't deserve what I did to her. I can see that."

Captain: "Now, for just a second I'd like for you to think

back about how his parents treated little Marvin and never let him have any feelings that weren't happy and positive. They were ugly to him and treated him unfairly, even though he didn't deserve it, just like you treated Jenny when she sighed."

Part: "Hmm... that's not a pretty thought; I don't like it and I sure as hell don't want to believe it. But now that you brought it up, I can't really deny it. I do treat her that way when I get upset."

Captain: "Thank you for understanding and admitting that it's true. I'd like to go one step further if I may. Is it possible that when you get upset with her you treat her worse than she treats us?"

Part, getting exasperated: "Look, this is not something I've ever thought about. I just can't imagine that's true; I don't lecture her for one thing."

Captain: "No, you don't do that, but you do curse her, yell at her, call her names, and even throw out veiled threats about leaving her."

Part: "That's not fair. I only do those things when she drives me nuts with her lecturing. I just explode because I can't take it anymore."

Captain: "I understand that you treat her so harshly only when you lose control. But you still treat her harshly just like our parents treated us. Think about it; she doesn't call us names, rarely yells, and never threatens to leave."

Part: "OK, already. It's possible I might be worse on her than she is on us. I don't want to think about it right now. I can hardly believe it anyway. I'll have to think some more on it later."

Captain: "Good. Now let's go back to the episode over Jenny's sigh about helping with dinner. I'd like you to really be open to seeing the truth about what actually happened. You just assumed that Jenny's sigh meant she didn't want to help because she was lazy or didn't care. And then you reacted according to your assumption. Was it possible that her sigh really had nothing to do with this, but was about what was going on with her at that moment? Wasn't she finishing an email at the time? Maybe she just didn't want to be interrupted until she finished. Maybe she was frustrated about something else and was just in an off mood. Maybe it had nothing to do with helping to fix dinner."

Part: "I never even thought of that. I guess I fly off the handle pretty quickly. I never gave her a chance to explain what was going on with her."

Captain: "Yes, you do seem to go off before getting the facts. You've got this habit of interpreting her irritation as being against us rather than just an expression of where she is in that moment. And don't forget that lots of times she's just reacting to some thoughtless or hurtful thing *you* said or did. At other times, she's just in a frustrated or anxious mood. In either case, there's no need for you to defend or protect us because from now on, I will handle these situations. I have handled a few of these recently and there was a much better outcome, don't you agree? There's no reason to *attack* her. Give her a few minutes and she'll be over it. She's not going to leave us or stop loving us just because she got momentarily irritated."

Part: "So I don't have to worry or get upset when she's irritated? There's no danger? Are you saying I don't have to protect us every time she gets irritated?"

Captain: "That's exactly what I'm saying. There's no danger. You can relax and maybe even try to understand the real reason she's upset. Maybe you can even learn to see things from her point of view when she's frustrated or irritated. Think about it; haven't you sighed or become irritated with Jenny sometimes? Hasn't she said or done something that bothered you? And it doesn't mean we are going to leave her or stop loving her just because you're a little upset, does it?"

It was important to get it across to the part that he was projecting his inaccurate beliefs about the sigh onto Jenny, and then *reacting to his projection*. The part needed to learn that he is fallible and that his interpretations were often mistaken. This doubt about his perceptions and the resulting crack in his armor were critical to re-educating and repurposing the protective part. When brought face to face with the light of reason and truth, the part began to falter and could no longer hold on to his fantasies and distorted beliefs. Achieving this is an essential step in healing a grievance or even a wound. This is only possible to see with a clear and unblended Captain.

Captain: "Thanks for understanding. Now, let's get to the real meat of the situation. You have a grievance toward Jenny because she lectures and makes us wrong 'all the time.' Is that right?"

Part: "Yes. She does it all the time and has been doing it for years and I'm really sick of it. I don't do it to her and I don't deserve it."

Captain: "I agree with you that nobody deserves to be lectured all the time, but I'm wondering just how often she really lectures us. Is it every day or once a week or twice a month?"

Part: "I don't know; sometimes it's several times a week. But for sure, it's always more than once a month.

Captain: "Can you see that her lecturing you occasionally is not all the time? Since we spend virtually all day, seven days a week with her, a few times a month is not that much. Actually, considering the time we spend with Jenny, her lecturing takes up only a tiny percentage of our time together. Isn't that true?"

Part: "Well, yeah, if you put it like that, I suppose she doesn't lecture us all that much. But it feels like it's all the time."

Captain: "Yes, you may *feel* like it's all the time, but the truth is, she lectures only a few times a year. It's very important to understand that what it feels like and what the truth is can be two very different things.

"So it seems like a part of your resentment and grievance against Jenny is based on something that isn't true. She doesn't lecture us all the time. In fact, she hardly ever lectures at all. Isn't that right?"

Part: "It's hard to believe, but when you put it like that, I guess you're right. It's kind of shocking to hear that she doesn't do it all that much. It really does seem like it happens all the time. And because of that, I've hated her and guarded our heart around her for several years. Have I been wrong all this time?"

Captain: "Yes, it's very possible you've been wrong about her. You've overreacted to her upsets and to her attempts to get us to understand her and her feelings. I sense that you're beginning to see the real picture. I know it's hard for you to accept that you've hurt her unnecessarily for years. You were trying to protect our little boy as best as you could with the tools you had. I truly appreciate all your efforts and join you in feeling sad that those efforts were misguided and ended up hurting Jenny. They also hurt our relationship and our attempts to have intimacy and connection. Now that you can see the truth about her lecturing, I'd like to explore those lectures and see if there might be another misunderstanding. Is it possible that most of her lectures are not really lectures at all, but merely attempts to get us to hear what she's trying to say?"

Part: "Maybe she didn't lecture that often, but I know a lecture when I hear one. When she spends ten minutes yammering about the same thing over and over and won't listen to a single thing I try to say, she's lecturing. And she refuses to ever say *anything* positive about us during her rant. And after five or six minutes of it, I'm ready to explode."

Captain: "Yeah, she can be pretty harsh and rigid when she

talks to us like that. I have two questions for you. First, why do you think she does that? Secondly, why do you think it bothers you so much that you want to explode?"

Part: "I think she lectures because she likes to drill it into our head how much she knows and how right she is. She says the same things over and over because she wants to make sure we get it. And it's her way of punishing us for saying or doing something she didn't like. And why do I get so upset? Wouldn't anybody want to explode if they had to listen to that?"

Captain: "I'm curious about just what it is she's saying that makes you so angry. Is she calling us names or screaming at us? Can you give me an example of a typical lecturing scenario?"

Part: "No, she doesn't call us names or anything like that, and she doesn't really scream that much either. A scene that happens over and over again is where she gets irritated with us over nothing and then I don't like it and get upset with her. Then she gets angry and keeps telling us things like we're not her ally because we have a reaction every time she is not one hundred percent pleased. She says that we can't be her friend as long as we don't give her room to have her feelings. Then she'll say something like she doesn't feel safe with us because we get mad at her if she's not perfectly happy. And she says these things over and over."

Captain: "OK, I get it. I'm wondering what you're doing while she's talking."

Part: "Well, a part of me is trying to listen, but another part is so sick of her lecturing that I just want to scream. I usually just sit there and take it. Sometimes I say, 'I'm sorry, OK?' or 'Look, I didn't get that mad at you. See, I'm listening.' Sometimes I tell her that there's no reason for her to have become irritated. All the while, I'm fuming that she's trying to shame and humiliate us. She treats us like a schoolboy who's done something bad."

Captain: "It sounds like she's trying to tell us something but you can't hear her because your anger and shame keep getting in the way. Is it possible that your body language and the things you're saying reveal that we're not able to listen or hear her? Maybe she's repeating herself because her feelings are hurt and she wants us to know that. She wants us to know what's going on inside her. Maybe she's not lecturing at all, but just trying to get us to understand her and empathize with her feelings. Have you ever thought that she just wants to connect and be heard at that moment, and *you* make it impossible for us to simply be there for her?"

Part: "If she wanted a connection, you'd think she could find a better way to do it than just yak at us."

Captain: "Maybe so, but remember she's upset and might not be at her best. Maybe she's trying the best she knows how considering the circumstances. Maybe her intention is not to punish us, but to be heard and understood. Maybe she just wanted a friend and ally to help and support her through her irritation and upset. Is that possible?"

Part: "Well . . . yeah, it's possible. Do you really think she was trying to be understood and not just trying to punish us by being stubborn and lecturing?"

Captain: "I'm sad that as the Captain, it's taken me so long to realize it, but, yes, I'm convinced that during all this time and all those 'lectures' she was just trying to get us to hear her, understand her, and empathize with her feelings. We've got to give her credit for not giving up on us. Think about it. She's hung in there for years trying to get us to be there for her and her feelings. She must really love us and believe that there's hope that we can change."

Part: "So you're telling me that all this time I've been resenting her and thinking she was bad for lecturing us when she was just trying to have her feelings and to be understood and supported? Are you kidding me?"

Captain: "No, I'm not kidding. I believe it's true, and I'm asking you to believe it as well."

Part: "Oh my God. If it's true, then I've made a huge mistake and have done Jenny a great disservice. How could I have been so blind and so stupid? How many times have I hurt her and prevented you from being there for her when she needed us? I gave her hell for just trying to be understood. I feel confused and ashamed of what I've done all these years."

Captain: "Please don't feel ashamed. You saw Jenny's irritation and her attempts to be understood as a threat when in reality she was just trying to get her needs met. Like all of us, you've done the best you could with the information and the resources you had at hand. When you came into existence, I was a little boy. I needed you to protect us then and you tried your best. And I know you've been trying ever since. It's just that you've never realized that once we grew up, we no longer needed you. You've never understood that as the Captain, it has been my job to protect us."

Part: "Maybe so, but you haven't done such a good job of protecting us. Every time somebody hurts us, you're nowhere to be found. It's always been up to me to do the protecting and defending."

Captain: "You're right about that. I've been missing in action and have never known how to protect us until now. Please trust me and know that I can take care of us from now on. In fact, I'm going to start by communicating with the exiled little boy you've been protecting. I'll get back to you later."

Captain to his exiled little boy: "Hello. I'm wondering if we could talk for a bit. I know I haven't spent much time with you all these years, but I want that to change. I want to get to know you and I hope you'll forgive me for neglecting you for so long. Can we talk?"

Because exiles have been hidden away in the basement of

our minds for so long, it is difficult for them to communicate in words as easily as other parts. Although exiles communicate mostly through feelings and body language, an aware Captain, using intuition and insight, can often give words to these nonverbal expressions, thus allowing the exiles to "talk." When trying to "get into" an exile, it's usually necessary to just sit quietly and let your mind drift back to your early days as a child and toddler, allowing memories to surface. Then encourage him or her to shift attention to the present moment and the feelings that are coming up.

Exile, after a few moments: "Yes, maybe, but I don't really know you."

Captain, tenderly: "I understand completely. I've acted as though you weren't there for so long. I think I was afraid of your strong feelings and how powerfully they could affect me. I didn't want to experience what you've gone through, so I just pretended as best as I could that you weren't there. I've left you to carry that burden all by yourself, and I'm so sorry I did that. I want you to know that, as of right now, things are going to change. From now on, I want you to share your burdens with me. I want to start protecting you and keeping you safe. You will no longer have to depend on those protective parts who just make things worse for you, keeping away the intimacy, love, and security you've always needed so desperately. Can you let me be there for you?"

Exile: "I just feel scared and alone all the time. I don't know how to trust. I just need someone to hold me and keep me safe."

Captain: "I'm so sorry I've left you alone all this time. I didn't want to feel all those scary feelings you've had to deal with. I'm ready now to let you share those feelings with me whenever you're ready."

Exile: "I'm not ready, but I feel a little hope that you might be there for me."

Captain: "I'll be there for you from now on and there's something I'd like to help you with right now. Does it scare you when Jenny gets mad at us?"

Exile: "Yes, I'm afraid she's going to hurt me. And I feel ashamed because if she's upset, that means I've done something wrong. I feel these terrible things over and over. It's been the same since I was a baby and a little boy. Every time somebody gets mad at me, I feel scared and ashamed."

Captain: "I hear you. It must feel so unfair because you didn't do anything to her. It's the protective parts that get her upset and then you have to pay the price with those terrible feelings. You must feel helpless to stop these awful fights between Marvin and Jenny. You need her love so desperately, and yet the protective parts keep attacking her, making her feeling unsafe and unable to love you the way you need to be loved."

Exile: "I want her love and I want to feel safe with her. And I want your love too."

Captain: "My love is yours from now on and our protective part has promised me that it will let me protect you from Jenny's anger. You'll see that once the protector is not making things worse, Jenny's upsets will not be scary. She's going to get mad at us sometimes and that's OK because if she starts lecturing, I will remove us from the situation until she calms down. I will not allow you to be hammered by her angry parts anymore."

Exile: "So I don't have to be afraid of her anymore?"

Captain: "No, my little one. You don't have to be afraid. You'll see that Jenny is a good woman who sometimes gets upset or irritated at us. If our parts don't make it worse, she'll usually get over it in a few minutes. She'll still love us and want to spend her life with us. It might be a little uncomfortable sometimes, but never unsafe for you. With me as your Captain and protector and Jenny as someone who loves us, you can now relax. Finally, you're safe and secure."

Exile, feeling hopeful: "I'm going to try my best to trust you and believe that I am safe."

Captain: "Good. I'll be talking to you soon."

It's important to understand that my exile was traumatized by angry parents who had little self-awareness and virtually no helpful information about how to raise a child. The fact that they were both very wounded themselves as children only made matters much worse. Because of this, my various exiles were deeply wounded and terrorized by neglect and abuse, leaving them filled with frightening memories and overwhelmingly negative emotions. In this session, those emotions and that deep-seated fear didn't come out and maybe never will. I can only try to gradually access my exiles *and* their feelings over time. It may take two more sessions or twenty, but each time I talk to one of my exiles I seem to get a little more comfortable in my own skin.

Interestingly, Jenny, and I'm sure many others are more successful at accessing the emotions of their exiles. Obviously, this can be an advantage when trying to truly unburden the wounded inner selves.

(This brings us to a note of caution here. It is possible that your exile has been so traumatized that uncovering it and the emotions it carries could result in you being re-traumatized and overwhelmed with frightening feelings. For this reason, if you suspect that you've been terribly wounded, it would be a good idea to seek counseling with an experienced IFS therapist.)

Back to my session and the Captain, who's once again speaking to the protective part.

Captain: "I've spoken to the exile and he's willing to let me protect him from now on. You can let go of that job you've held for so long. And now that you're seeing and accepting the truth about Jenny, you don't have to worry about her ever again.

"And just as importantly, you're becoming aware that most

of the time she wasn't really lecturing us so much as trying to get us to hear and understand what was going on with her and her feelings. She wanted us to understand that we hurt her in some way and to empathize with how she felt. Now you're learning that she is a good woman with a good heart who loves us and occasionally gets upset with us. And remember, she had parents who hurt her and left her wounded like us. You *do* see that, don't you?"

Part, softer, repentant, and more receptive: "Yes, I can see that she's a good person who was hurt by her parents. She's just been trying to get her needs met the best way she knows how. I'm done with grievances and hard feelings. But I have to say, there were times when she was just mean when we didn't deserve it. There were times when she exploded at us for no good reason. Those times hurt us and scared us."

Captain: "Yes, I agree she did do those things—not often, but they did happen. Please understand that Jenny is human and has also been wounded in her childhood. She's going to be overtaken by her parts occasionally and unfairly blame us for her painful feelings. But that rarely happens and doesn't mean she's stopped loving us or that she's going to leave. And remember, from now on I will take charge and get her to stop before the lecturing begins. You might feel *uncomfortable* when she gets irritated, but you're not *unsafe*.

"When she gets upset at us, instead of getting upset right back at her, I need you to stand down and maybe even help me focus on her feelings and what she needs. If she's upset, she needs something from us. Rather than defending by attacking or withdrawing, you can be there to help me figure out what it is she needs. Help me show her what it's like to have an ally and be loved, OK?"

Part: "Aye, aye, Captain. I'll do my best!"

It took just three sessions like this one to finally let go of my grievance toward Jenny about her lecturing me. Incredibly, the resentment is gone. I can talk with her about past conflicts and "lecturing" without having the slightest negative thought or feeling. When I think of those times now, I can see in my mind's eye how she was desperately trying, in the only way she knew how, to get me to *see* her, understand her, and empathize with her and her feelings. Knowing that she has her own troubles with protective parts, exiles, and emotional wounds make it possible to help her with my Captain whenever she needs it.

Please remember that my Captain is experienced and has had a couple of years and quite a few sessions to get the hang of talking to his parts and exiles. Your first session or two between your Captain and your parts might not go as smoothly as you'd like, but trust me, it will get better as you go along. And *any* session should result in increased self-awareness and maybe even a little growth. Over time, these sessions can become a powerful way to change yourself and your relationship. And the good news is that you can do them without your partner if he or she is unwilling or unavailable.

While solo sessions can benefit you greatly, you'll likely achieve better results with a wise, compassionate therapist or friend. But whether by yourself or with another, the attention, understanding, compassion, and insights from your dialogue could give your wounded and frightened exiles the validation and empathy they have always needed to feel safe, valued, and loved.

Chapter 20:

Hurt Feelings

I THINK IT'S SAFE to assume that virtually everyone on the planet has had their feelings hurt at one time or another. In fact, by the time we reach adulthood, most of us have endured hurt feelings hundreds, if not thousands of times. But what does it mean to get our feelings hurt?

In the language of Internal Family Systems, hurt feelings result from something that happens outside of ourselves that offended, frightened, shamed or threatened one of our hidden exiles. Our feelings may also be hurt when something happens that leaves our exile or inner self feeling small, neglected, unloved, or disregarded.

Unless we can remain in our Captains, the hurt exile will trigger our protective parts, which then react with an angry attack, a hostile or frightened withdrawal, a dissociative state where we can't feel or think, or a negative spate of internal dialogue. In the midst of these reactions are a temporary loss of wisdom and a closing of the heart. Hurt feelings are fertile territory for resentment and diminished emotional safety.

The reactions I've described are typical for most of us when our feelings get hurt and our protective parts get involved. However, there are other healthier ways to respond that involve either the Captain or a hurt exile that bypasses the protectors and responds directly to the "offender." A client and her daughter demonstrated how hurt feelings can be expressed through vulnerability and emotional honesty.

Several years ago, I worked with Linda, a smart, attractive single mom in her late twenties who had been raised by critical, unhappy parents. Because of her past, she tended to be a bit prickly and emotionally unavailable. During a session, she proudly shared an event from the day before. Tired and stressed after working all day, she'd finished cooking and let her daughter know that dinner was ready. After calling out a couple of times, a look through the screen door revealed her little girl still playing in the sandbox.

Flooded with frustration and anger, Linda yelled, "*Goddammit, Melissa. Get in here right this minute.*"

Dressed in her cute little jumpsuit and her tiny pink tennis shoes, Melissa bowed her head. With tears streaming down her cheeks, she trudged into the house and put her head against the refrigerator door. With hands hiding her face, she tearfully blurted out, "Mommy, you broke my feelings."

Thankfully, the three months of therapy had softened Linda's heart. She knelt down and wrapped her arms around Melissa. Through tears of her own, she responded, "I'm so sorry I broke your feelings, sweetie. I should never have yelled at you. Did it scare you?"

Without looking up, Melissa nodded. "You *scared* me."

"Mommy was just tired after working all day. It wasn't your fault and I was wrong to yell at you and scare you. You're a good girl, and I love you very much. Can you forgive me?"

After a few moments, Melissa nodded her head again, and then, in a cheerful voice announced, "I'm hungry."

Because Melissa responded straight from her exile with her true feelings of hurt, there was no anger or protective strategy directed at her mother. This allowed her mother to respond back without *her* protective parts getting triggered.

And because her parts were not involved, Linda was able to address her daughter's hurt feelings in a healthy, rational way. The heartfelt apology provided Melissa with acceptance, compassion, and closure, allowing the whole episode to be resolved and forgotten.

Now imagine for a moment that, through pouted lips, Melissa had angrily spewed out, "I hate you! You're mean." If that had happened, I seriously doubt Linda would have responded with a heartfelt apology. More likely, she would have grabbed her by the arm and yelled, "Don't you talk to your mother that way. Now say you're sorry, right now."

This would have hurt Melissa's feelings all over again, only this time, she would have to smother them while begrudgingly uttering, "OK, I'm sorry." Her repressed emotions would probably leave yet another sprinkling of shame, resentment, and anger in her young psyche. Further, Melissa's willingness to trust her mother with her feelings would erode, stifling her vulnerability, even with her own mother. The evening meal would have been an unhappy affair, and, more importantly, another brick in the wall between mother and daughter would have been laid.

How we respond to hurt feelings is of the utmost importance, especially in a love relationship where emotional trust and vulnerability are so paramount. In virtually all cases, the wise response to hurt feelings in a relationship is to become vulnerable and share the true emotions you're experiencing. Unfortunately, many, if not most adults in our country do not handle their hurt feelings that way. Men tend to react with either angry attacks on the offending person or stoically swallowing the hurt and acting like nothing happened. They have a hard time being vulnerable enough to admit that their feelings are hurt. Women, on the other hand, trained to be "socially appropriate," often restrain their reactions even though they feel the hurt.

It is hugely important for both partners in a love relationship to be open about their feelings, whether they are negative or positive. If your feelings are hurt, the wisest course of action (in most cases) is to tell your partner that your feelings were hurt as a result of something that just happened. It is counterproductive to say, "*You* hurt my feelings just now." When you say that, you're blaming your partner for your feelings and will likely trigger his or her protective parts, resulting in them becoming defensive, withdrawing, or outright attacking. And of course, that's the last thing you want to do. If you can stay emotionally honest and vulnerable when your feelings are hurt, there's a good chance that your partner will really hear you and respond with heart and empathy.

One morning after breakfast, Jenny commented with a little edge in her voice that I had washed only my plate, glass, and silverware, subtly implying that because I didn't do her dishes, I was somehow stingy with my time and energy. She followed her observation with, "When *I* do dishes, I do all of them, yours included."

Here, after I fixed breakfast, I was doing my dishes so she wouldn't have to. And she was giving me grief about it? I was offended by her response and had an exile that felt shamed for not washing her dishes as well as mine. I felt my protective part's anger at Jenny rising up in me, but I was able to restrain myself from acting on it. After breathing deeply a couple of times, I managed to be vulnerable and tell her what seemed to be happening inside me. "Honey, I was trying to save you a little work and you get upset with me! There's a familiar part of me that feels righteous indignation and wants to lash out at you, but I don't want to do that. Another part of me just feels hurt and maybe ashamed that I didn't do your dishes as well as mine.

I don't know, I guess I just feel hurt." (To dissipate my feelings and be done with the episode, I needed to be understood.) Without seeming to understand, Jenny responded, "Hey, I was just pointing it out. I wasn't judging you. It's just kind of weird, that's all."

Put off by the word weird and a lack of understanding, I had to take a deep breath to help me regulate my feelings. "OK, maybe it *is* weird. I learned to do it as a child, and I guess I'm still trying to please my mother. I don't see the harm in it, but if it bothers you, I'll do it differently. I just don't want you to believe that I'm selfish because I've occasionally taken care of only my dishes. It's just a habit."

Jenny continues, unaware that I'm just trying to be understood. "Well, I don't know that it bothers me all that much; it just seems a little weird for you to do your dishes and leave mine on the table." (Jenny is trying to get me to understand why she had an issue with me doing only my dishes while I'm trying to get her to understand why I do it and why my feelings got hurt. Neither one of us is getting our needs met.)

At this point in the interaction, it would have been easy for me to give in to an angry, impatient part that wants to attack Jenny with something like, "You're just impossible to please. No matter what I do, you're never happy or satisfied! For Christ's sake, what's the matter with you anyway?" I have allowed my parts to go off on her several times in our relationship and we always end up in bitter fights with lots of hurt feelings. I've learned the hard way that managing my parts and the negative emotions that go with them results in much better outcomes.

With my frustration rising, I take yet another deep breath while staying in my Captain. "Jenny, I understand that this behavior might seem a bit strange to you. I really do. But aside from that, I want you to understand that I got my feelings hurt and that I don't want you to believe I'm selfish."

Feeling at least somewhat understood, Jenny was able to respond to my request for understanding. "Marvin, I can see how you could get your feelings hurt. You were trying to help and I gave you grief about it. And as far as the selfish thing is concerned, we're all a little selfish at times. I think you have a very generous heart and it shows in lots of things you do and say. I don't think doing just your dishes makes you selfish at all." She laughed, "It just weird, that's all."

I laughed with her and the episode came to a happy ending.

Able to share my hurt feelings and receive a bit of understanding from Jenny, I was satisfied, my parts settled down, and no damage had been done to my exile or the relationship. That exchange was very different from what it would have been six years ago before we began our work. Back then, it would have gone something like this:

Jenny: "I noticed you only washed your dishes. What's up with that? I wash all of them when I do the dishes."

Marvin, probably responding with some heat in my voice: "Hey, what's that supposed to mean? You're giving me grief because I cooked breakfast and only washed my dishes? How many times have you fixed something to eat for yourself and never even asked me what I wanted? That's like the fucking pot calling the kettle black, isn't it? Millions of women out there would love it if their husbands did their own dishes. Obviously, you're not one of them."

Jenny, her protective parts ready to fire back: "That's just like you, getting all upset over nothing. I can't say anything without you getting your feelings hurt. I didn't mean anything by it, and now you're pissed off. Good job at being a grown-up, Marvin, because now *both* of us are pissed off. The whole day is ruined."

Needless to say, her prediction about the day would've been all too accurate. We've spent too many days and nights fighting over hurt feelings, all the while adding to our growing arsenal of mutual resentment.

Because a person's reactive parts are hypersensitive and tend to exaggerate or misinterpret "offenses," hurt feelings should be handled by either the Captain or a vulnerable exile. With their tendency toward righteous indignation, blame, and victimhood, the protective parts cause us to actually hurt our own feelings.

While working as a psychiatric nurse at a local hospital, my sister Anna was kidding around with another nurse we'll call Joanne. At one point, Anna laughingly said, "Joanne, you're such a character," and then tapped her on the shoulder with four little pieces of paper she had rolled up.

Immediately, Joanne's mood changed as she became deeply offended and even shocked. She blamed Anna for hitting and traumatizing her and was so upset she had to take the rest of the day off. Anna, who would not purposefully hurt or offend anyone, was mortified.

The next day, Joanne came back to work, and, after some discussion, she told Anna that she spent a long time the previous evening thinking about what had happened and why she had reacted so strongly. She finally got it that Anna had done nothing wrong and that her reaction was a result of being physically abused as a child by both her mother and father. It's not like they had punched her or beat her with a board; they had just slapped her occasionally and whipped her hard with a belt. She cried while telling Anna how sorry she was for overreacting.

In this situation, Joanne was able to become aware of the reasons for her overreaction, thus creating a good outcome. In virtually every love relationship, men and women frequently get their feelings hurt because of a sensitivity born of past experiences. Because they don't get to the root cause of their hurt feelings, they tend to blame their hurt on the partner.

A good example of how we hurt our own feelings and cause ourselves most of our misery in relationships happened a few days ago to a golfing buddy of mine. After a frustrating round of golf, Jack went home and walked around his five acres trying to shake off the lingering disappointment from his poor play. He brightened up a bit as he thought that maybe after dinner, he and his wife Susan could have a nice, relaxed roll in the hay.

After dinner, he decided to load the dishwasher as a token of appreciation for a good meal and also as brownie points to be used later that night. Because his stay-at-home wife took care of all the cooking and cleaning, Jack rarely needed to pitch in, but this time he wanted to help. After loading the dishwasher, he sat down and started reading the news on his computer, feeling good about helping out and looking forward to a little sensual dessert.

It wasn't too long before his wife came in and, with a bit of irritation, gave him some feedback about how the dishwasher had been loaded improperly. Jack slammed his laptop closed and screamed, "What? Are you kidding me? I take care of the dishes for you, and that's what I get? You're such a fucking perfectionist. Nothing I ever do pleases you. You're impossible. No wonder I never try to help out around the house. I try to pitch in, and this is what I get: a bunch of freaking criticism."

It would probably take a session to get to the bottom of his extreme reaction, but one thing's for sure; he *did* overreact. Should she have said anything negative about his efforts? It would have been much better to just smile, shake her head, and silently say something like, "He's such a guy." While it's true she could have handled it better, she certainly didn't deserve his volcano.

When Jack told me his story a few days later, he still wasn't clear about who was at fault for the painful episode. Although he was a little sheepish and embarrassed as he revealed his behavior, he evidently believed that her "nagging and criticism" provoked him and ultimately caused his reaction. In his defense, he said, "If she hadn't bitched about the way I loaded the thing, none of it would have happened. I'd have just read the news and we'd have gone to bed, made love, and everything would have been fine. She started it."

Jenny and I call that kind of argument "bullshit" because, while there's a kernel of truth to it, the notion as a whole is false. What he failed to let in is that if he hadn't overreacted, very little discord would have taken place and he could have still had his dessert. Everything would have worked out fine if he had responded with, "Ouch. My feelings just got hurt. I tried to help you with the dishes and you criticized my efforts. That hurts. I guess I just suck at loading the dishwasher."

With that honest response, his wife ideally might have said something like, "I'm sorry. I'm just a little weird about how things are stacked in the dishwasher. I didn't mean for your feelings to get hurt. That was actually very sweet of you. And there are a million things you don't suck at!" Of course, both responses are optimal and probably better than most of us would do on the spur of the moment, especially when a bit stressed. But with effort and some healing of sensitive, wounded exiles, we can learn to respond to hurt feelings without becoming victims or hauling out the heavy artillery. There *are* healthy, adult ways to protect yourself and to express your hurt feelings.

Reacting to our hurts with childish parts will seldom result in anything positive. Think about it for a moment; Jack was happily reading the news until his wife made the comment. After her statement, he was overtaken by angry, frustrated parts and attacked her with a verbal barrage, leaving her tearful and angry. His protective parts parlayed a little hurt feeling into a big fight, with pain and suffering on both sides. In other words, he hurt his own feelings and ruined his chances for a romantic evening. Of course, because he was completely overtaken by his parts, he was unable to see that the problem wasn't her comment; it was his *reaction* to her comment that caused the angry standoff.

Jenny and I have had so much trouble over hurt feelings that we developed a scale from one to ten to express not only our level of hurt but also the degree of egregiousness of the offending party. In other words, in the above example, we would probably concur that Susan's level of offense was no more than a one, and that Jack's level of hurt and reaction was a seven. In this case, it's easy to see that something's wrong. Because Jack's hurt was six points higher than the offense, we have to look underneath his reactions to see what's really causing the majority of his hurt.

Using the scale helps partners identify where the problem is so that it can be fixed. Over time, we learned to use this scale to express our level of upset, hurt, or anger. For instance, a mild annoyance or disquiet might rate a one or one and a half out of a possible ten. An upset that involved a few tears or raised voices might be a four, and if loud name-calling, cussing, threats, and door slamming came into play, then we're talking about somewhere closer to an eight or nine. This simple scale has become pretty important in our relationship.

If Jenny expresses her irritation with "that look" or a sigh, she's probably upset at a level of a one. Sadly, her one can cause me to react with a four or five. At the hint of her disappointment or disapproval, I might say—with an edge in my voice—something like, "What's going on? What have I done now? I didn't say anything to upset you."

Then she might tell me what upset her, and I might follow it with, "You're upset over *that*? I didn't mean *anything* by that."

And then Jenny would get more upset because I didn't give her room to even have a small feeling without minimizing or discounting it. We believe we should be able to have small upsets—a level of one, for instance —without the other partner getting upset and causing repercussions. We call it having a little wiggle room. Of course, if a partner gets a "little upset" every time we turn around, then that partner needs to look at what's going on inside him or her.

Certainly, if your partner is physically abusive, threatening, contemptuous, or calls you offensive names, then an appropriate protective or defensive reaction would be understandable and even healthy. In that case, it would be fair to say that your partner's offensive behavior certainly contributed to your distressing feelings.

This kind of thinking, however, can lead you down the slippery slope of blame. It is far better and more accurate to just assume that you are *always* in charge of and responsible for your feelings. Learning to manage your emotions even when facing challenging situations is a huge step toward personal empowerment and psychological growth.

Chapter 21:

The Natural Tendency to Blame Others

When an arrow does not hit its target, the marksman blames himself, not another person. A wise man behaves in the same way.

—*Confucius*

During fourteen years of counseling couples, I've rarely had clients start therapy by taking responsibility for the unhappiness in their relationships. Instead, they focused on the various ways their partners hurt, disappointed, or frightened them. While my clients could readily describe the flaws in their partners, they couldn't see how they contributed to the arguments, fights, and lack of passion and joy. They had no idea that they were actually causing much of their own misery and suffering.

This is understandable because it is natural to look outside ourselves for the source of our pain or distress. If we're walking outdoors and feel a sudden sting on our arm, we discover that it was caused by a wasp. We feel miserable from a cold we caught because someone came to work sick. We feel irritated by a nearby car with a horn that is blaring repeatedly. We feel scared while on a hike in the woods because we heard what sounded like a bear growling. In these and countless other situations, we can legitimately point to something outside ourselves that caused our feelings to be affected. This has been the case since our infancy. So, if our partners say or do something which scares us, makes us uncomfortable, or hurts our feelings, it makes perfect sense to believe that they caused our distress. Unfortunately, however, it's not that simple.

As with most human behavior, blaming falls on a continuum. Partners blame each other for everything from missing toothpaste caps to extramarital affairs. This chapter, however, is not about toothpaste caps or other minor inconveniences. Instead, it focuses on our habit of blaming our unhappiness, hurt feelings, anger, or lack of emotional safety on our partners because of something they've said, done or didn't do.

In other words, we're going to explore the phenomenon of blaming others for how we feel. We'll also examine how that kind of blaming affects our happiness, satisfaction with the relationship, and ability to create authentic love and connection. And, as you will see, blaming also stymies opportunities for our personal growth and evolution.

Working with your tendency to blame, however, can be like opening the proverbial can of worms. It can be painful, frustrating, and confusing to realize that you may have been blaming your partner for *your* shortcomings and feelings that come from *your* wounded past. Our egos *do not* like the idea of owning our flaws and hurtful behavior. But that is exactly what is called for if we ever want to change ourselves for the better.

100-Percent Responsibility

Sadly, neither Jenny nor I have been immune to the blame game in our relationship. Within a few months of our wedding, we'd already started our blaming and finger pointing. Of course, it didn't happen every day, but when feelings got hurt, the blaming wasn't far behind.

Even though this sort of thing can be a reflexive habit, it's important to understand that it is much more than that.

Blaming is a way to protect our egos by avoiding the shadow parts of ourselves that we don't like and can't accept. It's more comfortable to look at the faults of others because shining the light on our personal baggage can leave us feeling guilty, ashamed, or even frightened.

To help us resolve difficult issues where blame might be involved, Jenny and I developed a technique we called *100-percent responsibility*, which means that no matter what the other does or doesn't do, we are totally responsible for our feelings, reactions, and self-talk.

Following this rule left us no place to hide. We could no longer blame our feelings or our reactions on our partner, even if it was obvious that his or her error had a lot to do with our upset. This forced us to place all of our attention on the *reactive parts* within us, which presented the opportunity to explore and understand why we reacted the way we did.

Taking 100-percent responsibility also required us to "confess" our roles—no matter how small—in the upset, and then to apologize. When *both* partners do this, they will find that the negative feelings diminish or disappear entirely.

This process of taking responsibility may be one of the hardest things you will ever do. As we stated earlier, blaming others for our feelings and reactions is as natural as breathing. Blaming partners for our hurt feelings keeps us from having to look at the shame, guilt, or even fear of abandonment that's underneath those feelings. The protective parts that make up our "egos" don't want to admit that we are oversensitive, have faults, or could be wrong about anything. It takes time, courage, and ruthless determination to face our blaming and deal with its underlying causes.

I remember all too well an incident I'm not proud of that happened a couple of years ago. With some irritation in her voice, Jenny had asked me to turn down the volume on the television. Her irritation activated my protective part who instantly took the stage with distorted thinking and an emotional charge. My inner dialogue sounded something like this: "Everything I do irritates her. I can't even watch a football game in my own house. Just because she's a snob who doesn't like television doesn't mean that *I* shouldn't be able to enjoy it. I'm sick of her trying to boss me around. The TV wasn't that loud anyway. What's wrong with her that she's so irritable all the time?"

Under the influence of the offended part, I immediately turned off the TV and walked out of the room in a huff. As I sat on the bed and sulked in the company of my offended part, I just knew that she was responsible for my anger and hurt. If she hadn't been so irritable, I'd still be happily watching my program. It was obvious that her intolerance caused the whole thing, making me miss my game.

By keeping my focus on Jenny and her annoyance, I could completely ignore my childlike reaction. I didn't have to own the fact that I was acting like a pouty little kid and I didn't have to think about *why* I acted that way. Nor would I have to look in the mirror and face the fact that *I* was the major cause of my angry, hurt feelings. And finally, without the awareness and willingness required to look at and own my distorted thinking and behavior, there would be no possibility for me to understand and heal the underlying causes of my reaction. In other words, if I continue to blame, I'll avoid looking at my "stuff," continue to react like a child, and never have a chance to grow or change with respect to this issue.

Thank God somebody could act like an adult in our little tiff. After giving me a little time to sulk, Jenny gently reminded me of our agreement to take 100-percent responsibility for our feelings and behavior. Still heavily influenced by my upset protective part, I didn't want to hear about any agreement. I closed my eyes and did some deep breathing. I knew she was right, but I still didn't want to accept that I had basically caused the whole upset. I couldn't have made this mess all by myself! Was that even possible? Me? A grown, rational man and a therapist to boot? My ego-driven part was happy to answer those questions. "Of course you're not responsible for what happened. It was her irritation that caused the whole thing."

It took a few more minutes for my Captain to come online. It was a painful, bitter pill to swallow, but I eventually accepted that I had hurt my own feelings and blamed it on Jenny. I had caused myself to be missing out on the football game; Jenny didn't cause it! I did *not* want to believe it but I could see that Jenny had done virtually nothing to upset me. I was left with the agonizing realization that I had acted in such an immature and childlike way.

Once I finally accepted my responsibility for the upset, I could then focus my attention on why I reacted so strongly to such a minor annoyance. In that moment of clarity, it was painfully apparent that I had reacted negatively to Jenny's irritation many times before. This TV episode was just a different verse to the same old song; Jenny's displeasure with me was serious business. Because she got upset with me, she might not like me anymore and even worse, she might stop loving me. Then I would be abandoned and alone. Although it's an incredible leap, my protective part has believed ever since I was a child that if someone gets mad at me, there is a chance that they won't love me anymore.

This little incident with the television volume was a seminal event in my relationship with Jenny and my healing as an individual. I finally peeked through a crack in what I call my ego shell of parts and defenses. For just a moment, before the crack closed back up, I saw that it was possible that much of the misery and suffering I had endured in all my love relationships was self-inflicted. And also, for the briefest of moments, I had a glimpse of the pain I had caused my partners for all those years. Such thoughts are hard to stay with, and, predictably, I moved on to thinking about something else, eventually returning to watch the rest of the football game.

But something had changed. I'd seen something. I knew something. Now it was just a matter of time and many more verses. I'd taken the first, most difficult step on a road seldom traveled.

Although it wasn't true, over the next few months I continued to see Jenny as irritable, high-maintenance, and difficult to live with. The truth remained, however, that Jenny was the same loving, caring woman I'd fallen in love with. While her arguing and occasional irritation with me increased after our "in-love" phase, it certainly wasn't excessive by any stretch of the imagination. She was a good, easy to be with woman, but my unconscious, protective parts had her pegged as disruptive and argumentative.

My blaming her for my overreactions and hurt feelings wasn't fair to her at all. I finally saw that my anger and uncomfortable emotions came from my own wounded past and not from her little upsets. She wasn't causing my feelings! *I* was causing my feelings. What a revelation for me. I didn't like the idea at all at first, but with that new self-awareness, I began to make some changes to our painful little dance. Over time, I learned to take a few deep breaths each time Jenny expressed displeasure with me. I stayed present and didn't give in to defensiveness, blaming, or falling into a guilt spiral. Gradually, I was able to hear Jenny's words and attend to her feelings. By *responding* to her rather than reacting, I felt more powerful, more at peace, and more grown-up. Interestingly, it felt liberating to realize that I didn't have to get all worked up into an angry, guilty, shameful wretch every time Jenny got a burr in her saddle. I could remain calm, thoughtful, and even concerned about her issue with me.

With this new awareness also came another important revelation that I didn't like. Although Jenny had been implying it for three years, I could never understand that a lot of her irritation with me was caused by the way I treated her. It makes me cringe with regret now, but I finally had to admit that there were times when I disrespected Jenny, her ideas, and even some of her artwork. I didn't set out to hurt her, but a couple of my protective parts that had grown to dislike her were all too happy to give her a little grief from time to time. *There is so much to learn about ourselves if we can see past our biased perspective to the cold hard truth.*

Although I'd known for decades that I hated for anyone to be angry with me, I never realized how much energy I had expended to avoid another person's ire. I've placated, apologized, distracted, and occasionally groveled since childhood to keep the anger of others at bay. Working with Jenny on this issue each time we had a blaming episode gradually helped pry open that crack in my ego shell a little wider. I could see more clearly and retain a bit longer the truth that my fear of another's anger was a re-enactment of a little boy's terror of upsetting his parents.

As the truth kept banging me in the face, I had no choice but to accept that the real problem was with me and not Jenny's occasional irritation. Once I understood it and could accept it, I was able to take a closer look into my past for answers. Of course, I'd looked before, but never within this new context of owning my errant beliefs, my blaming, and my contributions to my own misery.

It didn't take a Sherlock to fit the pieces together. As a small boy, my mom and dad blamed me for things I didn't do. My dad was an anxious man and could easily get frustrated or irritated over normal sounds children make while playing. He often yelled and threatened us for offenses we were completely unaware of. I distinctly remember an event when he grabbed me by the arm and whipped me hard while I screamed that I hadn't done anything. After finishing his handiwork and dropping me in a heap of pain and tears, he found out that my brother had indeed broken the dish. He then proceeded to tell me that my whipping would be for general principles, all the while looking at me with an angry, unrepentant face.

Both my parents used slapping, whipping, shame, and humiliation to punish and control their three children. But for some reason, Dad seemed inclined to unleash the majority of his frustration and fury onto me and our dog. Although he wasn't always a pariah, I lived in terror of him. I remember feeling great joy the day our dog bit Dad after he had kicked her. I had to hide behind a tree so he couldn't see me giggling with delight. As I relived certain moments of my childhood, it became obvious that Jenny's irritation stirred up my memories of shame, terror, and feelings of abandonment.

Of course, it might seem ridiculous at first glance that I could experience such emotions over something as innocuous as an irritated request to turn down the television. It might *seem* ridiculous, but it happens every day in relationships all over the world. Let's face it; love partners can get bent out of shape over the strangest things. A psychiatrist friend of mine calls these minor upsets and the "he said, she said" episodes "emotional Jell-o." While in retrospect these little tiffs may appear silly, it can be important to look closely at what is going on beneath the surface. It's not important that you forgot to pick up cream for your husband's coffee; what's important is why he got so angry and blamed you for his upset.

Like millions of others, my firefighter parts became activated and attacked whoever "caused" uncomfortable feelings in me to be aroused. As long as I continued to blame Jenny for her bouts of irritation, I could never get to the wounds underneath my reactivity. Taking 100-percent responsibility helped me to focus on *my* contribution to the conflict. This new awareness allowed me to more clearly see beneath my feelings and behavior. Only then could I begin to see the truth about why I react the way I do.

Once I took responsibility for my overreaction to her request to turn down the television, Jenny was able to look at her role in the upset. Even though she had contributed only ten percent, when she accepted 100-percent responsibility for the dust-up, she accepted that she could have handled her irritation differently.

During our "courageous conversation," Jenny said, "If I had just touched you on the shoulder and said, 'Honey, could you turn it down just a little bit?' you probably wouldn't have reacted at all. Or I could have handed you the earphones and asked, 'Could you use these, sweetie? For some reason, the television is distracting to me.' I can see how I could have prevented the whole thing by presenting my request in a more relational way."

Of course, very little of this situation was really Jenny's fault, but if she continued to only see my contribution, she'd never learn the lesson that was there for her: waiting until you're irritated or angry to express your need or want is not the best policy. Also, by exploring what was really behind her irritation, she might discover its causes.

Once I saw through my ego's ironclad belief that I was mostly blameless in our fights and arguments, it became easier to accept the fact that I might be totally responsible for causing certain problems in our relationship. Although I still occasionally blame, I'm not able to hang onto it for very long. For instance, just a few days ago, I stretched a heavy-duty extension cord along the rock path from our front porch to the driveway so that I could vacuum my car. When I finished and began to roll up the cord, Jenny approached and asked me to leave it stretched out so that she could vacuum her car later that afternoon. She then got busy with other projects and forgot about vacuuming.

The next morning, while hurrying down the path to my car, with my mind a thousand miles away, I tripped over the cord and hurt my knee. My first response was a loud, "Goddammit, Jennifer." The thoughts that followed immediately were, "I left this cord out for her and look what happened. She didn't do what she said she would do, and now I've got a screwed-up knee." For a moment, I blamed her, not only for my hurt knee but for my angry feelings as well. I *was* happy and now, because of her, I was angry and upset.

Happily, it only took a minute and a couple of deep breaths for my Captain to come on board and see things from a more realistic perspective. While it was true that Jenny didn't do her vacuuming and remove the cord from the pathway as she intended, it was also true that *I* could have at least moved the cord off the path until she was ready. It was also true that if I had been looking where I was going, I would never have tripped over the cord. With just a little examination of the situation, it became obvious that my accident was more my fault than Jenny's. After realizing that fact, my negative feelings and self-talk about her melted, leaving me feeling a bit sheepish about the whole thing.

Like the extension cord caper, sometimes the roots of blame are not the results of ancient terror or trauma, but simply a habitual strategy to shift the responsibility for our upset feelings to someone else. Or we might be prone to blame an innocent partner for repeated upsets we had to endure as a child. For instance, the first time Jenny and I visited a museum, she became a little crabby after only fifteen minutes of viewing some paintings. Coupled with a few sighs, she commented, "How long does it take to look at a painting? You know, there's no place to sit down on this whole floor. I'm getting hungry." Her edginess signaled her irritation, and I assumed that it was directed at me.

Soon after, we left, with me feeling anxious and distant because she seemed upset with me. I also felt some irritation at her for being a "stick in the mud." It took a while for me to get out of my funk.

Later that day, we tried to sort through it. After the conversation, we used the 100-percent responsibility process to explore what was going on inside each of us. After some introspection, Jenny realized that she had blamed her unhappy feelings on me for my dawdling. She recounted her self-talk that included statements like, "Look at him. He's staring at each painting and acting like he's a connoisseur of fine art. Doesn't he know that I'm bored with all this? Is he doing this just to irritate me?" She then remembered being a small child accompanying her parents while they spent hours visiting museum after museum. To a six-year-old, the museums were boring and tiring, especially when she was hungry and thirsty and had to wait for what seemed like forever before she could get a drink or something to eat. To this day, she prefers to skip the museums when we travel.

When I looked at my part, I could see that, instead of being curious about Jenny and her feelings, I quickly blamed her for *causing* me to be anxious and for *making* me leave sooner than I wanted to. Jenny's complaint didn't cause my anxiety, and it didn't make me leave early. Distorted beliefs and anxiety from my childhood were stirred by Jenny's upset, causing me to make a premature exit.

Like my anxious dad before me, anxiety has prevented me

from empathizing with or understanding the feelings of others. Many times, I saw my dad's anxiety turn into frustration and anger if another's emotions or preferences interfered in any way with his plans or made him the least bit uncomfortable. Although I didn't like the pattern of behavior I was exposed to and certainly didn't want to emulate it, I ended up following in Dad's footsteps more than I realized. By taking responsibility for my part in the "museum caper," I could more clearly see how my anxiety had been causing distorted thinking and unhealthy, hurtful behavior for years.

Finally, no chapter on blame would be complete without a few words about how blame inevitably leads to victim/perpetrator roles. If my feelings are hurt and I blame Jenny for it, then I become the victim and she becomes the perpetrator. With my Captain inaccessible, I can't think clearly enough to assess the situation like an adult. Because my protective parts are "stuck in time," I experience Jenny as a disapproving parent and react to her as though I were a child. In this regressed state, I have no tools available except childish defensiveness, attacking or quietly disappearing into a fog of negative self-talk about how difficult and irritable she is.

Being a victim is a seductive role in committed relationships, because if you're a victim, you are absolved of responsibility, guilt, shame, and fault. It's much easier on the ego to feel like a victim than to deal with those uncomfortable feelings and thoughts. In our first years together, Jenny and I fought over who got to be the victim and who was the perpetrator. The other's offense was always more egregious than our own. Our fights were deadly serious then, but now seem rather silly.

Our tiffs often began with me shouting something like, "Well, you started it. If you hadn't gotten your panties in a wad over nothing, we wouldn't be fighting."

Then Jenny would chime in: "Yeah, well who's the most

upset right now? Who's doing all the yelling? You're the one who's making a mountain out of a molehill! You're the one who's managed to get me riled up. You just can't let me have a feeling that's not a hundred percent positive, can you? You want to keep me in a box so you'll never have to deal with my feelings."

I would then jump in, "There wouldn't even be a fucking molehill if you hadn't created one. I'm the one in a box, for God's sake. I can't do a damn thing without you getting irritated. Why can't you understand that you started the whole thing? I didn't do anything!"

And on it would go, lost in the Jell-o, with each of us vying for the victim role. Think about it; if I'm a victim, I'm blameless and get off scot free, even if I actually did contribute to the conflict. As a victim, I can soothe myself as I self-righteously lick my wound while pointing my finger at the perpetrator.

Although victims might derive some twisted pleasure or relief from their role, they'll never feel like adults or powerful people. The victim/perpetrator game is never a win-win situation, nor is it even a win/lose game. It is always a lose/lose game in committed relationships. Both people win when the two of them take the appropriate responsibility and accountability for their parts in the upset.

Blame Summary

Obviously, blaming partners for our hurt feelings, frustrations, disappointments, or anger is counterproductive. If greater intimacy, closeness, understanding, and connection are what we want and need, blaming is not the way to achieve them. If, on the other hand, we want more distance, more conflict, more resentment, and less emotional safety in the relationship, then blaming works every time.

Blaming not only fails to motivate others, it usually activates their protective parts, making them prone to not only resist, but to defend, attack, and return the blame. Blaming will never lead to the empathy, understanding, and love we're looking for with our partner.

While we may agree that blaming is not a useful strategy, we still do it. Blaming others for our negative feelings comes naturally for most of us and continues to be a way for people to avoid taking responsibility for their own emotions, behavior, and self-talk. It's easier to play the victim card and blame others for our unhappiness and painful feelings than it is to own and deal with our "stuff."

Even if your partner is a schmuck, there is a strong probability that you are making a contribution to your relationship troubles, which means that *you* are a part of the problem. So, at least some of your distress and unhappiness in the relationship is caused by *you and your own personal baggage*. Regardless of what your partner does or doesn't do, you have the power to change how you respond to him or her in any situation, and that's a good thing. You can stop or at least diminish your pain and suffering because you're not a victim, and your feelings are not your partner's responsibility. They are yours alone.

If your partner is not willing or able to change, you can improve the relationship by yourself. Trying to change a resistant partner is a fool's errand. Whether it's fair or not, changing the relationship for the better is up to you. Your relationship is a system and you are a part of that system. If you change, the system will change. Should you manage to cut down on your blaming and negative reactions, it will likely have a positive impact on your partner. If you can change, the odds are that your partner will follow suit.

Taking 100-percent responsibility for your part in a conflict without focusing on your partner's contribution is the best way to reduce your role in the blame game. Focusing *only on you* will enable you to work through the history that caused your protective parts to develop their penchant for blaming and reacting in the first place.

This is a powerful strategy, but it won't be easy. It will require a willingness to really look at yourself and how you are contributing to the problems in the relationship. In other words, you need to stop fighting and surrender to the truth about yourself. By going against the dictates of your ego and allowing yourself to be vulnerable, you can start accepting that *you* have room for improvement as well as your partner.

Using this strategy with an open heart and mind will reveal that your protective parts have been causing much of your suffering and misery for years. Granted, this strategy of owning your part is difficult, but it can go a long way toward helping you to become a better partner and person. When you're tempted to blame, it might be helpful to ask yourself this question: do you want to grow and achieve self-mastery, or do you want to make sure your partner knows how screwed up he is?

Chapter 22:

The Healing Apology

Since love relationships are so complex and can magnify a couple's emotional wounds, there are bound to be misunderstandings, arguments, and even occasional fights. These clashes will often cause one or both parties to experience anger, defensiveness, withdrawal, and hurt feelings. Because of this, it is crucial for partners to not only understand the need for apologies but to have the art and skill to apologize effectively.

Of all the phrases I've heard from books and movies, "Love means never having to say you're sorry" has to rank up there as one of the silliest. That phrase, from 1970s hit movie *Love Story*, is so far off base it's actually quite funny. Of course, the opposite of that silly slogan is true. Meaningful apologies are *essential* to smooth and repair hurt feelings, create trust, and reduce resentments in love relationships.

Because earnestly saying you're sorry requires vulnerability and an open heart, it can be good for you and your personal growth. Various religions have known for hundreds of years that confessions (apologies to a god) help a person release the burdens of guilt and shame from "bad" or unacceptable behaviors or even thoughts. Confessions and apologies facilitate the cleansing of the soul and instill a healthy humility. Because a heartfelt apology requires that we recognize our hurtful behavior and its effects on another, it helps us to become empathic. Of course, another benefit of apologizing is the potential repair of a rift in the relationship.

When hurt or offended by another, most people will experience anger, shame, being unloved, or a host of other uncomfortable feelings. But if—and this can be a big if—the offenders can quickly give a meaningful, heartfelt apology, the hurt partners may feel understood and soothed enough to regulate and calm their emotions so that, ideally, the rift can be repaired completely, leaving both parties even closer than before.

For many years, I facilitated weekly men's groups, learning much about the power of a felt apology as opposed to a contrived one. A good example took place one evening when "Bill" complained once again about his boring job and how his boss passed him over for a promotion. When Bill finished his complaint, "John" told him that his complaining would not get him anywhere and that he needed to get off his psychological ass and do something. John then told him that he was tired of listening to what sounded like a helpless little boy who was powerless to do anything to change his circumstances.

Understandably hurt, Bill yelled back with an angry, "Hey, *fuck you*. I didn't ask for your opinion."

John reacted with his own rising anger: "*Well, fuck you too.*"

I quickly suggested that everybody in the group take a couple of deep breaths and try to relax, reminding them that everything was going to be OK. I then asked Bill to tell the men in the circle what was going on inside him.

Looking across the circle at John, he spit out, "It's pretty obvious. I'm fucking pissed."

I encouraged Bill to close his eyes and take some more deep breaths while checking for other emotions underneath the anger. After a short silence, he shared his feelings of embarrassment and shame at being confronted like that in front of the group. He felt hurt that nobody understood how hard he had struggled with his demons around his job. For years he'd had fantasies about leaving the company and finding a better paying, more interesting line of work. And as a boy, he'd listened to his dad complain about being stuck behind an accountant's desk instead of doing something outdoors in nature. Although his dad had always wanted to be a game warden, he never did anything about it. Frustratingly, Bill had followed in his dad's unhappy footsteps. John's words triggered the shame Bill felt for his dad and for himself.

I then asked John how he felt after listening to Bill's explanation. "I'm feeling pretty much like crap right now. I never really thought about the hurtful feelings Bill has dealt with all this time."

I invited him to say something to Bill. He said, "Hey, I'm sorry for what I said. It was out of line, and I shouldn't have said that."

Although he felt better after the apology, Bill still experienced residual feelings that wouldn't go away. To facilitate more healing, I coached John on another apology.

John gave it another try. "Bill, it's been frustrating for me to hear about your struggles and dissatisfaction with your job. I've always wanted to help you but never knew what to say. Tonight, instead of helping and being supportive, I just dumped some of my impatience onto you. You deserved my understanding and not my crap. With all the problems *I've* got, I had no business giving you shit about your situation.

"When you've talked about your job thing before, I heard your words but never really understood the heartache and pain you've been going through. I'm truly sorry for my shallow and hurtful comments. Instead of supporting you and helping you find a solution, I criticized you and made things worse. I hope

I learned a lesson tonight, and again, I'm really sorry for what I said."

Apparently, that apology did the trick because as John talked I could see Bill's eyes moistening. Bill thanked John, explaining to the group that he felt much better. He actually crossed the circle to shake hands with John. Standing up, John wrapped Bill in a bear hug. After group, they talked and laughed with one another. An apology given with heart and skill can usually resolve a rift or conflict, often creating a closeness and intimacy that wasn't there before.

Not all apologies, however, are helpful. In fact, a poorly delivered apology with the wrong motivation can actually make matters worse. For example, I tend to blurt out an apology to Jenny whenever I've offended her. As I've mentioned before, I just can't stand it when she becomes angry with me, whether she attacks me or simply shuts down and retreats to her room and closes the door. I'm so distressed at Jenny's irritation that I immediately throw out an insincere apology with no heart or feeling. That kind of apology wrapped in urgency and tinged with a little anger is empty and does no good at all.

Just the other day, it happened for the umpteenth time. In a "constructive conversation," I mentioned that she could be a little difficult at times. Although I know that she hates to be called difficult, I mistakenly let it slip out, probably from frustration with the direction of our discussion. Anyway, she grew upset immediately and started in on me.

I quickly resorted to a typical apology. "Look, I'm sorry I used that word. Can we just let it go? I'm sorry, OK?"

"You're not sorry. You used that word just to hurt me. You don't care if you hurt my feelings; you're just sorry I'm mad because you don't like it when I'm angry. And you want me to just shut up and get over it so you don't have to deal with your own feelings. You're being sorry is all about you."

Although I knew somewhere inside that she was right, I continued with my well-worn, often repeated, dance of defense. "Look, I said I'm sorry. What do you want me to do, cut my wrists? For Christ's sake, do you have to get your panties in a wad every time I make the slightest mistake?"

It's amazing how my part uses almost the same words and phrases every time it gets triggered. Needless to say, my approach only added more fuel to her fire. She knew that my apology came from a protective part that was not the least bit interested in her hurt feelings or what was going on inside her at the time. There was no curiosity, no compassion, no understanding, nothing except the urge to stop her anger at me because it scared that insecure little boy, or exile, inside me. That frightened part of me had been hurt and emotionally abandoned repeatedly by angry parents. My reaction to Jenny's upset was strictly about protecting myself and that's what raised her hackles even more than my comment in our discussion.

Another example of an unhelpful apology happened to a client when her brother sold a painting from their mother's estate that meant the world to her. She'd spoken about the work of art many times over the years to her mother and even to her brother. When she confronted him about it, he blurted out something like, "Sorry 'bout that" with no empathy, no understanding, nothing. Finally, with tears coming down her face, she explained to him how she felt betrayed and how much it had hurt her. He accused her of being hysterical.

Then a week later, she mentioned her disappointment about the painting again. Dropping to his knees and with a voice dripping with contemptuousness, he "begged" her forgiveness for his "horrible" mistake. His apology felt like a dagger in her heart and hurt her almost as much as the loss of the painting.

While I believe that kind of apology is the absolute worst, there are others that are also ineffective and can exacerbate a situation. One that I call the "but apology" goes something like this: "Hey, I'm sorry, *but* don't you think you're overreacting just a bit? All I said was that your dress is fitting you a little tighter." Or "I'm sorry I said that, *but* you know what? You've said the same thing to me lots of times." Another gem is "Well, I'm sorry I yelled at you, *but* if you hadn't left the tools out in the rain, I never would have said anything and there would be no problem." If there's a *but* in the apology, there's probably a lack of understanding and sincerity; without those two things, the apology is bound to be ineffective.

Apologizing is a skill that many couples have never mastered. But it is not *just* a skill or a formulaic behavior that one can dish out when a situation calls for it. Authentic apologizing is also an art that requires access to the Self or Captain. To truly recognize and own what one has done involves vulnerability, understanding, compassion, and the ability to be in the moment.

What are the necessary ingredients for an apology that repairs the rift and leaves the hurt or offended party as whole as possible? First of all, it must be heartfelt. Apologizers should understand that their actions (or inaction) have caused pain or distress in another. That understanding should be communicated through words, tone of voice, *and* body language. Regret should also be part of an apology. It is also important to be specific about the exact harm inflicted. To summarize: an apology should be concise, heartfelt, demonstrate understanding and empathy, be specific, and hopefully include some sort of commitment to refrain from repeating the offending behavior.

Sometimes, if I can stay in my Captain, I can give an effective apology. Once, when Jenny and I were driving to Austin, a song came on the radio that was popular during her first marriage. Sadly, her husband killed himself a couple of years after she left him. It took her a long time to deal with all the feelings around the marriage, the divorce, and his suicide. While listening to the music, Jenny shared how she had danced with her ex to that song in the living room of their house. She'd mentioned him a fair amount over the couple of years we'd been together, and I always felt a bit uncomfortable talking about him.

As tears trickled down her cheeks at the end of the song, I said something very stupid: "God, Jenny that was twenty-five years ago. That's a long time to still have all those feelings."

Once again, my fearful exile had triggered a jealous part that instantly took over me, making it impossible to empathize with her feelings in the moment. Fortunately, Jenny's tears unlocked my heart and I was able to quickly access my better self. With my Captain in charge, I immediately realized that the song had stirred-up pain and heart-rending memories. I could also see that my judgmental comment and lack of support truly hurt her in a moment of need. I'd been thoughtless and insensitive at the worst possible time.

I said, "Jenny, you're right. My response was all about me and my jealous feelings. Neither my heart nor my Captain was anywhere around. When you heard that song, you must have felt so many different emotions and I wasn't there to comfort you or empathize with you like a caring partner. You needed connection and I gave you a cynical judgment. I acted like a jerk and I'm so very sorry, not only for my awful comment but also because I wasn't there for you. If you can forgive me, I would love to talk with you, either now or later, about that time in your life."

Although it took some further conversation and a little while for Jenny's hurt feelings to subside, she admitted that my apology helped her move past the incident with less resentment than she would have had otherwise.

So far we've looked at the art and skill involved in effective apologies and briefly explored ineffective ones. Now let's take a more complex look at apologies in love relationships. Jenny and I have a long-running disagreement about apologies—when they're appropriate and when they might interfere with personal growth.

As a little girl, Jenny's parents expected her to engage in strenuous piano practice, household help, and caring for five younger siblings. Whenever she failed to perform according to her parent's dictates, they criticized and often punished her even though she apologized profusely. So she learned early on that apologies didn't really make things better for her. And because her parents rarely, if ever, apologized to each other or to their children, it wasn't modeled for her as a child. Even when they did apologize, they continued to repeat the same hurtful behavior again and again. Her upbringing, plus the fact that she'd developed an avoidant attachment style, made apologizing difficult for her. By the time she left home at seventeen, Jennifer was definitely not a fan of giving or receiving apologies.

By the end of our first year together, I had apologized to Jenny dozens of times, while she had offered up one or two. Instead of saying she was sorry, Jenny frequently repeated a philosophy validating her aversion to apologies. In her mind, apologies were rarely necessary and could get in the way of personal growth. For instance, while chatting one afternoon early in our relationship, I happened to look down at her computer and noticed that she had received an email from an ex-lover. I thought we had an understanding that he would be off-limits now that we were married and I felt betrayed and angry. I wanted an apology but didn't get one because Jenny hadn't really agreed with our "understanding." She thought it was perfectly OK to have occasional contact with the guy and saw no reason to apologize just because I was insecure. Later, when things had cooled down, we discussed the situation.

Jenny said that if I weren't anxious about losing her, I

wouldn't have cared if she maintained a friendship with the guy. According to her, communicating a few times a year with a former lover who became a friend was reasonable. Jenny believed that if she apologized, she would be condoning my jealousy and admitting that her desire for occasional contact with her ex-lover was not OK. In other words, if she apologized, I would assume that my jealousy was understandable and appropriate and would see no need to deal with it. And if I didn't deal with it, we would both have to put up with it for the rest of our relationship.

Jenny went on to suggest that just because an apology is expected does not mean it is deserved. Expanding on that idea, she contended that an apology should be commensurate with the offense committed. So, if she believes that she's done nothing wrong, there's no need to apologize, even if the other person's feelings were hurt. And if she only committed an offense of a two on a scale of one to ten, then her apology should be small and short, even if I was terribly hurt. If I was deeply hurt by her minor offense, then it was basically my problem, and I should deal with it.

Jenny's point here is a good one. "Jane," a middle-aged client of mine, struggled for years with this very situation. Her husband "Don" was picky, to the point of being anal about everything around him. If she misplaced his pencil, moved his papers, ran the vacuum while he was reading, overcooked the eggs, or did any of a myriad of things that upset him, he expected an immediate apology. If he didn't get his apology, he stormed around the house cursing and yelling for a couple of minutes before settling into a period of angry silence. Because Don couldn't regulate his own feelings, he expected—and needed—Jane to do it for him.

In counseling, Jane quickly realized that her constant apologies allowed Don to avoid looking at two issues that were driving her crazy. She had allowed his pickiness and inability to regulate his anger to become her problems when, in fact, they were *his* problems. Over time, Jane learned to avoid unwarranted apologies while respectfully pointing out that Don could take responsibility for his extreme preferences and his temper. Of course, he didn't like it, but, after a few weeks, there was a small improvement in his expectations and behavior. Jane, meanwhile, felt empowered, relieved, and liberated. She'd quit her job as the "apologizer-in-chief" and the manager of his environment and his emotions.

 I tend to agree with Jenny's views on apologizing, but I do think that even when your "offense" is questionable, saying you're sorry can be helpful. A week ago, I asked Jenny to pick up some apples for me at the grocery store and thought I saw her nod in response. On her return from the store, there were no apples. When I mentioned my request to her, she said she never heard me ask for anything. I really wanted the apples, and, since our ranch is thirty minutes from the nearest store, it disappointed me and hurt my feelings.

 My protective part started a loop of inner dialogue about how she didn't care about me and how much effort I expend to please her. Of course, that part didn't consider that on most occasions Jenny buys what I want without me even asking. Parts aren't known for seeing things rationally.

 Feeling a little disregarded and hurt, I was looking for some sort of apology from Jenny to help me get over the feelings. After I mentioned that she had nodded when I asked her about the apples, she replied that she never nodded. When I shared that my feelings were a little hurt over the whole thing, she said that I was responsible for my hurt feelings, not her.

 Not only did her response fail to assuage my emotions, it also left me angry. I wasn't angry about the apples, I was angry about the fact that she wouldn't at least say she was sorry she didn't hear me and was sorry for my disappointment. Her legalistic response reflected no warmth or understanding of my feelings. A more satisfactory response would have been something like, "I'm really sorry I didn't come home with your apples. I didn't hear you ask for them and never realized that you needed them. I always try to think about what you might want from the store and this time I just didn't think about apples. I can see that you're hurt and disappointed and I'm really sorry it all happened the way it did."

In this "apology," Jenny would not be admitting to something she didn't do. She would not have to say that she was thoughtless or that she disregarded me. An apology would, however, help me with my feelings and repair the rift that was forming. This type of apology includes heartfelt words that convey that she cares for me and thinks of me when shopping, thus soothing me and helping to regulate my emotions.

When done well, apologies can do more than just make amends; they can convey to a partner that he or she is loved, valued, and appreciated.

In most cases, an effective, heartfelt apology can be given even when the offended partner is reacting from his or her own emotional wounds instead of what the other has actually said or done. For instance, shortly after moving to our little ranch, Jenny and I decided to dig up some cactus in a field close to our house. Jenny had never dug up cactus up by the roots and was struggling to use the tools effectively. Noticing this, I suggested a different way. With an edge in her voice, she retorted that she was doing just fine and if she needed any help, she would ask for it.

Her reaction stung me and I walked away in silence. What started out as a beautiful morning quickly shifted to an uncomfortable tension between us. When I returned to digging cactus, a protective part began an internal monologue complaining about how difficult it was to live with such an irritable bitch. After a few minutes of licking my wounds and angry, negative self-talk, I finally wound down enough for my Captain to enter the picture and see that I was definitely going in the wrong direction. I asked myself if that's how I wanted the rest of the day to go and the answer was, "Absolutely not."

With my Captain now in charge of the ship, I walked over and apologized for interfering with her process of learning things on her own. Although I had done nothing wrong, I hoped to salvage the morning by soothing her upset feelings. So the main purpose of the apology was to assuage her feelings and create a space where meaningful dialogue could take place in a safer environment. Sure enough, we talked for a few minutes.

Jenny explained that since her parents forced her to do things a certain way as a child, she disliked someone telling her what to do or how to do it. Her initial prickliness was a bit hard for me to swallow, but after her explanation, I understood and felt better toward her. So the apology started us on a road to repair, understanding, and peace between us.

Even if your contribution to a partner's hurt or anger is negligible, I believe it's a good policy to apologize in such a way as to assuage feelings and offer understanding, while at the same time maintaining your truth and integrity. Later, with both of you in your Captains, you can explore the situation in detail and hopefully uncover the real reasons for the hurt or anger.

For some men and women, this type of apology will be difficult because their underlying parts have grievances that have never been resolved. For instance, I had a client who, no matter how the "evidence" stacked up against her, she would never admit to any error or wrongdoing. If she'd erred, it was because of something her partner said, did, or didn't do. She refused to take responsibility for anything she did, so she never felt the need to apologize, driving her husband batty with frustration and later, with anger and even rage.

After working with this woman for several weeks, it became clear that her parents blamed her and even punished her for things she didn't do. They also refused to apologize to her, even when they had wrongly disciplined her. As a child, she developed an unconscious protector part that vowed to never accept anybody's opinion of her behavior or to ever apologize for anything that wasn't clearly 100 percent her fault. And since most disagreements and conflicts are the result of *two* parties who have been less than perfect, she couldn't apologize.

Summary of the Apology

To apologize is to express to another your awareness that something you've said or done has hurt or offended him or her and that you are sorry. This requires the strength to own your behavior, the wisdom to understand its effects on the other person, and the vulnerability to accept the blame.

To be effective, apologies need to be heartfelt, specific and should indicate that the apologizer understands what happened and its effects on the hurt party. By helping your offended partner feel heard and understood, your apology can soothe feelings, reduce resentment, and initiate forgiveness.

Apologies should never include "buts" and should never discount or minimize what happened. Apologizing is not an admission of guilt or shameful behavior. It is simply a heartfelt acknowledgment that one's words or deeds have triggered hurt or threat in another. With an effective apology, the offender is able to empathize with the feelings of the hurt party. When the hurt partner feels understood and empathized with, he or she can more easily forgive and forget.

To apologize is to reach out your hand to the other in an effort to reestablish closeness and good will. Ideally, a heartfelt apology can repair the rift between you regardless of who is to blame and even leave you feeling more connected than before the problem started.

Chapter 23:

Understanding Usable Love

Jack and Linda

THE CONCEPT OF usable love came to me years ago while counseling a middle-aged couple who sought therapy for frequent conflicts. Linda came into my office with a long list of grievances toward her husband, a moderately successful car salesman. She tearfully described him as basically ignoring her, treating her like a piece of furniture while he spent most of his time at home glued to the television or his computer. According to her, he did nothing to help around the house, even though she worked and brought home a paycheck just like he did. Through tightened facial muscles she said that his offerings of attention and affection were saved for those times when he felt sexual.

Linda noticed the marriage going downhill six months after the wedding. With the honeymoon phase over, Jack began to criticize Linda for everything from her clothes to her cooking and even accused her of having an affair with her boss. And there were the times when his unresolved anger turned into a hostile silence that might last twenty-four hours. In our session, she also mentioned that his drinking occasionally got out of hand, leaving him belligerent and spoiling for a fight. Weekly happy hours with his buddies became happy evenings, with him getting home at ten or eleven, wanting a little quickie with his tired and irritated "honey." Linda described herself as a "stand-by-your-man" kind of woman, but her commitment was seriously eroded by the time she came to see me.

In a joint session, Jack defended himself. First, he discounted or minimized what Linda had said. "You're painting a picture of me that's not true." Looking over at me, he continued, "That's not the way it is, OK? I have a social life and knock down a few beers with my buddies on occasion; so what's the harm in that?" Next, he excused or tried to make allowances for his behavior: "Yeah, I get mad sometimes and let off a little steam, but I have a stressful job and I'm not perfect." Finally, he pointed to her behavior: "Linda yells at me too. And she never initiates sex. I don't even think she likes me. How am I supposed to deal with that?"

With Jack shaking his head, Linda continued. "When the two children came along, he left it to me to take care of them, feed them, get them to school and all of that."

Jack interrupted. "Look, this is not fair. I play with those kids and I try to be a good dad and a good husband too. I'm not perfect, but I'm also not the monster that you're making me out to be. The real truth is that there's nothing I could do that would ever please you, so what's the use?"

After more laments from Linda, Jack tried to soothe her, reminding her of all the good times they'd had and actually saying that "things weren't really all that bad". By the end of the counseling session, I could see that things were indeed "that bad."

Not willing to be "guilted and shamed" again, Jack skipped the next therapy session. Linda ultimately moved out.

A few days after she left, Jack made an appointment to see me. He came into my office looking tired, disheveled and beaten. He was extremely upset about losing his wife and children, telling me that he couldn't live without them. With tears moistening his eyes, he softly said he would cut his arm off if that's what it took to get them back. In fact, Jack spent virtually the entire meeting letting me know how much he loved and needed his wife. He used the remaining minutes of the session trying to convince me that Linda's leaving wasn't his fault.

He finished with, "I swear I tried to be what she wanted. I know I wasn't perfect, but neither was she. She hurt me in so many ways I can't even tell you. She didn't respect me; she wasn't nice to me; and she hurt my feelings a lot. But I still love her and don't want to lose her." With a loud sob, Jack exclaimed, "And I love my children so much."

After Jack left, I sat there with my heart aching for him and for Linda. They believed they loved each other, but neither one was able to feel loved by the other. How could they spend years living together without knowing what they were doing to each other? How could something as powerful as love become so weak and impotent between two people?

If your love doesn't influence the way you think, feel, and behave, then it won't be of much use to your partner. Love gets its power and potential only when it flows through the eyes, lips, ears, hands, heart, mind, and actions of a human being. It is up to us, then, to make sure that our love is expressed in ways that are actually meaningful, even useful, to others. Saying we love our partner is nice but doesn't really do him or her much good; our true feelings are expressed through our tone, attentiveness, body language, facial expressions, words, and actions. And certainly, this applies to loving our children as well as our partner.

To increase the usefulness of our love for a partner, we need to consistently treat him or her with understanding, validation, empathy, caring, and appreciation. Not every moment, mind you, just consistently. Remember how you felt inside when you fell in love with your partner? You had *feelings* of love coursing through you. You felt moved and touched by the mere thought of your lover. Although many years may have passed since then, it's still possible to *feel* love for your partner. In fact, if you don't feel that love, it's not going to have much impact on your partner, no matter what you do. Going through the motions of caring behavior without feeling them in your heart comes across as empty and loveless. That's why usable love is about *being* more than it is about *doing*. Without feeling loving, no list of communication skills or "to-do lists" will ultimately matter.

As you might have guessed, this is not some variation of a Hallmark card kind of love or any other sort of gooey sentimentality. Usable love is muscular, powerful, and will absolutely have a beneficial effect on loved ones. It is not something to be celebrated or observed a few times a year; it is a living process going on between two people that can change their lives forever. For most of us in the North American culture, giving this kind of love will require a certain way of being, feeling, and acting that is beyond our current level of development and maturity. If we are terribly anxious, afraid of intimacy, filled with resentments, critical and judgmental, self-centered, or have a hardened heart, we will need to do some work to remove these obstacles to love. Facing our demons and making the effort to heal and grow through one or more of these in the name of love is one of the noblest things we could ever do.

I believe there are particular qualities of love that are universal and true for everyone and every culture. In other words, when two people are in a romantic, committed relationship anywhere in the world, these qualities make their love more usable to each other. When you read some of the attributes of usable love below, there should be no surprises. It makes perfect sense that every sane person would want to be treated according to those qualities by a partner who loves them.

Please understand that you can't be expected to be or act loving every minute of every day. You *are* human after all, with human frailties and your own unique set of personal baggage. As you gradually make the changes required to give usable love, you'll find that loving your partner (and others) gets much easier and will feel so much better than relating the old way. Of course, you'll never be perfect, but as you become strengthened, empowered, and enlightened, your love can be expressed in ways that will make a huge difference in your life, as well as that of your partner.

Creating Emotional Safety

With all the craziness in what often seems like an upside-down world, we all need a safe place where we can feel supported and loved. We need a "home" where we belong and can just be ourselves. We need a place where it's safe to share our thoughts and feelings without fear of repercussions and reprisals. Ideally, our love relationships should provide us with a sanctuary that is supportive and nourishing.

To be that sanctuary, there will be times when we have to put aside our own needs, wants, and feelings so that we can be there for our partner. Unfortunately, extending ourselves in this way doesn't come naturally for many of us. Just to *notice* how our partner is feeling often escapes our attention. And when a partner is feeling anxious, sad, or even angry, it's important to support him or her with empathy and understanding. Obviously, this can be a real challenge when your partner is disappointed or angry with *you*. This has certainly been true in my case. It's been a struggle for me to stay calm and present when Jenny gets angry with me. I'm better at it now, but it's still a stretch.

As I said, it won't be easy; learning to give another real, usable love is not for the fainthearted. Learning how to regulate your own feelings so that you can be there for your partner in their times of need is a skill and an art of self-mastery that you can learn as you put into practice what you read in this book.

Seeing Your Partner

In the movie *Avatar*, the lovely human/creature from another planet looked into the eyes of the protagonist and told him that she could *see* him. When she said that, the audience knew exactly what she meant. Maybe because she had special powers, she could see into his heart, his essence, and the kind of man he really was. She saw his good intentions and his sense of social justice and concern for her environment, her culture, and her planet. She saw his inner conflicts and his struggle to do the right thing. She *knew* him. She saw him as an individual apart from her. And one could tell by his expression that, at that moment, he felt truly seen and known. His essence, his true self, his very being, felt visible to her.

Unfortunately, many of us see our partners almost exclusively in terms of how they affect *us*. By looking at our partners through self-referential eyes, we mostly just see the parts of them that make us feel good or bad. In other words, a wife might describe her husband to friends as someone who is patient with her, remembers her birthdays, and helps out with the house and kids. The point here is that she is seeing and describing the parts of him that relate to her. She's not describing him as an individual separate from her wants and needs, but as the husband role he plays in their relationship. This way of seeing involves looking at a person through the eyes of self-involved interest. My experience tells me that the average couple sees each other through these eyes most of the time.

Another, even more unhealthy way of seeing one's partner

is through the prism of negative projection. Under the spell of this unconscious, defensive phenomenon, a husband could unwittingly project his angry, critical mother onto his wife. So, when his wife gets a little upset, his unconscious mind takes over, seeing and reacting to her as though she were his threatening mother. He cannot see a good, loving woman who is temporarily upset. Instead, he's relating to her as a distorted projection of his unconscious. And of course, in this case, his wife will not feel seen or understood.

I once told Jenny that a real-life example of this repeatedly occurred with a previous client of mine. As a child, his wife was exposed to a stern, judgmental, and frequently angry father who had a tendency to give long, heated lectures to his children for any transgression. Because he tolerated no rebuttals, back talk, or even looks of anger, my client's wife learned to shut down her feelings and go inside. So, in their marriage, every time he wanted to talk to her about an issue, especially if there was an edge in his voice, she was gone emotionally and unable to hear what he was saying. Because he had some tendencies that resembled those of her dad, her unconscious reacted to my client as though he were him. In those instances, she wasn't seeing her husband; she was seeing her dad, and because that protective part of her mind had no concept of time, she regressed into a child whose only option was to "go away."

To get the idea of projection across to my clients, I have often used an example of a German shepherd dog that bit me as a child while I was riding my bike. For several years after that incident, my heart raced with fear when *any* German shepherd got near me. It didn't matter whether the dog was nice or not; if it was a German shepherd, I didn't want it anywhere around me. My unconscious had projected the dog that bit me onto every other similar dog.

Listening and Hearing

I'll never forget that first session with an attractive, middle-aged woman who began our meeting by telling me about her fears of getting older and her problems with a disinterested husband. Right in the middle of the meeting, she stopped talking for a moment, and then broke down and cried.

After a few seconds, she composed herself and apologized for the tears. "I'm so sorry. It's just that I'd forgotten how it feels to have someone listening to me and actually hearing what I'm saying and maybe even caring."

Everyone wants to be heard and understood. It's a basic human need. Sometimes the most loving thing you can do for a friend or lover is to listen to them and care about what they are saying.

Before becoming a therapist myself, I'd been a client in several therapy sessions with different therapists to deal with various issues, especially my anxiety. Out of more than two dozen meetings, I remember only three or four. In one of those memorable sessions, I shared some difficult and traumatic experiences I'd had as a small boy. As I described a time my dad beat me with his belt, I looked up and saw a tear coming down the cheek of my therapist. She looked at me with compassion and empathy and said, "Marvin, you were abused. That's just so sad." That moment in therapy happened many years ago, but I can still remember how transfixed I was by her reaction. She heard me.

Several things can get in the way of hearing and appropriately responding to a partner who is sharing. Sometimes the listener is not able to "be there" for the partner. Once, many years ago, after watching the movie *Fried Green Tomatoes*, I broke down in the car, weeping profusely. I was overtaken by grief after seeing on screen the kind of connection and friendship I'd never had.

A friend with me at the time responded with, "Should we call somebody?" She didn't know what to do and didn't understand that I just needed to let out my feelings. A simple touch on the shoulder or saying, "Something really got to you" would have been all I needed. Too often, partners feel like they need to fix something when all they need to do is just *be there* for their loved ones. Sometimes, words aren't even needed at all, just your full, heartfelt attention.

Another thing that can get in the way of hearing is the ego or protective parts of the mind. For instance, a client of mine gently told her husband that she would really like it if he touched her genitals more softly and slowly as a prelude to sex. She added that she's very sensitive in that area and anything more than a soft touch begins to hurt very quickly.

That's what she said, but the husband heard something different. He heard that he didn't measure up and that he wasn't pleasing her, which meant that she didn't like having sex with him because he was basically inadequate. Listening with a protective part rather than his rational adult, he told her he'd never had any complaints before and that the foreplay was totally for her benefit in the first place.

Her request quickly became all about *him* and his wounded ego and nothing about her or her needs and desires. In other words, he wasn't able to hear her.

A similar example of letting a protective part get in the way of hearing happened recently when a friend of mine told her husband that his comment about her weight hurt her feelings. His response was, "Well, you hurt *my* feelings yesterday when you said I'm just a couch potato who never wants to do anything anymore." His defensive grievance prevented him from hearing her or "getting" that he'd hurt her feelings. He couldn't empathize or imagine how she must have felt. Instead, his response told her that he couldn't care less about her hurt feelings.

Sadly, although he might have cared very much about her in the recesses of his heart, he was unable to access that part of himself because his feelings were hurt from the day before. So, instead of a heartfelt apology and a closer connection, their protective parts argued angrily, went to their corners, and ended up causing both partners to feel unloved and disrespected. All because he couldn't *hear* that he'd hurt her feelings.

Providing Special Experiences for Your Partner

Before going to sleep, Jenny likes to lie with her head on my lap while I gently stroke her hair and back for twenty minutes or longer. At first, this seemed like a lot of work for me to go through when I'm sleepy and tired. We had some fights over my reluctance to give her this very important attention that she needed and wanted. Over time, I realized that giving this physical attention to Jenny was an act of love. I learned to overcome the obstacles in the way so that I could enjoy giving her the pleasure, relaxation, and feeling of being special and loved by stroking her. She'd rather have this than flowers, candlelit dinners, or jewelry.

If she strokes my hair and back, I experience it as being pleasant, but not much more. However, if she puts on some make-up and wears a sexy outfit, I know she's doing it for me, which makes *me* feel loved and valued. I appreciate it when she cooks or cleans the kitchen, but I love it when she dresses up and acts a little flirty.

Providing special experiences for a partner is a wonderful way for your Captain to make your love usable. Find out what your partner really likes, and then make it happen every week or two. It's always nice to do it as a surprise and to do it for no reason except that you love your partner and want him or her to experience joy and pleasure.

Cherishing Your Partner

My father-in-law owns a silver-grey Porsche that he cherishes. Although the car is fourteen years old, it looks brand new, without a single scratch or blemish. He drives it occasionally, but most of the time it sits in the garage on top of a white carpet. He hand washes the car twice a month whether it needs it or not. He even wears a shirt with a Porsche insignia on it and has a subscription to a Porsche magazine. The guy is nuts about his car.

If someone can feel that way about a machine, doesn't it make sense that we could also feel that way about our spouse? Trust me; if the typical American couple felt that way about each other, we wouldn't average a million divorces every year. Can you imagine how much joy and happiness marriages could provide if each partner cherished the other and treated them accordingly?

When we cherish a partner, we feel deeply grateful and blessed that we get to spend our lives with them. We notice the uniqueness of their inner and outer beauty. We treasure their smile, their laugh, and their touch. Being with them brings joy and happiness to us. Of course, when they disappoint or make us angry, we will feel differently and might even see them as an adversary, but in a healthy relationship that negative state of mind will be short-lived.

If you can't cherish your partner, something must be in the way. Maybe he's hurt you and you have grievances. Maybe you've discovered that she's just not your cup of tea. If something is in the way, my advice is to find out what it is and do something about it. If you have grievances, this book will teach you how to work through them. Importantly, if you don't like your partner, there's a good chance it's because you've been hurt by them. Once you clean up the hurts, you might feel very differently. You won't know for sure until you've removed the pain and the resentment from your system. If you get clean and still don't like them, it might be time to move on to someone that you can truly cherish.

Treat Your Partner with Dignity and Respect

You would think that two partners in a love relationship would naturally treat each other with dignity and respect. And, of course, you know as well as I do that many, if not most couples struggle to do this consistently. Daily stresses, anxieties, grievances, different priorities, power struggles, and a host of other challenges can result in partners either treating each other unkindly or with disinterest.

It's understandable that when stressed, anxious, or angry, partners might act in hurtful ways toward their loved ones. It's understandable, but not acceptable, and not in keeping with the notion of usable love. If you want your love to be useful, it's important that you learn to regulate your emotions to the extent that you can be angry and still treat your partner with respect. In my view, it's OK to yell out that you're so angry you could bite a nail in two because that's about you and your anger. It wouldn't be OK, however, to yell "I can't believe you did that! That's so stupid," because that's about your partner and it's not OK.

It's important to remember that we are not our partners' teacher, boss, guru, or adversary; we are supposed to be their friend, lover, confidant, cheerleader, and sponsor. And love demands that we treat them that way as much as possible.

Remember, you are not above or below him or her; you are peers. It doesn't matter if you're taller or shorter, heavier or thinner, better looking or homelier, more or less educated, more or less socially adept, more or less intelligent, or more or less rational. What matters is that you and your partner treat each kindly and as co-equals. The partner you've chosen to love and be with is a human being with feelings and should be treated accordingly. It's important to realize that when you're in a discussion or even an argument with your partner, how he or she feels toward you after all the words have been exchanged is usually far more important than the points you and your part were trying to make.

I've known several couples whose sniping, bickering, and subtly contemptuous looks left me feeling uncomfortable around them. I couldn't help but notice a pall of tension and negative "vibes" that seemed to fill whatever room they were in. And yet, if you asked them if they loved one another, I'm sure they would swear that they did. Sadly, their habitual way of interacting created a mostly negative interpersonal space between them that became "normal."

To me, this kind of pessimistic sparring can create tiny nips and tears in the fabric of each partner's self-esteem, emotional safety, and positive feelings for the other. And, of course, it would have the opposite effect of usable love because it is hurtful and keeps both partners on guard most of the time.

It's really quite simple: if you want more closeness, connection, and intimacy with your partner, treat him or her with more kindness, dignity, and respect.

Supporting Your Partner's Emotional, Psychological, and Spiritual Growth

Love [is] the will to extend oneself for the purpose of nurturing one's own or another's spiritual growth.

M. Scott Peck, author of *The Road Less Traveled*

The surest way for you and your partner to grow in your relationship is to create emotional safety for both of you by being gently, but completely honest with each other, even when it hurts. At this juncture, it is important to understand that we are important people in our partners' lives, and in all likelihood, our opinions and feedback about them are taken seriously. Giving them the room to grow and even supporting them in the process is, without question, a critical form of usable love.

The majority of us are likely to agree that expressing love in these ways will impact loved ones in a very positive way. Surely, if partners consistently expressed their love through kindness, cherishing, seeing, hearing, and so forth, the level of intimacy and connection in their relationships would improve immensely. If most of the people on the planet agree with this, why don't we all put it into practice? *This* is the quintessential question that must be asked and then answered.

Chapter 24:

Men and Their Struggles with Love

MEN AND USABLE LOVE
The last stanza of a poem by Etheridge Knight speaks volumes about so many relationships where a man couldn't be present, intimate, or connected with the woman he loved.

> *this poem is for me*
> *and my woman*
> *and the yesterdays*
> *when she opened to me like a flower*
> *and I fell on her like a stone*
> *I fell on her like a stone*

I can still remember the morning when I first met Brenda. I was relaxing in my office, gazing out the window at an energetic sparrow that was bouncing around the branches of a nearby tree when a loud knock at the door jolted me from my reverie. I opened the door to a thirty-something-year-old woman whose pretty face was drawn and tight. She tried to smile as she glanced past me while we introduced ourselves.

As she sat down, with her slender, boyish figure and close-fitting jogging outfit, I could almost imagine a teen-aged girl there before me. But when she spoke, it was with the tight, restrained voice of a woman who had been holding back for some time.

Brenda's agitation was so strong and close to the surface that my relaxed feelings quickly shifted into an uncomfortable tension in my stomach. Although I'd never seen her before, I had this vague feeling that she was angry at me.

A couple of questions were all it took to get her started. Brenda came ready to talk. "First of all, I want you to know that I've been to see several other therapists over the past few years. Whatever they were trying to do with me didn't work because here I am with the same song and the hundredth verse. I'm getting tired of going through this same old story, having to spill my guts to some stranger, and watching whatever new hope I might have clung to get dashed to pieces one more time. I don't even know why I came here. I guess I'm just desperate enough to try it again. Besides, I don't know where else to go or what else to do."

Previous experience working with clients like Brenda told me that trying to help her could prove to be difficult and stressful. Still, I could see that she was in pain and I truly wanted to be there for her in any way I could.

Although Brenda's demeanor and conversation led me to believe that her childhood must have been less than ideal, it was her current relationship that was on the front burner. As is often the case, the first few months of her marriage to Stephen were like a fairy tale. They went skiing in the Rockies, sailing in the Bahamas, and shopping in New York. Through it all, he was romantic, attentive, and thoughtful.

Brenda, an emergency room nurse, had met her future husband at the hospital where she worked. Stephen, an established physician, had just invented and patented a medical device that had a lot of promise on a large scale. A couple of years into their marriage, demand for his device increased, as did his considerable wealth. Unfortunately for Brenda, demand for his time also increased, as did his stress level. He gradually became more and more available to his business and less and less available to Brenda and their baby girl. Brenda told me that she started out being a wife and turned into a "glorified nanny and household manager."

Stephen traveled extensively, making deals and meeting with people who could be important for his business. Gradually, the reunions with Brenda after his trips became less animated and romantic. Over time, Brenda sensed that he was becoming detached and withdrawn. Little gestures of affection like hugs, kisses, and touches, so plentiful in the beginning, became less and less frequent. Brenda said she gave their sexual relationship five stars in the first year, three in the second, and by the end of the third year she was saying, "What sexual relationship?"

"Lately, if we have sex at all, it's like he's not with me," she said. "He doesn't seem to see me, feel me, smell me, or taste me. It's like I'm not there and he's just going through the motions until he gets off. Afterward, I feel empty and, I don't know, kind of used and dirty. It's not a good thing anymore."

It wasn't that Stephen was abusive to her, she said, he just didn't appear to find her attractive or interesting anymore. He became aloof and distracted to the point where having a sustained conversation with her seemed like such an effort. If she made a comment about his unavailability, he would just pat her like a puppy and say that he's just been a little tired lately. If she persisted, he got upset and talked about how hard he was working to provide her and their child with the best of everything.

It was true that he gave Brenda pretty much whatever she wanted. She lived in a large home in the middle of two incredibly landscaped acres. She had a part-time gardener to tend to the yard and all the flower gardens. For her thirty-eighth birthday, Stephen let her pick out a brand new red sports car that she had always wanted. She took tennis lessons and went to a spa once a week for facials, massages, and yoga. She went shopping until her huge closet was stuffed with new clothes and shoes. She had the freedom and the means to do whatever pleased her.

When she finished naming all the wonderful things Stephen had given her and all the resources he had placed at her fingertips, she said that I must think she's one of those spoiled, rich women who want to have their cake and eat it too. "It's hard enough to admit this to a therapist who's supposed to listen and not judge. I *really* hate to bring this up to Stephen after all he gives me," she said, "Besides, he's got his plate full, and the last thing he wants is a needy wife nagging at him for more attention. But I can't help it. I'm lonely. I don't feel loved. I'm not happy, and I think I'm getting depressed. How's that for a little rich girl who has everything?"

After a few more sessions, Brenda's trust in me increased to the point that she could actually express the hurt feelings and not just talk about them. Several times, she cried off and on throughout the hour. She grieved the loss of what she once had with Stephen and for what she had hoped to have with him for years to come. She talked about the isolation she felt. Although the attention and comfort from her friends helped, it wasn't the same as getting it from her former *best* friend—her husband.

I could see that some of Brenda's profound sadness was likely percolating up from unresolved problems in her childhood, and it was obvious that her feelings of rejection and disconnection with Stephen were painful and emotionally wounding. But there was more than just sadness.

One afternoon, Brenda came into my office so angry that I suggested she beat a pillow with an old tennis racket I kept in the closet for such a purpose. I placed an empty chair a few feet in front of her and told her to imagine the chair was Stephen. I invited her to look at the chair and say whatever came to mind as she beat the pillow.

She started slowly but then began beating the pillow with such force that I was momentarily taken aback. Her face was red as she cursed and shouted at "Stephen," yelling things like, "You hurt me. Why don't you love me anymore? How dare you treat me like this? Who do you think you are?"

After a minute or so, she collapsed, crying in a heap on the rug. She'd been carrying so much anger and resentment that she was afraid of letting it out around Stephen for fear that she might explode and say or do something she'd regret.

Toward the end of the session, I asked Brenda if she was feeling better. She smiled and said, almost sheepishly, "Yeah. And I feel a little stronger, too." I could see the relief in her face from venting her pent-up emotions.

As she left, she said, "That was good. I needed to do that."

At her next session, Brenda said that while things hadn't improved at home, she'd felt better after the past session. She joked that she should tell her tennis instructor to bring a pillow to her next lesson so she could beat the hell out of it.

During our time together that week, we talked about her options with the marriage. She said that she was clear that a divorce was the last option she wanted to consider, but neither did she want to spend the rest of her life with Stephen if something didn't change.

I asked Brenda to pretend that Stephen was in the empty chair across from her and then to tell "him" what it was she really needed from him that she wasn't getting in the relationship.

"Well, I feel kind of silly talking to an empty chair, but I'll try. OK, here we go." Brenda took a deep breath and leaned forward in her chair. "Hello, Stephen. I'm glad you're here because I've got some things to say to you. And I want you to listen, OK? I want you to hear me. First of all, I'm lonely." Tears started coming down her cheeks. "I don't feel close to you and I don't think you feel close to me. In fact, it seems that your way of loving me is to just put up with me.

"When I share something with you, I don't think you really hear me. When I touch you or caress you, I'm not sure there's any sort of reaction inside of you at all. When I look into your eyes and your face, I don't see connection or warmth, just a blank look. Sometimes I feel like I'm yelling and beating on a wall and you're on the other side, but you can't hear me.

"I know that you're nice to me sometimes and give me things. I know you try at times. But my friends and my dog are nice to me, too. Being nice is not enough. I know that something's missing between us. I feel it in every cell in my body.

"You're just not there. I feel like I can't get through to you, no matter what I say or do. When you walk through the door, it's like you become a kind of zombie. There's nothing inside I can share with or relate to or love. It's like you're a box, but there's nothing on the inside.

"I need you to be *with* me, to open up and let me see what's inside. I'm your wife; you can trust me. I want to be with a warm, feeling, human being." Brenda sat back in her chair, shook her head, and cried softly.

She asked me if I would see her husband a couple of times and then maybe they could come in together for a while. Although I doubted he would consent to come in, I told her it might be worth a try.

To my surprise, Stephen called me later that week to set up an appointment. Several days later, this man I'd heard so much about was sitting a few feet in front of me. It's always interesting to have spouses describe their mates and their behavior for weeks and then to meet that spouse in person. Most of the time, my clients' perceptions of their partners seem pretty accurate to me.

Stephen, however, seemed more friendly and approachable

than I had expected. With his longish, perfectly combed, graying hair and his casual but expensive-looking slacks and shirt, he had the appearance of a distinguished gentleman in his late forties or early fifties. His easy, confident smile was that of a man who was comfortable in his own skin.

After a few minutes of guy talk about sports and his medical-device business, we eased into the apparently troubled waters of his marriage to Brenda. I asked him what it was like to live with her.

"Well," he said, "first of all, I'm not sure why I'm really here. But if I can help Brenda get to a better place, then that's what I want to do. Now, to what it's like being with my wife. She can be a handful at times. She has these emotional swings where she's animated and happy with everything and then the next day, she's moody, sullen, and quiet. In those times, she gets irritable and upset over nothing. Then there are times when she just mopes around the house or lays on the couch for hours watching television. Sometimes I wonder which wife I'll be coming home to." Stephen seemed genuinely perplexed over his wife's erratic moods and her tendency to overreact to seemingly trivial situations.

I asked him if he and Brenda ever talked about why she was sad or upset.

"Of course we've talked about it," Stephen replied with a hint of agitation. "When she first started acting like this, I would ask her what was going on. She wouldn't tell me. Then, after a few months, she started implying that everything was my fault. I didn't talk to her or listen to her enough. I didn't take her seriously. I wasn't interested in her. A few times she's even questioned my love for her. I'm not a psychiatrist, but I've thought for a while that she's dealing with hormone issues or some kind of a mild bipolar situation. I don't know how else to explain her attitude and behavior. I mentioned it to her once and she got upset, saying I was trying to shift all the responsibility to her so that I didn't have to change."

As our conversation continued, I began to sense that Stephen's ability to be empathic and compassionate had long since been covered over by life experiences and maybe even emotional wounds in childhood. I asked Stephen how he responded to her when she started blaming him for some of her problems.

"Well, like any guy would do, I guess. I get pretty upset inside, but I still try to assure her that I *do* take her seriously and *am* interested in her. I tell her regularly that I love her." Stephen's frustration was beginning to surface. "I even started bringing her flowers from time to time and picking up little things for her when I'm away on a trip. She might be pleased at the moment, but it doesn't last. It just seems that whatever I do, it has never been enough. It's just not enough.

"And if you want me to tell you the truth, I'm getting pretty fed up with the whole thing. The things I give her and the effort I put into that marriage and she's not satisfied? What woman wouldn't want to have what she's got, for God's sake? She can do anything she wants. She's got anything in the world she wants and she's not happy with me or the marriage? Come on, you've got to admit that it's ridiculous. And to be honest with you, I'm tired of this whole goddamn mess." Stephen's confident, easy going demeanor gave way to frustration, bewilderment, and finally, anger.

I asked Stephen what he was feeling.

"Isn't it obvious? I'm angry. Come on," he said a bit testily, "can't you see I'm pissed off?"

I told him that what I could see wasn't as important as what he could see. Since it was just the first session, I decided not to go any further into his anger. As he began to calm down, I asked him if he really felt it when he assured his wife that he loved her. He admitted that most of those times he probably hadn't felt much of anything and that saying, "I love you," had usually been an attempt to make her feel better and improve her mood.

I asked him if he still loved her.

"There was a time when I could have answered that with no hesitation," he said. "When I first met her at the hospital, she was bubbly, energetic, and a great nurse. By the time we started dating, I already had strong feelings for her. She seemed like the good-hearted woman I'd always wanted to settle down with. I fell pretty hard for her. I loved her more than I could have imagined. It was just wonderful.

"Gradually, she lost her zest. She became someone else. Someone I didn't feel very attracted to. I'll admit that the feelings of love don't come around as often as I would like. You know, with her always being so unhappy and negative about everything, it's been hard to work up many positive feelings toward her.

"And I certainly couldn't find many good feelings when she would get angry with me and start attacking me for not caring about her and that whole thing. If I'm honest, I'd have to say that I've gotten pretty tired of that lately. I'm not sure how much I love her anymore, if I love her at all.

"Don't get me wrong; I'm not saying I want a divorce. I want to love her and I want to make her happy. I'm just not feeling very optimistic right now."

Stephen went on. "What I can't understand is how she could resent me or get angry with me so often. You know, what have I done to her? I don't go out chasing other women. I don't drink or gamble to excess. I usually come home after work. And, my God, I couldn't be more generous with her. She has her own credit card to go shopping with. I frequently surprise her with a gift. I take her on trips and cruises. She takes tennis lessons and goes to the spa with girlfriends. She has a gardener, for God's sake. She's free to do anything she wants. It's like *Alice in Wonderland*—nothing makes sense anymore. All I know is, if somebody did all that for me, I would be so grateful and so pleased and so happy, I wouldn't know what to do."

When Stephen showed up for therapy the next week, he again expressed frustration, confusion, and ambivalence about the relationship. He hinted that this was probably his last time to see me. Because of that, I decided to gently confront him. I said that while a chemical imbalance could indeed be contributing to Brenda's behavior, there was a good chance that the relationship dynamics weren't meeting some of her important emotional and psychological needs.

He was not very receptive when I went on to tentatively imply that maybe his way of relating and attempting to love Brenda could be contributing to her unhappiness. I told him that it was possible that he had unwittingly been throwing a lot of material things into the marriage while skimping on his personal involvement. I continued that this kind of generosity by itself didn't create the conditions for trust, connection, or intimacy. I suggested that it was possible that his efforts to care for her didn't result in a love that Brenda could use to soothe and nourish those parts of her that craved emotional intimacy. And no matter how elevated her standard of living, without usable love, there was a good chance that she would become lonely, depressed, and frustrated.

Unfortunately, Stephen didn't return for further counseling. I did continue to see Brenda for several more weeks, however. Her continuing work in therapy helped her to understand that her emotions were quite normal for the situation she was in and that she wasn't a spoiled little rich girl. On her last visit, Brenda told me that she had an improved awareness of her situation and that she understood herself and Stephen better than she ever had.

She realized that it wasn't Stephen the person that she was upset with, it was *how he related* to her. She said, "He's a good man. I don't hate him or even blame him anymore. It's certain parts of our relationship that I'm not happy with. And although they are very important parts, I feel better about him than I have in a while."

She understood that if things were going to change, it would most likely be because *she* changed and altered the way she interacted with him. It was a real challenge but she was ready to accept it for now. She wanted to stay in the relationship if there was any hope at all that things could get better.

Although like Stephen, a lot of men can be nice and even generous at times, the fact remains that when called upon to engage in one-on-one intimacy, many of them respond like a fish out of water. While there are certainly exceptions, the unfortunate truth is that far too many males find it difficult, if not impossible to be *in relation* with their female partners, their children, and others in their lives. This is perhaps the greatest hurdle that males have in their quest to give and receive usable love. And because it has such an incredible impact on attempts at romantic love, I'd like to explore what being *in relation* means and why males have such trouble achieving it.

Chapter 25:

Men and the Struggle to Be in Relation

BEING IN RELATION describes a living, in-the-moment, naturally occurring process between two people. This living process engages each person in the give-and-take, back-and-forth movement of feelings, ideas, thoughts, touch, empathy, compassion, and warmth. Throughout the process, there is a felt sense of connection, vulnerability, and openness that could only happen in the presence of emotional and physical safety.

In this safe and supportive space, as defensive walls are lowered, hearts are free to dance and play, laugh and sing, and cry and grieve. Even difficult feelings of anger and frustration can be appropriately expressed, contained, and resolved relationally within this process. Not only are all feelings OK, but they are also honored and seen as a necessary and authentic way to share what is happening inside two people within a given moment. It is this kind of honesty and mutual sharing, this kind of knowing, and this kind of acceptance of each other at the moment that begets true intimacy.

Although there are many ways to give and receive usable love, this living, in-the-moment process is its heart and soul. It is here, more than anywhere else, that authentic love can be nourished, revitalized, and celebrated. Again, to be in this relational space, walls *must* be lowered, and hearts *must* be opened. There is no other way.

I like to imagine that this kind of intimacy is like two parallel but separate streams moving across the countryside, and then suddenly coming together to merge and form one larger stream. These two streams, joined together as one, wind their way across the landscape. At some point further down, a boulder or change in the terrain diverts the bigger brook back into separate, individual streams. The two individual streams, now renewed and replenished by the exchange of waters and nutrients, move once more across the land as separate entities until some new change in the terrain brings them together again.

In my experience as a therapist, a husband, a father, and a male, I've noticed that women are more likely to engage in this kind of connected intimacy than most men. Notwithstanding the many exceptions, I believe that the typical male might handle the streams running close together or side by side, but his masculine conditioning and his psychological defenses will likely prevent him from joining with his romantic partner to make a combined stream of open, in-the-moment, emotional intimacy.

This disparity in the ability to be intimate is one of the great challenges of modern love relationships. Starting early in life, little girls are naturally drawn into a world of interpersonal relationships where they laugh, cry, and endlessly talk while sharing intimate feelings and thoughts with their girlfriends. By the time they are grown, a large percentage of women have experienced at least some emotional intimacy with their mothers, girlfriends, and others in their circles of friends. Quite naturally, they expect this level of intimacy to continue with the men they choose to spend their lives with. Tragically, like in the poem, "Belly Song," millions of women "open to their man like a flower, only to have him fall on her like a stone."

Instead of becoming best friends and confidants, far too many men remain almost like strangers who are uncomfortable and unskilled in the realm of feelings, listening, sharing, connecting, empathy, commiseration, and compassion. Although most women make valiant efforts to adjust and accept whatever level of intimacy their men can manage, on the inside they are often left with feelings of loneliness, disappointment, and even resentment. In many cases, over time, their unmet needs for intimacy and connection lead to episodes of unhappiness, depression, anxiety, and finally despair and hopelessness.

This is perhaps especially true of so many contemporary women who no longer have extended families nearby to meet their needs for closeness, connection, and emotional intimacy. And today's working women who juggle careers, housework, children, and husbands have less time to spend sharing and connecting with girlfriends and peers. With fewer opportunities to get their emotional needs met outside their primary relationships, women could certainly use a little empathy, compassion, understanding, and intimacy from the men they live with. This sort of usable love could make a significant difference in their lives, but, sadly, it is too often unavailable from their husbands and boyfriends.

It's no secret that a large percentage of men find it difficult to engage in the kind of connection and intimacy that typical women have experienced and have come to expect from their romantic partners. Hundreds of magazine articles, books, television shows, jokes, and conversations have featured this particular issue that has perplexed so many men and women for so many generations. I believe this is a critical problem with enormous implications, not only for romantic relationships but also for politics and societies at large. Although there is possibly a biological component, I believe that gender conditioning and the preparation that men go through on their respective journeys toward manhood is the fundamental cause of their struggles with emotional intimacy and connection. And if you are a woman reading this, my hope is that you will gain at least a little more understanding and compassion regarding men and why they think, feel, and behave the way they do.

Chapter 26:

Men and Their Emotions

THROUGHOUT HISTORY, PROVIDING for family and community has always been the major responsibility of men. Certainly, women have also been providing for their families for millennia, but they had other essential roles as well. Because providing has always been a major and primary role for men, it has been taken seriously by the various cultures. Whether it's taught through initiation, rites of passage, the military, sports, games, or schools, young males have been conditioned psychologically, mentally, and physically to bring home the bacon. As they grow into adults, males have been establishing and proving their manhood for millennia by dragging home a deer, a fish, a paycheck, or whatever else their particular culture has dictated as necessary for survival.

During this time, males have been expected to put their bodies and even their lives at risk to provide for their families, tribes, villages, and nations. In seaside villages throughout the world, men have boarded their small boats and ridden the waves of the oceans in a search for the fish to feed their families. These men have always known that dangerous storms could appear from nowhere, creating mountainous waves capable of sending them and their boats to the bottom of the sea. Each time they go out, they accept that it could be their last. And yet they joke, sing songs, and happily do the job that was waiting for them when they came of age.

Similar scenarios have been repeated in every culture the world over for millennia. Generations of coal miners have risked cave-ins and black lung to provide for their families. From loggers working the forests of the Northwest to roughnecks hanging from the oil derricks of Texas, men have risked life and limb to provide for their loved ones. From the monotonous assembly lines of factories to the drudgery of crunching numbers in windowless offices, men have persevered and got the job done. It's important at this point to recognize that while their gender conditioning diminished their emotional availability, it was considered essential preparation for men's quest to provide for their families.

A negative outcome of this gender conditioning is that, in too many cases, men have learned to equate their worth as human beings with their ability to produce and achieve. With their eyes constantly on the results, they become focused on the outcome and often miss the joys and inner satisfaction of the process. They learn to compare their achievements with those of other men and to judge themselves harshly if they don't measure up. Most men take great pride in the work they do.

My work has helped me understand how men of all ages depend on their jobs and businesses for their identity and sense of worth. Several out-of-work men I've counseled wept as though they had lost the love of their lives. I wonder how many men have gone to their graves secretly feeling like failures as human beings simply because they didn't make enough money or have the right kind of job.

To protect their loved ones, their gods, their villages, their way of life and their countries, countless men have, in the process of doing their duties as males, made the ultimate sacrifice. So many millions of young men, with their futures still in front of them, had their lives snuffed out by swords, bullets, and bombs. They have died in the heat of the desert, in the frigid snows of foreign lands, gone down with their ships in the middle of the oceans and languished alone with their wounds in some killing field far from home. Other men, called lucky by some, have returned home with parts of their bodies and their selves lost forever in some battle for control of a hill or remote beach. Millions of other brave fighters have gone back to their families, hoping to put the hell they've endured behind them, only to discover that it won't go away. For too many of these men, the nightmare memories of war, with its trauma and heartbreak, make normal living and loving almost impossible.

As part of their responsibility to their loved ones and society, men have also been thought of as expendable during various crises. For instance, when the *Titanic* was sinking and there weren't enough lifeboats for everyone, it was decided that women and children would be first to get on the little boats. If there were any spaces left, then the men would be allowed to board. Over one thousand three hundred men slipped into the icy waters to die as the ship fell to the bottom of the sea, while their wives and children drifted off to safety. Although it may be seldom talked about, every man knows that if such a time comes, he will be expected to risk his life or give it up if required to save the women and children in peril. It has always been "women and children first." That's just the way it is and men accept it.

Historically, women, peers, and older males have often served as enforcers who keep watchful eyes on boys to ensure they conform to rigid masculine roles, behaviors, and emotional expressions. Behaviors by males that have resembled anything feminine or less than masculine have traditionally been discouraged through the use of shame, embarrassment, and ridicule.

I can still remember a scene in high school that taught me how unsafe it was to show sensitivity. One morning as I approached the school grounds, I heard shouts and yelling and turned to see a small crowd gathered in a circle. As I made my way to the edge of the group, I saw Tom, a classmate of mine, in the middle of the circle. Several of the guys and even a couple of girls were taunting the boy, calling him names like sissy, queer, and girlie. One of the guys moved into the circle and tried to start a fight by pushing and slapping a visibly shaken Tom. Thankfully, a teacher happened by and interrupted the emotional lynching of this terrified young man.

Although I was just a bystander, I remember being stunned and frightened. Tom's crime was exhibiting "feminine" qualities like sensitivity and tenderness. He was "different," and that apparently wasn't OK. That morning in the schoolyard was only one of a thousand different ways I got the message that my vulnerable, sensitive feelings wouldn't be tolerated by the world I lived in.

Interestingly, just last week I wore a pink shirt to the golf club and one of the guys came up behind me and playfully hugged me around the neck and called me sweetie. Men learn to walk whatever narrow road of masculinity their particular culture has built. In far too many cases, the price for staying on that road has not only been their ability to feel and express their own emotions, but their capacity to love in an intimate, connecting, and usable way.

While boys in every culture are born with the natural capability to experience and express a full range of emotions, the masculine conditioning they receive in the various respective "boot camps" gradually grinds away at their vulnerability and sensitivities. The all-too-familiar "boys/men don't cry" becomes a mantra that is indelibly imprinted on their brains.

To avoid the feelings that might bring about the tears, boys learn to ignore not only their own vulnerable emotions but also the tender emotions of others. In time, they go from ignoring to not even noticing that the feelings are there. Unfortunately, this process of selectively disowning one's own emotions can ultimately result in feelings that are so buried, they can't be retrieved. Once their vulnerable emotions are hidden away, many men find that the predominant feelings they have left and are allowed to express are aggressive ones like anger and frustration.

Bereft of their tender feelings, males may become inured to their own hurts, pains, and emotional needs. When this happens, of course, they also tend to become inured to the hurts, pains, and emotional needs of others, including their loved ones. Empathy and compassion then become difficult to experience or even comprehend. Gradually, almost inexorably, the pervasive masculine conditioning walls off the sensitive, heart-infused inner self and makes reliance on cognitive, left-brain influences the norm. Thus, millions of men are making decisions, taking actions, and participating in relationships in business, medicine, politics, armies, religions, schools, churches, the media, law enforcement, and families with precious little of the natural wisdom and compassion of the heart to serve as a compass. While it is true that there are many exceptional men who are deeply informed by their hearts and contribute to humanity in incredibly positive ways, it seems that too many male players upon the various stages of the world are engaging in unfortunate, negative behaviors and decisions that arise from their protective parts and masculine conditioning.

Rites of passage for boys in various cultures throughout the ages are quite interesting and, in extreme instances, have included such brutal experiences as scarifying large parts of the body, beatings, traumatic fear, and excruciating pain. Although delving into the masculine rituals of exotic, faraway cultures would likely prove compelling, I believe it would be more relevant and helpful to examine modern gender conditioning in postindustrial cultures like the United States.

Rather than enduring physically painful and heavy-handed rituals and rites of passage, males in more modern cultures learn their gender roles through psychologically effective messages that pervade the environment they grow up in. These teachings about becoming a *real* man are delivered to the boys by parents, siblings, peers, teachers, clergy, star athletes, politicians, television, movies, comics, video games, Internet, newspapers, talk show radio, and magazines. And, because the messages are so pervasive and ever-present, the concept of manliness, with all its expectations and proscriptions, becomes a part of a boy's psychological makeup. Even college fraternities have hazing to "prepare and initiate" new members into their fold.

Young males learn the masculine code as effortlessly and naturally as they learn their language. Although these messages have accomplished the goal of instilling in most males the ability and willingness to protect, provide, and procreate, the unintended consequences of this gender conditioning have taken a toll on men and their relationships. The ability to engage in usable love that includes emotional intimacy, tenderness, sensitivity, empathy, and compassion has unwittingly been compromised in countless males through this conditioning process. It seems as though the baby was thrown out with the bath water.

One of the older books dealing with the differences between men and women is John Gray's *Men are from Mars and Women are from Venus*. Although I found his book to be helpful, I don't think men are *from* Mars; I think men are *sent* to Mars for their masculine conditioning and their basic training in real manhood.

Have you ever seen a little baby boy cooing and giggling

as he looks into his mother's eyes? Or a three-year-old boy laughingly protest as his dog licks him in the face? We've all seen little boys with skinned knees and tears running down their cheeks running to Mommy for soothing and comfort. Before they were "sent to Mars," males felt and freely expressed a full range of emotions, but, when they returned, they were different. Their capacity to feel and express tenderness and receptivity had been squashed. Their ability to empathize and be curious about another's feelings had been compromised at best and completely destroyed at worst.

Even though women have access to more warm and fuzzy hormones and may have certain brain attributes that provide them with an advantage over men in the emotional department, these biological disparities fail to explain why most men are so different when it comes to feelings. Let's face it; a large percentage of men have been hurt by their cultural and gender conditioning. This has compromised their ability to function as loving, caring, fully functioning human beings in a love relationship. I can't recall the name of the movie, but I remember a scene when John Wayne's character was handed a baby; he held it out away from his body like it was some kind of strange, foreign object. It was funny but revealed a lot about the masculine culture being presented. And although men like that might appear strong and powerful, right below the surface many of them wrestle with loneliness, anxiety, confusion, and a feeling of disconnection from everything around them. If they stay distracted with work, sports, sex, or whatever, then they can get through another day.

While it's true that more recent generations of males are less likely to follow the John Wayne images of masculinity that their fathers and grandfathers were exposed to; it's also true that they have no clear cultural role models for what a man should be. Many modern young men are no longer willing to go through life as lonely, mechanistic, and disconnected shells of what they could have been. While they are beginning to resist the old, rigid ways of determining manhood, they haven't necessarily gravitated toward a masculinity that advocates vulnerability and connectedness. Although these "new men" are still in the minority, I believe that it's possible that someday this nascent shift might become a tidal wave of positive social change. In the meantime, there are still cultural messages out there that are affecting our boys and young men in unhealthy ways.

Although there is definitely a shift taking place in the consciousness of the world, the masculine code and way of thinking still have a powerful grip on the throat of civilization. You need to look no further than typical politicians, military leaders, corporate cultures, and much of the media. Although there are exceptions, these men (and some women) are inclined to use questionable or even Machiavellian means to achieve their ends. Think of the degradation of our planet, the perpetual wars and conflicts going on across the world, the immoral disparity between the rich and the poor, the political in-fighting and backroom deals, and the unending "defense" and military expansion.

Let's look at a few of those messages that have deeply influenced males for generations:

Men are brave and fearless.

Men are in control and take charge.

Real men appear cool.

Men are expected to know the answers.

Men take action and make things happen; they never give up.

Men are the real breadwinners for their families.

Men are not emotional and don't cry.

Men must protect their honor and the honor of their women.

Men take risks to achieve the expectations placed upon them.
Men are strong and can take care of themselves.
Men compete and win, succeeding despite the odds.
Real men get the girl, are virile, and are great lovers.

If we stop and think about it, most of these criteria for manhood are sensible and, up until recently, have been necessary for most societies to survive and flourish. Even in today's world, many of these messages are still needed to prepare young males for the various masculine roles they will play as adults. Problems arise, however, when boys and young men have no wise and available fathers or mentors to translate and interpret the messages into reasonable, measured beliefs and behaviors.

Let's imagine for a moment how young boys, bereft of those wise elders, might interpret those messages for males based on movies, comics, peers, video games, and other such providers of cultural information.

Real men do it even if it's dangerous because real men are never afraid. Being afraid is unmanly and even cowardly.

Real men are in control of themselves, the situations, and the people around them at all times because men are responsible for everybody and everything.

Real men act cool and look cool to others no matter what the situation or how they feel inside.

Real men always have answers and they are always right, because men are supposed to just know.

Real men take action and get it done, no matter what it takes, even if there's collateral damage to the environment or people.

Real men are the main providers for their families. Being productive is synonymous with manliness. Losing one's job or failing at business is humiliating and unmanly.

Real men are tough, individualistic, and unemotional. Not

only do they not show or express sensitive, vulnerable feelings, but they also don't even allow themselves to experience them on the inside. Tears show weakness, are feminine and are to be avoided at all costs.

Real men must protect their honor and that of "their" women, even if it involves aggressive action or violence. Signs of disrespect are not to be tolerated, no matter what.

Real men are unafraid to take risks. They drive fast, shoot from the hip, and engage in risky behaviors to prove that they are masculine.

Real men are strong and invincible. They ignore pain, avoid the doctor, always open the pickle jar, and don't need any help with anything. (The characters that John Wayne played often perfectly embodied this skewed idea of manhood.)

Real men must compete and win at all costs. The outcome is much more important than the process. There are winners and there are losers. Every game, every enterprise, every activity could involve some form of competition and, therefore, must be a proving ground for one's masculinity.

Real men get the best girls and are sexual athletes. They can always get it up, do it again right away, and have tools big enough to please any woman.

Real men are masters at lovemaking and seduction and, therefore, rarely have to take no for an answer.

Unfortunately, these uninformed, exaggerated, and occasionally distorted interpretations have had unintended, negative consequences for millions of men and their families. By following this masculine code literally, or in an exaggerated fashion, countless men have learned to interact with the world around them in mechanical and emotionally repressed ways. With emotional intelligence compromised, they struggle to recognize and communicate their own feelings. This then leads to an impaired ability to deal empathically with the emotions of family and friends. Unable to achieve closeness and nonsexual intimacy with wives, children, and others, men have difficulty deriving pleasure or meaning from interactions with them. This has caused many men to be overly attracted to competition, production, or other pursuits that might involve solitary participation, like porn or watching sports on television.

Because their interior, emotional lives are so hidden, a significant number of men often become alienated from their inner selves and may seem like strangers to their coworkers, friends, and even their own families. How much can you really know about an emotionless person? (I've worked with many a man who told me that his dad was basically a stranger to him.)

The masculine code, with its vague and poorly translated messages, often results in males comparing themselves to each other to determine their own sense of masculinity. This frequently leaves men uncertain and insecure about themselves and their manhood. That insecurity, coupled with the masculine code, creates in men an excessive need to be right and to feel like they are in control of the people and the situations that surround them. For the same reasons, they are overly competitive and feel an exaggerated need to come out on top. It doesn't matter whether it's to gain the advantage in a business deal, win an argument, get control of the remote, be victorious in video games, or defeat opponents in sports activities like golf, tennis, or bowling. They can even get overly competitive in games like Monopoly, charades, or Scrabble.

It could truly help matters if influential people in the culture could reinterpret and teach a more measured and reasonable masculine code. Imagine how different our men would be if the following amended messages were taught and followed by fathers, mentors, politicians, popular icons, and sports heroes:

There will be times in your life when, in order to protect yourself or your loved ones, you may be called upon to do something that frightens you. It's OK to be scared, but if it's something you really need to do, then momentarily set aside your fears and do it anyway. Bravery is not the absence of fear but doing what needs to be done in spite of the fear you're feeling.

There will be certain instances, especially in a crisis, when a man may need to rise to the occasion by using his strengths, creativity, and wisdom in an assertive manner to assure a good outcome. He must understand, however, that a wise man knows there will be times when his best contribution will be as a team member and not a leader.

Being cool is very different than acting cool. *Acting* cool is about looking good, wearing the latest styles, using the latest phrases, and walking with the right swagger. And it's about hanging out with the right people in an effort to be popular while hiding the fact that you feel inadequate and insecure on the inside. *Being* cool is about being easy and comfortable in your own skin, doing the things you enjoy, and treating yourself and others with respect and dignity.

There will be countless times when you will be called upon to answer questions, fix things, settle disputes, and solve problems. A wise man will prepare intellectually, physically, and emotionally so that he can be of help to himself and others. He knows, however, that no amount of preparation will prepare him to always know the answer. A real man knows when he doesn't know and has no trouble admitting it.

A man's actions should be thoughtful and informed. Although we are expected to be "men of action," there are times when doing nothing is the smartest and most productive course.

If he is physically and mentally able, it is a man's responsibility to do an honest day's work to support himself and his family. An honest day's work may take many forms, however. Men who choose to be elementary school teachers, professional dancers or nurses are no less manly than those who are fighter pilots, coal miners, or plumbers. And it may even be that staying home and taking care of the children while his spouse works could be a man's most important contribution. There also may be times when, beyond his control, a man loses his job or becomes physically unable to work. This in no way is a reflection on his worth as a human being or his standing as a man.

Real men cry. Sometimes they cry out of grief while other times they cry when they are overcome by joy or when something is so beautiful it brings tears to their eyes —like the birth of their babies or making love in the moonlight. Crying is as natural for men as it is for women and is an acceptable way to express strong feelings. Even frustration and deep disappointment may bring tears. In fact, tears of frustration are much better than aggressive actions taken in the heat of anger. There are times, however, when men must hold back their tears and emotions so that they might accomplish the task at hand or appear strong and in control for others who depend on them in the moment. Crying is not feminine—when a man cries, he cries masculine tears. In loving relationships, real men can be vulnerable, tender, sensitive, and compassionate. Occasionally, there are even times when it is appropriate for a man to let down his guard and express his feelings of neediness and helplessness.

Since men are often physically stronger than women, they are expected to protect themselves and their female partners from real harm. Protecting their honor, however, can be a confusing and slippery slope that can lead to unnecessary fighting, injury, and even death. Others, especially men who've been drinking, can be rude and thoughtless. It's not your job to straighten them out and teach them a lesson. A wise man can ignore those things and move along.

While many men take careless risks to prove or shore up their masculinity, real men take only calculated risks, whether for adventure or fun or because they must do it to save themselves or others from harm. It is never manly to *prove* anything by gambling with your life.

Men are often expected to handle jobs and situations that require heavy lifting. Although a man's additional strength allows him to help out whenever necessary and appropriate, his extra power does not mean that he is expected to be Superman. His strength does not mean he can do anything, nor does it make him immune to disease, pain, or any normal human need.

Succeeding and reaching your goals can be an important and satisfying part of your life. However, it is important to realize that material success is only a part of being a successful man. *How* you succeed and how you behave with family and others is even more important.

Real men understand that successful sex with another is a two-way, mutually pleasurable, mutually enjoyable experience. Healthy seduction does not involve misleading, exploiting, coercing, or deceiving another. And sex is not a stage upon which you must perform to prove yourself. Rather, sex is an opportunity to let go and celebrate yourself and your partner as you create a safe place for both of you to enjoy the experience.

Hopefully, someday these and other similar messages will become an essential, everyday part of a boy's journey into conscious manhood. If that would only happen to cultures across the planet, imagine how it could impact our relationships, politics, environment, and international relations. While there would still be conflicts and problems in such a scenario, I truly believe that a world populated with compassionate and emotionally available men would be a much better place for us all to live. It would be a world where joy, peace, usable love, and respect for one another might just have a chance to grow and flourish in the lives of people everywhere.

Most men do the best they can considering that their natural ability to feel and express their emotions has been compromised by families and cultures determined to make them *real* men. I have had the privilege of working with literally thousands of males in my practice in workshops and conferences across the country and have seen the pent-up pain and hurt hidden by decades of stiff upper lips and stoic personas. I can only imagine that millions of men in our country go through their daily lives working, watching TV, playing sports, and engaging with their families *as though* everything was just fine.

Although they might not admit it, right below the surface too many of these men wrestle with loneliness, anxiety, confusion, and a feeling of disconnection from everything around them. If they stay distracted with work, sports, sex, or whatever, then they can get through another day.

A month before my dad died, I visited him in a nursing home. His broken hip became infected, leaving him unable to walk. When I entered his room, he was reading. I asked him about the pile of books beside his bed and he answered by saying that he read to keep the bad thoughts away. I felt so sad for him, knowing that he'd spent his whole life struggling to keep those bad thoughts at bay. I can only imagine that his childhood, with a mentally unstable mother, his stint flying fighter planes in World War II, and working decades at a boring job left him with plenty of bad thoughts.

Emotional wounds and unexpressed feelings tend to generate the kind of unhealthy thinking that plagues so many males in the world today. It's just tragic that these men suffer in silence for so much of their lives. If they could just uncover their feelings and deal with the issues and memories from their pasts, they could heal or diminish the wounds and stop the bad thoughts. Instead, they suffer and unwittingly cause suffering for those around them as well.

Many a woman has opened herself up to a man, only to be heartbroken when she discovers that he cannot return her love, vulnerability, warmth, or affection in a meaningful way. Emptiness and loneliness await the woman who shares her emotions with a mate who can neither receive her feelings in a healthy, validating way nor express his own emotions.

Years ago, during a layover in Chicago, I sat at a pub, listening to a table of guys talking about a golf game they had apparently finished that morning. I noticed that they weren't listening to each other. One of them said something like, "I can't believe I sunk that putt from twenty feet. It had so many breaks it could have been a snake!"

No one responded. Instead, another guy announced that he hit the best drive of his life on the third hole.

Again, there was no response, except for a third fellow lamenting about how badly he'd scored that day. No response.

The guys were talking, but no one was listening. Their remarks weren't even being acknowledged with a polite, "Wow," or, "That's fantastic." There were five men at the table, and, without them realizing it, each one of them was alone.

For me, that scene epitomized the plight of millions of men in this country. They are alone, each encapsulated in his own little cocoon, unable to connect with anyone outside it. I see it every time I play golf at my club. Men either make attempts at humor or talk about trivial things and virtually no one is listening or the least bit interested unless they try to one-up what has just been said.

Unfortunately, this way of relating is not limited to the golf course. I've worked with many wives who complained that their husbands couldn't seem to sit still for a conversation about something meaningful to them, whether it was their feelings about work, their weight, or their situations with family or friends. The husbands would sit there with their eyes glazing over, glancing at a computer or newspaper next to them, making the wrong comments, or just trying to wrap up the uncomfortable session by fixing whatever their wives were upset about. By the time the "conversations" were over, the wives felt a lot like the guys at the pub—alone, not heard, not seen, and definitely not understood.

A friend of mine tried to get her husband on board by announcing that she had something important to share. Asking him to sit down, she then explained to him, in as nice a way as possible, that she was feeling lonely and disconnected in the relationship and needed him to open up and really talk to her.

His response was classic: "OK, what do you want me to say?"

Frustrated, she responded by saying, "Just tell me how you're feeling, like right now. I want to know you and connect with you on a deeper level. I'm lonely."

Looking baffled, he replied, "I feel fine. Honey, I don't know what you're talking about; we're doing great. We connect all the time."

"No, "she said. "You don't understand. Just because we snuggle on the couch and watch television together or share a bed doesn't mean we're connecting. Connecting is about sharing our deepest thoughts and feelings with one another. And we don't do that."

He grinned and started massaging her shoulders. "Honey, that's what you have girlfriends for. You know I'm not good at that kind of stuff." Without realizing it, he was "falling on her like a stone."

What so many men don't understand is that a woman wants that "kind of stuff" from the man she loves and lives with. She wants her man to truly *see* her for who she is and not just for the role she plays. She wants him to see her as a woman and a person in her own right who has dreams, desires, needs, doubts, and fears that she would love to share with him. She wants him to genuinely listen and *hear* when she shares something important to her. She wants him to be curious about who she is underneath her role as his wife, and to ask questions so he can learn more about her. She wants to be understood and appreciated as a person with many roles and responsibilities that require daily effort and attention. She wants her man to caress her and look into her eyes with warmth and genuine affection for her as a human being. And she yearns to know what is really going on inside *him*, what makes him tick, and who it really is that she's living with.

Women want more than a one-dimensional John Wayne character or a Vulcan like Mr. Spock. A woman can't be truly intimate or emotionally connected with either of those types because there's not enough of him available with whom to be intimate. Both intimacy and connection are *felt* experiences that depend on the back and forth of thoughts *and* feelings between two people.

Most men and many women mistakenly confuse or conflate the meanings of intimacy, connection, attachment, and closeness. In *The Art of Intimacy,* Dr. Thomas Malone and Dr. Patrick Malone describe closeness as a feeling a couple get when they snuggle on a couch with some popcorn and a good movie. According to this father-son team of psychiatrists, second honeymoons in Hawaii, candlelit dinners, and sexual fireworks all create closeness more than intimacy. Sharing the reassuring phrase, "I love you," celebrating anniversaries, and giving gifts are ways of creating and maintaining closeness. Like a warm massage, closeness calms and soothes the tired, frayed nerves and muscles of a relationship. The authors suggested that closeness creates order and stability in a relationship while serving as a foundation for intimacy, which can be the catalyst for growth and change.

Intimacy, on the other hand, differs greatly from closeness. Intimacy, the format through which healing and personal growth takes place within a relationship, demands intellectual and emotional honesty between two partners. That requires lowering defenses, facing the risks, and becoming vulnerable with each other. Intimacy is not about hiding from or coddling each other's unhealthy sensitivities and "buttons." Instead, it's about sharing a ruthless pursuit of the truth about oneself and the relationship. There's your story, and there's my story, and then there's the Cold, Hard Truth.

Unlike closeness, intimacy can often cause chaos, leading to the disruption of a peaceful stalemate. Intimacy moves things and shakes them up, looking for little white lies created to protect the emotional wounds and fearful places of both partners. Although it can be painful and difficult, true intimacy fosters the kind of closeness, healing, and self-awareness that allows two people to love each other with psychological muscles that are rarely used. Like closeness, intimacy is an integral part of the matrix of love.

Intimacy sets the stage for the vulnerability and deep honesty between partners that makes connection possible. It's crucial here to understand that connection is very different from attachment. We can be attached to each other like Velcro® and yet not be connected at all. Couples who are attached but not connected are usually lonely and unfulfilled. Without the intimate, reciprocal sharing of thoughts and feelings, the relationship becomes stale and empty.

Sadly, many men, and some women as well, have strong defenses against being vulnerable. To share their deepest thoughts and feelings would be risky and even frightening. Instead, they prefer the closeness and attachment that assuages their fears of abandonment or being alone. The rub comes in when men remain satisfied with closeness and attachment, while their mates are dying inside from the loneliness and emptiness that comes from a lack of intimacy and connection.

Admittedly, it's a long road to get from repressed emotions and a defended heart to openness and vulnerability. Protective parts, created by the family of origin and the masculine culture, must be diminished or re-educated. Obsolete, distorted beliefs about feelings, women, sexuality, and the masculine code must be changed. A man's heart, so underused in our culture, must become a compass that guides him in his relationships and his inner world. Although success in a career may be important to a man, it shouldn't be nearly as important as his relationship to his mate, his children, and even to himself. To be truly successful, a man must live from his heart-infused Captain and not his protective parts.

Although we've devoted several pages to the issues of men and how they contribute to the lack of usable love in relationships and the problems of the world, it is important at this point to not throw the baby out with the bath water, even though there might be lots of people who would like to. We must understand that men, like women, do pretty much the best that they can, given their level of development, their gender conditioning, and their biological and psychological makeup.

Blaming men for their individual and collective shortcomings is not helpful, nor is it completely fair. What is needed at this juncture is an acute awareness and understanding of the dilemma that modern males face, and how it contributes to the troubles of families, cultures, and the environment. With such an understanding, it will be much easier to cobble together a bit of compassion and empathy for men and their current situation. And it is exactly that kind of attitude from others that will foster the safe and supportive environment every male needs to climb his particular mountain of personal growth and positive change.

After seeing mostly female clients for my first year of practice and listening to their litany of complaints about the men in their lives, I was further convinced that most men out there needed some serious help. It was at that time, however, and for that reason, that I decided to focus my career on men and specialize in their issues. I wanted to understand what made them the way they were, and so, I counseled dozens of men in my psychotherapy practice and worked with thousands of males in weekend wilderness workshops across the country. Among these men were doctors, preachers, plumbers, oil men, professional athletes, airline pilots, computer programmers, poets, singers, judges, lawyers, businessmen, construction workers, and psychotherapists.

Many of the men who participated in the weekend gatherings or came to see me in my office had never been to therapy, had never read a self-help book and had never been interested in personal growth. While their ages varied from seventeen years to seventy-nine, their reasons for seeking change were similar. Most of them were motivated to seek help because they felt threatened by some sort of crisis involving their health, careers, or relationships. They were simply unprepared psychologically or emotionally to deal with these sorts of crises. I remain awed by the courage and perseverance these men showed in their willingness to be vulnerable and to confront long-buried feelings of hurt, fear, rage, and grief in their journey to become better human beings, husbands, fathers, and friends.

In time, I realized that meeting in groups was definitely the best way to help men change. So I started a men's group that met once a week and lasted for twelve years. Although some men came and went, several were regular members for the entire time. Having marched through the same gauntlet of gender conditioning throughout their youth, these men soon learned that they had much in common with each other.

In general, they were competitive, distrustful, afraid of exposing their fears and vulnerabilities, and, if pushed, prone to verbally aggressive behavior. There was also a certain self-centeredness that came from excessively monitoring themselves and their behaviors to ensure that they measured up and lived according to the masculine code. Their conflicts between who they really were on the inside and who they were *supposed* to be on the outside led to internal upheavals and dialogues that had too often kept their focus on themselves instead of others.

A major goal of the men in the group was to jettison certain internalized gender messages that had crippled their ability to be authentic and intimate with their loved ones and friends. They wanted to learn whatever it took to feel their real feelings and to give and receive usable love.

After working with them for a while, I came to understand that the gender conditioning these men had endured was not so different from brainwashing on a national scale. Of course, it's not the result of some clandestine conspiracy; it's just an indirect way that our country prepares boys to be men. But because it's so informal and disseminated by so many different people in so many different ways, it's easy for the messages to be distorted and exaggerated. When this happens, many of the naturally occurring, positive human qualities are unwittingly discouraged and stunted.

Our job in the group was to basically deprogram the men so that they could replace the inappropriate messages embedded in their psyches with new, more life-affirming and relational ways of being. Once this process took place and the natural, emotional selves of the men resurfaced, the results were amazing.

Jed was a tall, handsome young man of thirty-three with

wavy black hair, a slender build, and a classic, clean-shaven face. His stated purpose for joining the group was to deal with his impending divorce and to become a better person and father than his own dad. Although he could be funny and frequently made the group laugh, Jed was basically a troubled, serious man with an aggressive nature and a quick temper. The members liked and respected him but they also were quietly intimidated by his outbursts and tendency toward verbal aggression. In fact, it was that kind of behavior that prompted his wife to file for divorce after only a year of marriage and shortly after his daughter was born.

He was devastated by the failure of his relationship and the loss of his wife. But he was especially distraught about being separated from his baby girl. When his wife moved across the state soon after the divorce, it became difficult for him to spend time with his little daughter. And even though he was willing to spend the nine hours for the round trip to see his daughter, his wife made it difficult for him to see her at all.

Jed was determined that if he ever had another chance as a husband and father, he'd never make the same mistakes again. Because of this, he was motivated in the group to learn new, less aggressive ways of relating and dealing with his feelings.

During his first three years of concerted effort in the group, Jed spent a lot of time unlearning some of the distorted cultural messages about being a real man. Through processes, conversations, and interactions, Jed gradually began to open up and allow his full range of feelings to surface in front of the other men. The rigid walls and defenses he'd built to protect himself were finally coming down. With his newly discovered vulnerability, he let himself weep from the sadness over the loss of his wife and daughter. Rather than withdrawing in stunned silence, or, worse, ridiculing his tears, the men in the group comforted him and empathized with his feelings.

The release and the relief Jed felt was palpable. The "masculine" dam that had held back his tears ever since he was a small boy finally gave way. In time, he grieved the hurts and pain of his childhood and the loving dad he'd never had.

As he felt and expressed his emotions like never before, Jed's anger and aggressiveness began to diminish to the point that he could manage them much better. He could now deal with frustration without immediately going into anger. It was truly an amazing experience to watch this man change before our very eyes. His taut, angular face had softened and his body language became relaxed and non-threatening. He even became one of the leading peacemakers in the group, helping others find the true feelings hiding behind their conflicts and frustrations.

With his newfound emotional awareness and maturity, Jed was able to meet and attract Linda, a lovely young woman who eventually became his wife and best friend. Although some problems developed in the marriage, Jed continued to work on his issues in group and take what he learned back to the relationship. Within a couple of years, they had Thomas, a little blue-eyed baby boy. Using the group as a support system and a safe place to continue learning about emotions, intimacy, and usable love, Jed became the husband and father he'd always dreamed he could be.

This was wonderfully demonstrated by a story Jed told the group when little Thomas was about three years old. Apparently, Thomas had been sleeping in the same room as Linda and Jed since he was born. Thinking it was time for the boy to sleep in his own room, Jed put Thomas to bed in his own little bedroom. Although he was tired from a long day's work, Jed played a game with Thomas, read him a story, kissed him goodnight, left a little night light on, gently closed the door, and then quietly went to the other room and fell asleep with Linda.

After about thirty minutes of much-needed sleep, Jed felt his covers being pulled off him, and, as he looked up, there was Thomas, saying, "Daddy, I want to sleep in here." Groggy and tired, Jed got up and carried his son back into his own little bedroom and told him that he was going to have to take away his favorite stuffed shark if he didn't stay in his bed. He tucked him in bed once again, read him another story, and then went back to Linda and his own bed.

This time he had just fallen asleep when, yet again, he felt the covers being pulled off to the sound of, "Daddy, I want to sleep in here with you."

Again, Jed carried his son back to his own room. He took away Thomas' shark and told him the teddy bear was next if he didn't stay in his bed and go to sleep. Sure enough, the whole scenario happened again, and the teddy bear was taken away.

The fourth time it happened, Jed put on some clothes, picked his son up and carried him out to the car. They rode around the neighborhood until Thomas fell asleep. Jed then went back home, put the sleeping Thomas in his own little bedroom, tucked him in, and then finally, exhausted, returned to the master bedroom where Linda was fast asleep.

This time, thankfully, Thomas slept through the rest of the night. Within a few nights, he was adjusted and sleeping well in his own bed. Although there may have been many different ways of handling that frustrating situation, Jed managed to accomplish what needed to be done without hurting his son or adversely affecting their relationship.

This story is significant because it shows that an impatient, angry man with few relational tools can become a loving, sensitive husband and father with a little help, some guidance, and a lot of work and effort. I believe that, like Jed, most males want to be more emotionally available and empathic and they want to give that kind of usable love to their families; they're just not able to do it with their current level of awareness and development. And most unfortunately, the information, the support, and the effective help they need to make the necessary changes are rarely available. Sadly, our culture has few roads that can lead a man to personal growth and emotional availability.

Chapter 27:

Men and Sex

YEARS AGO, I had the privilege of attending a talk by psychiatrist Scott Peck, author of the mega best-selling book, *The Road Less Traveled*. Interestingly, the only thing I remember from his presentation was the simple statement that went something like this, "If a couple tells me they have no problems in the bedroom, they're lying." While there may be many exceptions to his pronouncement, I believe that, for the most part, what he said was true.

Having great, passionate, pleasurable sex with the same person for years can be daunting for several reasons. Of course, a couple can engage in many types of sexual experiences that use fantasy, domination, submission, and countless other ways of creating excitement and variety. But perhaps the most meaningful, satisfying, and fulfilling sex involves vulnerability, intimacy, and connection. Unfortunately, as we've mentioned earlier, those three things are difficult for most men to achieve and share with a mate.

Modern males have an interesting history when it comes to the sexual arena. For millennia, men have been conditioned by their societies to be effective, enthusiastic procreators. Virtually all cultures, from tribes and villages to huge, postmodern societies, have in place certain rituals, rites of passage, oral traditions, jokes, symbols, and teachings to prepare men to be adequate, if not overly functioning, in the world of sexuality and procreation. With few exceptions, it has been in society's best interest to ensure reproduction among its members. Our culture is no exception.

With no information to the contrary, many males believe all the hype, feeling anxious and inadequate about their manhood and themselves as sexual beings. They then spend untold energy and efforts throughout their life spans, trying to prove that they are real men, complete with sexual stamina, size, and skill. Unfortunately, the emphasis is on how *they* are measuring up and not on the pleasure, joy, and meaning their lovemaking partners might receive. While males may show interest in their partners' satisfaction, ("Was that as good for you as it was for me?") much of that attention is about how her pleasure reflects his sexual prowess.

In addition to all the messages about the sexual criteria to achieve manliness, young males are bombarded with images of attractive and scantily clad females that, together with their exploding hormones, fuel their fires and sexualize them at an impressionable time in their lives. After fantasizing about, and masturbating to, these glamorous, stimulating images hundreds of times during their youths, males often become sexualized to them by the time they reach eighteen. Because this sexualizing process is psychologically imprinted and stable, it is probable that these images will be a significant source of sexual ideation and stimulation for the rest of their lives.

As these young men marry and have families, the natural aging process will likely diminish the physical proportions and perceived beauty of their female partners. This increasing disparity between their wives and the sexualized ideals of their youth has created problems for countless husbands and boyfriends over the generations. I've spoken to many a man who has become disenchanted with his wife or girlfriend simply because her looks began to deviate from the ideal he had grown to appreciate as a youth.

Although we, as a society, chastise these men and impugn them as shallow and immature, they were unwittingly sexualized by a culture that failed to counter all those luscious female images with sufficient messages of wisdom about the joys and value of inner beauty, emotional intimacy, and usable love. I'm not implying that these messages weren't around; I'm just saying that, in the world of men, they were infinitesimal when compared to the barrage of sexy female images.

I've also had conversations with many men who told me that adjusting to a monogamous relationship after the sexual freedoms of bachelorhood was a difficult transition. It was perfectly acceptable, if not encouraged, for a man to "sow his wild oats" and acquire some experience while single, but on the day of his wedding, he was expected forever after to focus his sexual energies and desires on one person only-his wife. This profound and immediate change in his sexual attitude and behavior can be daunting after the "in love" phase has worn off. Whether it is the male ego, evolutionary influences, cultural conditioning, or a combination of these and other factors, many men find it challenging to be comfortable with the restraints of monogamy. (Interestingly, some women find monogamy challenging as well.) This leads us to a fascinating supplement to countless men and their quest for sexual excitement, release, novelty, and satisfaction.

Finally, even the briefest examination of men's sexual issues would be incomplete without a word or two about pornography. While females account for a small percentage of this shadowy enterprise, not surprisingly, the research has shown that males are the overwhelming patrons of porn. In the United States alone, the porn industry racks up over $13 billion per year in revenue, which is more than Major League Baseball, the National Football League, and the National Basketball Association combined.

On the surface, there seems to be a good reason for its powerful attraction and resulting popularity. We don't need research to tell us that using pornography can bring intense pleasure and instant gratification. And it's virtually effortless, convenient, relatively inexpensive, anonymous, and free of misunderstandings and expectations. And let's not forget that you don't get STIs while looking at pictures or videos. There is also a type of porn to fit every man's particular fantasy, no matter how imaginative. In many ways porn can be a user-friendly, pleasurable path to bring about the release and relief of orgasm. And it does so at the viewer's pace whenever he wants it.

There is a darker side to porn, however, and many authors and groups have more than sufficiently addressed those concerns. My interest here is to touch on the correlation between the negative effects of masculine gender conditioning and the use of pornography. As we have previously noted, societal preparation for manhood can unwittingly alter a man's naturally occurring emotional self to such an extent that it is hardly functional. By the time a man has made it through the gauntlet of masculine conditioning, he is often basically unsuited for authentic, relational intimacy and emotionally usable love. Dog paddling and splashing around in the shallow waters of porn seems much easier and safer than diving into the deep waters of emotions and felt intimacy.

Because their vulnerable feelings have been hammered down by so many different sources throughout the culture, many men may feel threatened when tender emotions rise to the surface. Since the very nature of real intimacy and usable love requires those feelings to be part of the equation, men often feel anxious, inadequate, and just plain uncomfortable when their partners look to engage in those special moments of honest, face-to-face sharing and intimacy. And because, on some level, he knows that he's not giving his partner what she really needs and wants, he will tend to avoid those special moments.

If his partner desires those special, intimate times to be part of her sexual experience, he might begin to see sex with her as something he can't live up to. The pressure and expectations to perform emotionally are enough to gradually kill his sexual buzz. This is where pornography becomes a viable alternative to his marriage bed because it's easy; there are no expectations, and he doesn't feel inadequate or like a failure in the eyes of his mate. Although porn is neither intimate nor connecting, it's OK because he's unable to do much connecting anyway.

In my therapy office, I've worked with a surprising number of men who consistently choose porn over the lovely, interesting women in their lives. This even happens in cases where the women make it obvious that, although they don't get all the intimacy they would prefer, they could still enjoy sex and would like to have it as a part of their lives.

In a somewhat different scenario, a man may not notice or care that his sexual relationship with his wife is unsatisfactory to her. He just wants and expects regular sex. He's so shut down that he doesn't even understand what she wants and needs from him. As his nonsexual intimacy and communication skills are virtually nonexistent, she no longer feels close to him and loses her desire to share her physical and emotional bodies with him. And so she begins to suffer from an increasing number of "headaches." With such a strong desire for sex and no place to express it, the man turns to the ever-beckoning world of pornography.

Unfortunately for too many husbands and boyfriends, pornography has become a way of life. For them, this sad and solitary substitute for intimacy has become the harbor where their ships of sexuality are tied. Without compasses or the skills to navigate the ever-moving and sometimes turbulent waters of intimacy, these men rarely turn their vessels toward the spontaneity of the open seas, preferring instead the safety and predictability of the harbor.

The important thing to remember here is that those unfortunate men didn't start out that way. As little boys, their potential included a bright, wonderful future complete with loving, meaningful, and intimate sex lives with the special persons in their worlds. With well-meaning, but imperfect parents who emotionally hurt them and a society that inadvertently misinformed them about the nature of sexuality and masculinity, these wounded males have wandered about, unwittingly drifting into alluring pitfalls that stole their attention and ensnared them for life. With their potential for usable love and the joys of emotional intimacy so far out of reach, countless of these men follow each other down empty, lonely, and soulless roads that lead to nowhere.

Chapter 28:

Healing Your Wounds and Opening Your Heart

WORKING ALONE IN a Relationship
If you want to improve your relationship but your partner isn't interested in growing or working with you, please don't be discouraged. There is hope for you and the millions of men and women who have mates unable or unwilling to engage in the kind of transforming work we address in this book. It *is* possible to open your heart, improve your connection, and decrease your loneliness without directly attempting to change your partner. This effort would be required of you even if your partner was willing to do his or her own work.

By focusing your attention on your own needs and the unhealthy strategies you've used to get them met, you can learn a new way of relating to your partner. A wise but unknown person wrote, "You can't change what's going on around you until you start changing what's going on inside you." That kernel of wisdom couldn't be more applicable than when it comes to love relationships.

As you begin relating to your partner in a powerful, straightforward way without blaming, shaming, complaining, or criticizing, it's very possible that he or she might see you in a different light. By attempting to get your needs met in a healthy, honest, and non-hurtful way, your partner will likely feel safer and less prone to be overtaken by protective parts, thus changing the negative cycle of your parts against his or her parts.

Just remember that when you stand up to your partner and refuse to accept hurtful behavior, you are not acting *against* him or her, but *for* yourself. It should not be a battle or a war but a positive, self-affirming strategy that protects you and your exiles from pain, threat, and unfair treatment.

Mary, a middle-aged female client, recently described her husband as someone with a tendency to be critical, angry, controlling, and verbally aggressive when he's not happy with her. When Steve started in on her, Mary would typically regress into childlike behaviors like emotionally collapsing, acting passive-aggressively, or even dissociating. As a child, her protective parts had learned fearful, avoiding strategies to protect her from aggressive, punitive parents.

Recently, much of Steve's criticism had been focused on her "substandard" work with the laundry, dirty dishes, and other failings around the house. Implying she was lazy and inept, Steve rarely missed a chance to point out her mistakes and deficiencies.

I invited Mary to do a role-playing scene where I would be an angry Steve and she would respond as usual. She agreed and gave me some hints about how Steve talks to her when he's upset.

I began as an agitated Steve with a raised voice. "Who has ever heard of a wife who seldom cooks, rarely cleans the house, and never does laundry until it's falling out of the hamper? What is it with you anyway?"

Mary, playing her usual self, apologized by saying, "I know I could do better. Time just gets away from me. With my work schedule, helping Lisa get ready for school, and then helping her with her homework, I can't seem to get it all done."

In a contemptuous voice, I answered, "So you have a job and one kid and you're overwhelmed? What about all those working wives out there with two jobs and three or four kids to take care of? They seem to get it done just fine."

Mary sighs. "I'm sure they're out there. I just don't know how they do it. Do you have any suggestions?"

Me: "That's your department. You need to figure it out. Maybe if you didn't spend so much time reading or talking on the phone with your girlfriend, you could get a handle on things."

Mary, resignedly: "Maybe you're right. I'll see if I can do a better job of staying on top of everything."

As we talked about her responses, Mary conceded that based on past experience, it was unlikely that her conciliatory and passive responses to Steve's mistreatment would ever change his behavior. Without some sort of adjustment on her part, Steve would keep on believing that he is right about her ineptitude or laziness and would continue to vent his frustration in unhealthy, hurtful, and unproductive ways.

Mary confessed that she seldom confronted Steve about his behavior because she was so afraid of his anger and disapproval. As her therapy progressed, however, her fear diminished, and a welcome sense of power began to take its place. After only eight weeks of therapy, she decided that she was ready to face Steve with her truth.

Before that critical moment, however, Mary and I did a session where we role-played again so that she could practice what she wanted to say to him. I invited her to create an intention that was in keeping with her new way of seeing her partner and her relationship. After some thought, Mary decided that her intention when confronting Steve was to create more connection and intimacy between them. To do that, she knew that she had to have at least a grasp of what his real needs might be, which probably had little to do with her housekeeping habits.

I invited Mary to see that Steve likely had two concurrent problems: he didn't know what his real needs were and he used hurtful, unproductive strategies to meet "needs" that were actually just preferences. We discussed the idea that when unmet preferences are perceived as needs there are usually negative overreactions. It was also important for her to see her husband as a fellow traveler whose hurtful behavior was caused by his wounded parts and his lack of awareness. Seeing him as the enemy would only end up hurting both of them.

When addressing our needs or the needs of our partners, it is important to understand the difference between the "needs" of our protective parts and the real needs of our exiles and essential selves. In the above scenario, Steve's protective parts "need" Mary to keep up with certain symbolic duties so that he can feel loved and valued. His flawed thinking probably goes something this: if his wife keeps the house clean and cooks meals for him in a timely and predictable manner, then she obviously loves and appreciates him. If she doesn't, then she no longer loves him. Thus, when the house is neglected, he feels unloved and his resulting attachment anxiety causes him to lash out at her.

Mary's submissiveness tells Steve's parts that their demands are legitimate and that she is, indeed, remiss in her duties. As long as his parts can maintain the boss-employee relationship with Steve's wife, they will have the misguided belief that whenever she complies, he is loved and secure.

Steve's exiles and his essential Self, however, need very different things than his protective parts. Like virtually all people, Steve's essential Self has a need for true intimacy, connection, and love. His Self doesn't need Mary's acquiescence or other symbolic demonstrations of his power over her. He doesn't need respect generated by her fear of him and he doesn't need to have his ego stroked. Underneath his bluster and judgment, he needs the real thing; he needs Mary's heartfelt love that is based on who he really is, not something he coerces out of her with his power over her.

Somewhere in Steve's subconscious, he knows that Mary's compliance is not love and never will be. He knows his strategies aren't working to get him what he truly needs. He just doesn't know how to relate to her in such a way as to generate authentic intimacy and love.

Before Mary could help Steve and his needs, it was important for her to know what her own needs were and to set in motion a healthy, productive strategy for getting those needs met in the relationship. Then she might have the free attention to imagine what Steve's real needs might be. She could then empathize with his feelings about not getting those needs met.

Of course, to do this she would have to deal with, and drain off, much of her resentment and anger that had built up over the years. We had a session where Mary used the plastic bat and beat the hell out of the pillow while yelling at an image of Steve.

When she finished hitting the pillow, she cried briefly before smiling and saying, "Wow, that's exactly what I needed. I should have done that long ago."

A few days after the session, Steve arrived home already frustrated because an employee had done some shoddy work that reflected poorly on the whole team. When he saw Mary, who had been home from work for half an hour, sitting at the computer, he started in on her. Although Mary couldn't remember exactly what was said during the episode, she shared the basic gist of what happened.

Steve, in a loud voice: "*What are you doing*? The breakfast dishes are on the counter, there's no dinner being cooked, and you're sitting at the computer looking at emails. I thought you were going to try harder to make this a home instead of a house where we just happen to live together. This is just not working!"

Mary, looking up from her computer: "You're right, Steve; *this* is not working. Yelling and blaming me for your frustration isn't going to work anymore. In fact, it obviously never worked. As long as you keep doing it, you're not going to get what you want or what you need from me."

Steve, taken aback by Mary's assertiveness, replied, "Now, you wait just a minute—"

Mary interrupted: "No, Steve, *you* wait a minute. I don't want to talk about this until you've calmed down."

Frustrated, Steve yelled, "I *am* calmed down. If you've got something to say, just say it!"

Mary spoke evenly and without emotion, "I'm going to rustle up something for dinner and, later, after we've eaten and Lisa is in bed, I'd like for us to talk if you're interested."

Steve, still frustrated, "Jesus Christ, what is it with you all of a sudden? It's about that therapy you've been doing isn't it? So now you're going to get all uppity around here; is that it? You're going to get your mojo?"

Mary responded, "I'm going to fix dinner now, and if you're interested, I'd love to talk to you later this evening."

Deflated and a little shocked, Steve sighed with resignation. "Yeah, OK, whatever. Call me when you're ready for me to eat."

After Lisa was down for the night, Steve wandered into the kitchen to find Mary finishing up with the dishes. He grabbed a dish towel and even dried and put away a glass and a couple of plates.

Disturbed by what might be said in the upcoming "talk," Steve quietly asked, "So, what is it you wanted to talk about?"

Suggesting they talk in the living room, Mary told Steve of a Native American talking stick process where the person holding the stick does the talking and the other person listens.

(I'd shared this process with Mary in one of our sessions because Steve had a tendency to interrupt.) He agreed to try it. With a ruler as the talking stick in her hand, Mary began: "I want to start if that's OK with you."

Steve nodded and took a deep breath.

"First of all, I believe that you are a pretty good husband and a good father to Lisa. You're a dependable provider and that's important to me. But what's more important is how you treat me when you get upset or frustrated. Your yelling, criticizing, and contemptuous behavior hurts me, scares me, and kills my feelings for you. I've had enough of it. I'm not your whipping post and I'm not going to tolerate it anymore. If you want to live with me, you're going to have to stop it. It's that simple. I understand you might slip up a few times in the next couple of months, but basically, I'm done with you disrespecting me and blaming me for how you feel."

When Mary paused, Steve reached out for the talking stick. "Mary, I'm not that bad. Like you said, I'm a good husband and I'm very good for Lisa. I even help her with her homework sometimes. I just lose it once in a while and get a little rowdy."

Mary reached for the stick and Steve relinquished it. "I didn't say *you* were bad, Steve. I said that you did hurtful things when you 'lose it.' You need to understand that when you lose it, you're losing a lot more than just your temper. You're losing my love and my respect for you. You're losing my ability or even desire to connect with you, be close to you, or even have sex with you. You're losing me as a friend. You're losing your partner, Steve, and I know you don't want that. But that's what happens.

"Each time you yell at me and treat me like I'm beneath you, a little bit more of my heart closes to you. This has got to stop if we're ever going to have a chance to be a happy, loving couple.

"I'm not your employee or your disobedient child. I'm an

adult who is your co-equal in this marriage, and I want to be treated as such. I have a need to be respected and to be treated with dignity, even when you're frustrated. I also have a need to feel close to you and to be connected with you and I can't have either one as long as you treat me the way you do.

"And it doesn't matter if it's twice a week or once a month. When you yell at me with your frustration and contempt, my heart closes and I go away. I know that's not what you want, but that's what happens."

Steve blurted out, "But I don't mean to hurt—"

Mary interrupted: "Wait; I've still got the stick. I know it may take some time to break this habit, but if you treat me badly again, we're going to have another talk. It's got to stop, Steve. That's all there is to it."

Mary told me that the discussion continued for another half-hour while Steve minimized what he'd done and accused her of being too sensitive and not giving him a chance to have his feelings. She said that she stood her ground until he finally agreed to change his behavior and, if he couldn't, to see a therapist.

Of course, this vignette between Mary and Steve will be different for different couples. Some men may be understanding and apologetic while others might react with even more disrespect and anger when confronted. Still others may threaten to end the relationship. All an offended partner can do is to remain non-blaming and positive while staying strong and firm in his or her intention to be treated with respect. *Every* time a partner is disrespected or treated poorly, he or she should respond with an appropriate message that the behavior is unacceptable.

The important point here is that Mary, with a newly found strength, became a change agent who altered the course of her relationship. Once Mary and Steve discovered what they really needed from the relationship, they could then create effective strategies to meet those needs.

Taking responsibility for your needs and using healthy, non-toxic approaches to get them met will almost certainly improve your relationship. It's also true that giving usable love to your partner can increase his or her sense of safety and diminish the armored impediments around the heart. The inner strength and power that comes from doing this work will allow you to be a change agent as you stand firm in the face of your partner's protective parts.

Because different partners have different wounds and personalities, the approach to effectively deal with them will have to be tailored to fit. Regardless of whether they are passive, aggressive, anxious, obsessive-compulsive, passive-aggressive, or just plain difficult to live with, the best strategy to deal with them will always be handled by the Captain.

If you're faced with a disruptive or passive partner and want things to change, it's important that you start by setting a realistic goal. For instance, your goal might be to get more of your needs and wants met while helping to increase your partner's self-awareness and emotional growth. Then you need to have a plan to help you meet that goal. Your plan might include stopping your partner whenever he or she is being disrespectful or hurtful to you. Then you might tell them how you'd like for them to behave toward you. Tell them what works for you and what doesn't. Be clear, concise, and consistent without being *against* your partner. Try to be *for* yourself and *for* your partner.

By understanding what's beneath your partner's behavior, you can more easily have compassion for their inner world and the struggles they are going through. Always remember that, believe it or not, partners are doing the best they can considering their emotional development, awareness, genetics and so forth.

Your empathy for their inner turmoil and unhealthy attempts to protect themselves will help them to feel seen, safe, and supported. This creates the conditions for a partner to trust enough to be vulnerable and emotionally honest. Being critical and hostile toward a loved one will only drive them deeper into their toxic, unhealthy patterns of behavior. By being the best partner you can be, you'll be ensuring that your loved one will move closer to being the best partner that he or she could be.

Chapter 29:

Understanding Healing

AFTER GETTING THIS far in the book, it should be obvious to you that emotional wounds and an armored heart take a tragic toll not only on one's love relationship but on one's life as well. I believe that owning your brokenness and then working to heal it must be the greatest love of all. And, I might add, it is the most usable form of love you can give to your partner, your children, your friends, and even your planet.

If a conflicted couple seeks counseling, the therapist will often focus on teaching conflict resolution and healthy communication skills. When done well, this type of therapy can be helpful and may even be all the couple needs to "get along" and create increased harmony in the relationship. However, the underlying reasons for the conflicts are frequently not addressed by this emphasis on the *symptoms* of the problem. In many cases, the counselors haven't done the deeper work on themselves, making it almost impossible to take their clients where they've never been.

Jenny and I believe that teaching behavior changes to a couple is only a small part of the healing process and in many cases is even unnecessary. One can be taught to be "nice" and appropriate, but kindness is an attitude and cannot be taught; it simply wells up from an open, unfettered, and loving heart. Our experience has demonstrated that real healing takes place when partners remove or diminish the impediments protecting their hearts. Once this is done and the heart is more open, most partners can naturally communicate and relate to each other with kindness, sensitivity, emotional honesty, and vulnerability.

As healing takes place, partners will be more aware of their lovers' feelings and will want to speak their truths in a relational way, without anger, shaming, or blaming. And conversely, they will be able to hear a mate's feedback or requests for change without becoming defensive. In the language of IFS, healing takes place when the Captain befriends the protective parts, validates their efforts and reeducates them according to current reality. The Captain can then create a trusting relationship with the exiles, paving the way for them to open up and express long-buried thoughts, emotions, and stories about traumatic and hurtful experiences from the past. This expression unburdens them from the painful, emotion-laden memories they've been carrying. Once this happens and the overwhelming feelings have dissipated, the exiles can begin to feel safe, loved, and valued. And importantly, there will then be no need for the protectors to react defensively or close the heart.

While there are currently many approaches to help individuals and couples struggling with emotional wounds and closed hearts, we believe that IFS is the most efficient and practical path available today. And because it is so user-friendly, IFS can even be employed in some cases by an individual or couple without the presence of a therapist. In this section, we will demonstrate how this powerful and pragmatic way of using the mind to heal itself can lead to wholeness by removing the obstacles to a loving and open heart.

Healing yourself from past psychological wounds and hurts is a lot like going to a gym to lose weight and get fit. Joining the gym and getting a workout schedule is the first step, but it takes more than that to change your body into what you want it to be. You have to actually go to the gym and regularly work out according to your schedule. You can't just walk by the entrance or go in and sit while you sip a protein drink and chat with others about the benefits of belonging to a gym. If you want results, you'll have to actually lift the weights and use the exercise machines. In other words, you'll have to expend the right kind of effort and energy in places that give you results.

In the same way, if you want to *heal* your broken heart and emotional wounds from the past, you can't just focus on the symptoms and learn a new language of healing and psychology. To heal your heart and change yourself from the inside out, you must address the wounded self that is deep within. That soft, frightened, vulnerable self is usually burdened with overwhelming feelings that have been repressed or blocked for years.

According to IFS, there are often several wounded areas that have each created a distinct, vulnerable inner self or child in the mind. For instance, I had one inner self or exile that was wounded by repeated shaming and humiliation. I had another wounded inner self that was hurt, frightened, and traumatized by a physically and emotionally abusive father. I had still another exile that developed attachment issues because my mother rejected me and angrily took her love away each time I displeased her. So I had three different wounded selves that needed to be addressed separately. This is important because each of these exiles or inner selves had their own protectors that interfered with my attempts at intimacy, connection, and love.

Many men may struggle while working with their exiles because of the aforementioned cultural conditioning that makes vulnerable emotional experiences more difficult for them. For instance, when the Captain is asking the exile how it feels or what it was like to have gone through those hurtful and even traumatic times as an infant or child, the exile may be unable to express tears or tender, vulnerable emotions. Without the bodily expression of those long-ago feelings of pain, fear, rejection, abandonment, or other types of abuse, it will be more difficult to have the *corrective emotional experience* that can help to heal the wound.

Because of this, a man's Captain must be patient, tender, and attuned to his exiles, giving them whatever time and support they need to finally feel safe enough to become vulnerable. Even if he can't get to the feelings and tears, it will be enormously helpful to address and befriend those hurt places that have been banned to the basement of his mind. Just making repeated contact with an exile can be healing.

This stuff really works, but like at the gym, you'll have to put out some effort and energy. Unlike the gym, however, this work will usually require some courage along with dedication and intention. If your relationship is one of the most important things in the world to you, doesn't it make sense that you would want to do whatever it takes to make it fantastic? Imagine for a moment what it might be like to finally look at yourself and your partner through the eyes of joy, exuberance, and total acceptance. Imagine future years together, sharing the deepest kind of emotional intimacy, connection, and felt-love you had in your early romantic period. Love is all the things the poems and songs say it is, but *only* when it comes from an open and unfettered heart. You can give yourself this remarkable gift if you do the work!

Chapter 30:

Getting Started

IF YOU DECIDED to seek therapy to help you with the wounds and issues that trouble you, limit you, or make consistent intimacy and connection impossible with your love partner, you would probably want a therapist who was skilled, compassionate, wise, non-judgmental, and concerned about your well-being. To find this person, you might ask friends and family for recommendations or you could scour the internet for a therapist in your area with stellar reviews. Of course, after reading this book, you might decide to try an IFS therapist to see if this powerful therapy could work for you.

On the other hand, your adventurous spirit might just decide to give your Captain a try as your therapist. If you choose this route to begin your journey, there are a few things you might want to consider before starting.

An Essential First Step

Before your Captain can be an effective change agent in your relationship, he or she will have to not only be strong, but clear about the cold, hard truth between you and your partner. Your Captain must be able to confront your protective parts with that truth while remaining gentle, understanding, and compassionate. And remember, if your parts are holding grievances and resentments against your partner, it's very likely they are clinging to similar issues left over from childhood.

You can't move forward until those grudges and perceptions have been cleaned up. In fact, just cleaning up your past and current grievances will result in some important emotional healing. This kind of deep forgiveness and understanding will likely involve some patience and hard work by the Captain. Protective parts that for years have seen your partner as an unsafe, hurtful adversary may not change their perceptions easily. As a first step toward forgiving and letting go of our grievances toward each other, Jenny and I remind each other of a truth that's been mentioned in earlier chapters: "Everybody is doing pretty much the best they can, considering their cultural conditioning, their genetic makeup, their childhood experiences, their knowledge, and their levels of self-awareness." Whether we like it or not, that *is* the cold, hard truth.

If you think about it, no one in their right mind would want to be miserable or to make others miserable just for the sake of being mean. We believe it's true that men and women do the best they can, in spite of their emotional and psychological wounds and the strategies their protective parts have adopted to survive in the world. Certainly, it can be difficult to see your partner through these understanding and forgiving eyes, but you might at least think about the *possibility* that we're all doing the best we can. (Actually, this way of seeing is not being generous; it is being realistic.) If, over time, you can learn to see this truth about your partner, it can help you begin the process of diminishing and eventually eliminating any bitterness or negative beliefs you harbor against your mate. And if you've been in an unfulfilling relationship for a while, it's very likely you've got some resentment and grievances toward your partner.

Doing a "session" between your Captain and your relevant protective parts is a great place to start the journey toward seeing your partner with new eyes. You can do the sessions by yourself or with a trusted witness such as a friend or therapist. It is probably not a good idea to do these angry, grievance sessions with your partner because of the strong feelings harbored by protective parts.

If you choose to do a session by yourself, your chances of success are greatly increased if you begin by letting your protective parts air their grievances toward your partner out loud. During this process, let your parts have free rein to yell, curse, blame, and flail about until they have spewed out all of their thoughts, feelings, and beliefs about your partner and his or her behavior. Although your Captain can interrupt from time to time, it's a good policy to let the part vent until it is done with its initial outburst.

It is important to understand that before the Captain can be effective, he or she must be completely separated and unblended from the protective part. When working with a part, you might remember that it has always had your best interests at heart. The part was formed to protect you and although it might cause you and your partner misery and suffering, it is always trying to help. Therefore, to be effective with the part and to gain its trust, the Captain must recognize and appreciate the part's intent and efforts to protect. Being angry or unappreciative toward the part will sabotage your efforts to transform the part's attitude and behavior.

After the part vents and feels heard, the Captain can begin to gently confront and redirect it toward reality. Once the part can no longer deny the obvious, the Captain, through interactive dialogue, can begin the task of reeducating and repurposing it by revealing the truth about the resented partner. After successfully dialoguing with your protective part, you are then ready to approach the vulnerable, hurt exile with compassion, caring, and curiosity. There is an example of such a session on hostility and forgiveness in the chapter on anger.

When I went through this process for the third or fourth time, I came away with a much different picture of Jenny. Instead of seeing her as a difficult woman who was irritable and nearly impossible to please, I saw her as a lovely woman who was basically generous, caring, and often kind, even though she had been terribly wounded as a child. I saw how much of her "irritability" had been caused by my lack of attention, my hurtful pokes at her, and the tendency to pull my love away whenever I became upset with her. I saw a wounded woman who had made heroic efforts to love me in spite of her wounds and my shortcomings as a partner. Finally getting it and realizing the truth brought tears of appreciation, respect, and a newfound love for Jenny. Was this the woman I'd been living with for seven years? Could I have been so blind? I still remember the shudders I felt as I understood that the answer to both questions was an emphatic *yes*.

Although my parts can still get triggered from time to time, my reactions are less hurtful and my recovery time is usually minutes instead of hours or days. And the great news is that, once I'm back in my Captain, I'm able to see and love Jenny for the marvelous person she really is. By going through the sessions, I gave myself an amazing gift. I was now living with a woman I deeply loved and respected. I often feel the kind of "in love" emotions I did in the first few months of our relationship, except that these feelings are now based on Jenny as a whole person and not just a romantic fantasy. Of course, this transformation was wonderful for Jenny, but it was even better for me. It took some time and effort, but with Jenny's help, I managed to change the way I thought, felt, and acted. Love was finally a stable and palpable part of my emotional and intellectual life. I now understand that this is what healing looks like.

Healing can also take place when you stop in the middle of

an argument and ask your mate for a time out so that you can both cool off and get back in your Captains. Healing takes place when, although it feels like the hardest thing you've ever done, you reach out your hand to demonstrate to your partner that you are ready and willing to end a painful stalemate. Healing occurs when you realize and admit that beneath your anger is a hurt feeling and a need to be understood and comforted. It can be healing when you realize and confess that underneath your jealous accusations are feelings of fear and insecurity. Healing takes place when you finally accept that your hurt feelings are usually caused by your interpretation of events and that those interpretations could be all wrong. In other words, you start growing the moment you realize that *you* are causing most of your misery and suffering.

It is also healing to recognize whenever you (or your partner) have shifted into a protective part. Once you realize that you've shifted into a part, you can take deep breaths and ground yourself so that you can return to your Captain. It also can be healing to learn that you are not your parts and your partner is not his parts, either. Parts are merely sub-personalities that have temporarily taken over. Of course, it is healing to appropriately stand up for yourself and to insist that you be treated with dignity and respect.

All of these and other "micro-healings" begin to change our attitudes and our behaviors toward ourselves and our partners, leading to increasing emotional safety, connection, intimacy, and a felt sense of love. Every moment spent with a partner is an opportunity to open your heart and to treat him or her with love and respect. Every moment is an opportunity to really listen with your eyes, your ears, and your heart. Every moment is a chance to see your loved one as a person who, underneath their hurts and wounds, is very much like you, needing attention, understanding, and love.

Whatever you do to help you achieve self-mastery is healing. Removing impediments from your mind and heart so that you can think, feel, and behave in more compassionate and loving ways is healing. Another tool for healing is to use this book as a resource after you've read it. Even though I wrote the book, I often read a particular chapter when I'm struggling with something in my relationship. For instance, when my feelings get hurt and my protective part is clinging to its story, I might go to the chapter on hurt feelings and read it. By the time I'm halfway finished with it, I'm feeling much better, seeing more clearly, and back in my Captain. It helps to be reminded about emotional honesty, truth, and integrity.

Some of the attributes and tools needed to achieve emotional healing are self-awareness, courage, desire for change, attention, focus, patience, and determination. Because it requires these tools and a lot of effort, most people will never attain the transformation and metanoia we've talked about in this book. My hope is that these pages have informed and inspired you in such a way as to make this journey a reality for you. You can do it! You can become the person you were meant to be rather than the one you were programmed to be by unwitting parents and an unhelpful culture. Self-mastery will allow you to live in the world and your relationship with integrity, emotional honesty, and an open, compassionate heart. It's your choice.

The Greatest Love of All

From the very beginning, this book has been about love. We have talked about the ways love can be stunted or even killed by the vestiges of emotional and psychological wounds from infancy, childhood, and hurtful experiences from the past. Like flowers competing with invasive weeds, love for a partner cannot flourish in the midst of grievances, hostility, and negative projections. It is up to each of us on the path to wholeness, intimacy, and connection to become aware of the wounds we carry. And we need to understand how our wounds will harden not only our hearts but can harden the hearts of our partners as well. And with that understanding, we must do whatever it takes to free ourselves from those toxic, ancient beliefs and behaviors posing as our protectors. Only then can we give ourselves and our partners an unfettered heart filled with usable love. To willingly be shaken and threshed to the core for love is not only heroic, but as I said earlier, it is without question simply the greatest love of all.

Marvin spent fourteen years as a psychotherapist focusing mainly on couple relationships and the struggles men have to be emotionally honest, aware, and present. Because of his own personal struggles with relationships, Marvin has had a lifelong interest in emotional and psychological healing as a way to a deeper experience of intimacy, connection, and love. Far too many couples miss out on the incredible power, security, and inner joy that love can bring simply because their emotional baggage gets in the way.

By following the path described in his new book, *The Conscious Road Home*, Marvin and Jenny have learned how to truly love each other and build a relationship they always wanted. The fights, the blaming, the arguments, and the resentments have faded into the past, replaced with emotional honesty, affection, mutual respect, appreciation, and a love that is *felt* every day.

Marvin has appeared on the Oprah Winfrey show, ABC's 20/20 with Hugh Downs and Barbara Walters, PBS and BBC prime time specials, and has been featured in the New York Times Sunday Magazine. He also wrote the book *Angry Men, Passive Men: A New Approach To Healing For Husbands, Fathers, And Friends,* published by Random House.

Jenny has had a lifelong interest in relationships and emotional healing. She has been especially dedicated to discovering processes that create true and lasting change. Her interests in spirituality and psychology have spurred her to take full advantage of many opportunities to explore how true emotional healing is made possible with a special emphasis on how healing can happen in a relationship.

Website: ConsciousRoadHome.com
✉Email: marvin@consciousroadhome.com
❋Facebook: @themarvinallen
❋Twitter: @TheMarvinAllen
❋Instagram: @marvinlallen

Made in the USA
Monee, IL
18 March 2021